GoldMine® 6 For Dummies®

Cheat Sheet

D1317184

The GoldMine Basic Toolbar

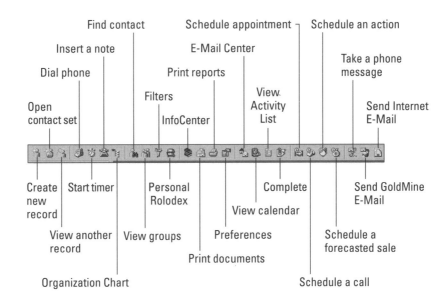

Find contact
Insert a note
Dial phone
Open contact set
Filters
Print reports
InfoCenter
E-Mail Center
Schedule appointment
View Activity List
Schedule an action
Take a phone message
Send Internet E-Mail

Create new record
Start timer
Personal Rolodex
Complete
Send GoldMine E-Mail

View another record
View groups
View calendar

Organization Chart
Print documents
Preferences
Schedule a forecasted sale
Schedule a call

✔ **Create new record:** Enter new records into GoldMine. You're prompted to enter Company, Contact, Phone, and E-mail information.

✔ **Open contact set:** This icon is for GoldMine users who have more than one contact file or database. It brings you to the Contact Set Database screen, where you can choose what contact file you want to open.

✔ **View another record:** View two or more contacts at one time.

✔ **Dial phone:** If you have a modem and telephony software, clicking this icon dials the main phone number of the contact record you're currently viewing.

✔ **Start timer:** Time your call or activity with this icon. A timer starts and is displayed at the bottom of your GoldMine screen. To stop or reset the timer, simply click Edit Timer.

✔ **Insert a note:** Automatically stamp a new note with the time, date, and username in the main Notepad.

GoldMine® 6 For Dummies®

Cheat Sheet

- ✔ **Organization Chart:** Opens the Organizational Chart to the left of the contact record.

- ✔ **Find contact:** Quickly locate the desired contact. The Contact Listing window opens, which allows you to search for the contact by simply typing in the name.

- ✔ **View groups:** Quickly view all of your previously created groups or build a new one.

- ✔ **Filters:** Activate a filter or build a new one.

- ✔ **Personal Rolodex:** Lets you easily enter and retrieve all your personal phone numbers. This listing is unique to each user.

- ✔ **InfoCenter:** Access the cumulative knowledge of all your GoldMine users in the InfoCenter. Search on a topic or keyword, or add some of your own knowledge for everyone else to use.

- ✔ **Print documents:** Go directly to the Document Management Center. Do not pass Go. Do not collect $200.

- ✔ **Print reports:** Enables you to choose from the standard GoldMine reports or ones you have modified or added.

- ✔ **Preferences:** Change your own user preferences, including alarms, colors, Internet options, toolbars, and much, much more.

- ✔ **E-mail Center:** The one-stop shop for all your e-mail needs.

- ✔ **View calendar:** View all of your scheduled activities for the day, week, month, or year. Need to see what everyone is up to? This is the place to start.

- ✔ **View Activity List:** See all the activities you have completed, or scheduled, break it all down to calls, actions, others, to-do's, appointments, and what is open or closed.

- ✔ **Complete:** Select this icon after you have finished an activity. If you just completed a call, complete it and now it's history!

- ✔ **Schedule appointment:** Display the contact you're going to see, click this icon, and enter the details.

- ✔ **Schedule a call:** Display the account you need to call and select this icon. You're led directly to the Schedule A Phone Call screen.

- ✔ **Schedule an action:** Display the right account and then select this icon to schedule almost any activity that isn't an appt, a phone call, or a forecasted sale.

- ✔ **Schedule a forecasted sale:** Keep track of all your potential sales.

- ✔ **Take a phone message:** Send an instant phone message to the right user.

- ✔ **Send GoldMine E-mail:** Send an internal e-mail to another GoldMine user about the current contact. Whatever you send will be tracked as a history item.

- ✔ **Send Internet E-mail:** Send Internet E-mail to the current contact and everything is kept in history.

For Dummies: Bestselling Book Series for Beginners

GoldMine® 6

FOR

DUMMIES®

GoldMine® 6

FOR

DUMMIES®

by Joel Scott

Wiley Publishing, Inc.

GoldMine® 6 For Dummies®

Published by
Wiley Publishing, Inc.
909 Third Avenue
New York, NY 10022
www.wiley.com

Copyright © 2003 by Wiley Publishing, Inc., Indianapolis, Indiana

Published by Wiley Publishing, Inc., Indianapolis, Indiana

Published simultaneously in Canada

For general information on our other products and services or to obtain technical support, please contact our Customer Care Department within the U.S. at 800-762-2974, outside the U.S. at 317-572-3993, or fax 317-572-4002.

Wiley also publishes its books in a variety of electronic formats. Some content that appears in print may not be available in electronic books.

Library of Congress Control Number: 2002110289

ISBN: 0-7645-0845-8

Manufactured in the United States of America

10 9 8 7 6 5 4 3 2 1

1O/RZ/RS/QS/IN

About the Author

Joel Scott is president of the Computer Control Corporation, with offices in New England and in Southern California. Since 1991, Computer Control has been a dedicated GoldMine dealership, designing and installing literally thousands of customized GoldMine systems. While there are hundreds of GoldMine dealers worldwide, Computer Control Corporation has been awarded GoldMine's prestigious Top10 dealer status every year since 1996.

Mr. Scott is an authorized GoldMine and GoldSync technician as well as an authorized trainer for GoldMine. In that role, he has trained thousands of students in every corner of the country since 1992, and he is a well-known national speaker on GoldMine, CRM, and client retention.

Author's Acknowledgments

Three years ago, GoldMine Software Corporation merged with Bendata, a company well known for Help Desk Software. Since that merger, the two companies have been known as FrontRange Solutions Inc. While GoldMine software continues to evolve, the company itself is now very different.

The one constant has been Natalie Burdick. While her title has changed more times than I can count, I think of her as the product manager for GoldMine. In that role, Natalie has helped me with software previews, explanations, criticisms, and a kind word now and then. Although I have already thanked her publicly, there's no harm in doing so again here.

This is the third version of *GoldMine For Dummies*. Each time I have gotten invaluable assistance from almost everyone on Computer Control's staff. Jill Messier has helped me with virtually all the art in this book and that's a task that inevitably requires her to do each figure at least three times while I change my mind about the text.

Mike DeLisa, our head trainer, is my unofficial editor. Long before any editors at Wiley see my work it has to pass Mike's scrutiny. His critical input always makes the final product better.

Both Don (DJ) Hunt and Doug Castel have helped me with some of the new and more technical features. It often takes me a good deal longer to understand the significance of some of GoldMine's latest innovations than it does them.

Bob Woerner and Christine Berman from Wiley have once again exhibited the patience and humor always needed for one of these productions. Thank you both.

And, finally, I want to thank the hundreds of readers who have called or e-mailed me with comments on the previous two editions. Many of your constructive comments have now found their way into this latest edition. Keep those calls and e-mails coming.

Publisher's Acknowledgments

We're proud of this book; please send us your comments through our online registration form located at www.dummies.com/register/.

Some of the people who helped bring this book to market include the following:

Acquisitions, Editorial, and Media Development

Project Editor: Christine Berman

(Previous Edition: Nate Holdread)

Acquisitions Editor: Bob Woerner

Copy Editor: Jean Rogers

Technical Editor: Karen Telese

Editorial Manager: Leah Cameron

Media Development Supervisor: Richard Graves

Editorial Assistant: Amanda Foxworth

Cartoons: Rich Tennant, www.the5thwave.com

Production

Project Coordinator: Maridee Ennis

Layout and Graphics: Joyce Haughey, Jacque Schneider

Proofreader: TECHBOOKS Production Services

Indexer: TECHBOOKS Production Services

Publishing and Editorial for Technology Dummies

    Richard Swadley, Vice President and Executive Group Publisher

    Andy Cummings, Vice President and Publisher

    Mary C. Corder, Editorial Director

Publishing for Consumer Dummies

    Diane Graves Steele, Vice President and Publisher

    Joyce Pepple, Acquisitions Director

Composition Services

    Gerry Fahey, Vice President of Production Services

    Debbie Stailey, Director of Composition Services

Contents at a Glance

Table of Contents

Introduction

● ●

*Y*ou finally decided to get your professional life organized. Good. You
bought and installed a copy of GoldMine, or your boss decided to buy it,
installed it on your computer, and then told you to figure out how to use it.
Or maybe you recently upgraded to GoldMine Business Contact Manager
version 6.0 (GoldMine 6.0), and you want some help with the new features.
If any of these cases apply to you, *GoldMine 6 For Dummies* is for you.

GoldMine is the good, strong medicine needed by people who are constantly
disorganized. It even works for people who are already well organized but
have more to do and more to remember than is humanly possible. Use
GoldMine correctly, and your associates and clients will be convinced that
your desk is always neat and clean, and that you'll never let something fall
through the cracks. Use it incorrectly, and you could mess things up even
faster and more efficiently than ever before.

With some of the new tools that several independent companies have
recently developed, you can now use GoldMine to deliver not only organizational benefits, but also as the basis for a real business process and intelligence system. I discuss this throughout the book.

Every few years, FrontRange Solutions, Inc. (the company that has taken over
GoldMine Software Corporation) releases a new version of GoldMine. These
versions have recently been numbered 2.5, 3.0, 3.2, 4.0, 5.0, 5.5, and 5.7. In
between these versions, GoldMine releases updates, called builds. At the
time this book was written, version 6.0 was about to be released. Therefore,
GoldMine 6 For Dummies is based on GoldMine 6.0 as it was released to beta
testers in the summer of 2002.

You can check to see what version you are using by choosing Help➪About
from your main menu.

How to Use This Book

I've tried to organize this book so that the chapters progress logically from
the most basic skills you need to the more advanced topics. You should be
able to comfortably read the book from start to finish (maybe with one or
two breaks). On the other hand, this book is a reference, and each chapter is
designed to stand on its own.

You'll get the most benefit from this book by reading it while you're sitting in front of your computer with GoldMine on the screen. You can easily convince yourself that you've "got it" after reading a paragraph or two, but there's just no substitute for trying it yourself to make sure you really understand.

Conventions Used in This Book

GoldMine offers more than one way to access menus and to perform various tasks. You can choose from a menu, click a toolbar button, click an icon, or right-click and choose from the shortcut menu that appears. In this book, I try to provide the easiest method to accomplish a particular task. If you find another way you like to accomplish the same task, by all means use it.

I often instruct you to make a selection from a menu. If I tell you to "choose Edit⇨Preferences," I mean "from the Edit menu, choose Preferences."

Some GoldMine terminology occurs frequently throughout this book. The following is a quick explanation of the most common terms I use:

- **GoldMine main screen:** Whenever you have an account or a record in front of you, you are looking at the main screen. The main screen contains the main menu, the main toolbar, and most of the static data (names, addresses, phone numbers, and so on) for each account.

- **Main menu:** As with most Windows applications, GoldMine has several pull-down menus that contain virtually all of GoldMine's basic functions. The main menu sits at the top of the main GoldMine screen.

- **Main toolbar:** This is a collection of customizable icons that can also trigger most of the vital functions within GoldMine.

- **Local menu or toolbar:** Many of the secondary windows you access have their own menus or icons that are local or specific to that one window.

- **Taskbar:** GoldMine has a series of customizable, icon-based shortcuts for performing various functions.

Foolish Assumptions

I assume you have some basic computer and Windows skills. If you don't do Windows, you need to get yourself up to speed in this area. Find a local class or seminar, or get one of the *Windows For Dummies* books on your version of Windows. Regarding GoldMine, however, I assume you just landed from Mars and need to start using GoldMine today.

I also assume you have a basic understanding of database concepts. If you're comfortable with fields, records, files, folders, and how they relate to each other, you'll be fine. If this is already sounding bad, you can seek help at most community colleges, local computer training facilities, or your local Authorized GoldMine Training Center. (See the FrontRange Web site, www.frontrange.com, for dealers and training centers.)

If you're going to be your own GoldMine administrator (backing up files and assigning user names, passwords, and access rights), you need to really understand records, files, folders, and networks. If you just want to be a good day-to-day user of GoldMine, make sure you understand what a file is and how to locate one using Windows Explorer.

How This Book Is Organized

This book has eight parts. Each part stands on its own, but you're best off if you at least skim through the basics before you dive into the more complex material.

Part 1: GoldMine BCM Basics

This part gives you an overview of what GoldMine is all about and provides a tour of the GoldMine main screen. You also find a discussion regarding setting user preferences and default values.

Part II: Managing Contacts

In this part, I explain how to enter new records into your GoldMine database and how to easily locate existing records. You also get more details on screen functions and a discussion of the information that goes into the Notes, Contacts, Detail, and Referral tabs. In addition, I show you the little-known shortcuts for finding records really quickly. The new Search Center comes into play here. In this part I also discuss the Organizational Chart, which has been continually enhanced.

Part III: Managing Activities

Here you find out how to schedule activities for yourself and for others and how to check on things that have already been scheduled. After activities are scheduled, you need to complete them in some fashion — I show you all five ways to do that. If you are in sales or sales management, you will also want to visit Chapter 11 in this part. I also discuss filters and groups, which are methods of selecting bite-size chunks of your data, in this part.

Part IV: Managing Documents

Three basic types of documents are discussed in this part — Word documents, e-mail, and faxes. You also find a discussion of linking external documents to their related records in GoldMine.

Part V: Organizing and Distributing Information to Your Team

The InfoCenter, a great place to store and from which to disseminate company information, is discussed in this part, as is the entire Statistical and Reporting Center.

Part VI: Customizing GoldMine

This part deals with changing field labels, adding new fields and field views, and lookup lists. GoldMine is very customizable and can be set up to perform just the way you want it to. This part also contains a chapter on getting data into and out of GoldMine.

Part VII: Advanced Stuff

This part deals with accessing your data when you aren't connected to your local area network. For those who travel or those who manage people who don't work in the main office, this part is a must-read. This part also deals with Automated Processes and the Opportunity/Project Manager. It also contains information on the new My GoldMine window and the new GM+View tab.

If you want to integrate GoldMine with either Outlook or a handheld device such as the Palm Pilot, you find chapters on these topics in this part. And finally, this part contains a few thoughts on how best to use GoldMine to improve your business.

Part VIII: The Part of Tens

In this part, you can read about the ten best add-on products I know, and you get my own listing of the ten most significant new features in GoldMine 6.0.

Icons Used in This Book

This icon indicates an action that could potentially be dangerous to the health of your database. You're given proper procedures to avoid problems.

This icon lets you know that some particularly geeky, technical information is coming up. You can usually skip this if you want.

This icon indicates a slick shortcut or timesaver.

This icon points out important information or concepts that you shouldn't forget.

GoldMine 6.0 contains everything the prior versions contained and then some. This icon indicates a feature included in 6.0 but not in prior versions.

Where to Go from Here

If you've already lived with GoldMine for a while, you may just want to pick and choose topics from the Table of Contents. Chances are that almost every chapter has some tidbit for you, so when you have a chance, thumb through the rest of the material. Start giving some thought to how GoldMine might enhance your business life and then make it happen.

If you're a first time user, I suggest you go through Chapters 1, 2, 4, 8, 9, and 10, at least. These chapters give you a solid introduction to the very basics of living with GoldMine.

If you have questions or constructive comments and want to contact me directly, please send me an e-mail at dummy@ccc24k.com.

Part I
GoldMine BCM
Basics

The 5th Wave   By Rich Tennant

"Well, she's fast on the keyboard and knows how to load the printer, but she just sort of 'plays' with the mouse."

In this part . . .

A little planning goes a long way toward the success of any project. This part provides you with some of the basic building blocks needed to set yourself up for a successful implementation. In addition to a general overview of what GoldMine can do for you and how to navigate the main screen, this part also contains a discussion of user preferences.

You can probably ignore the user preferences if you just want to play a little at the beginning. But, if you're really serious about getting the most out of your investment, put some time into Chapter 3 and use the preference settings to fine-tune GoldMine to your own best advantage.

Chapter 1

GoldMine: An Overview

In This Chapter

▶ Discovering everything that GoldMine can do

▶ Investigating a few of the things GoldMine isn't designed to do

▶ Planning a successful project

▶ Providing training: The key to success

GoldMine 6.0 (also called Business Contact Manager or BCM) is a tool for sales, marketing, customer-service people, and their managers. In fact, GoldMine is for *you* if you ever have contact with customers or with business prospects. Right out of the box, GoldMine lets you track all the basic information you need to manage your client relationships.

In the late '80s, my company was growing a bit too fast and was getting a little out of control. I began searching for some kind of tool that could help us sustain our growth without causing additional pain. I chose GoldMine because it

✔ Prevents us from forgetting to return phone calls

✔ Ensures that we remember all our appointments

✔ Provides a central place to store all client information

✔ Links all our documents to clients' records so we can't lose proposals anymore

✔ Makes sure that we all get home for dinner on time every night

The developers at FrontRange Solutions, Inc. (formerly GoldMine Software Corporation) don't really know the special needs of your business; your work may require some fields or functions that just aren't there. For example, you may want to track your competitors on a particular account, but you discover that the field isn't available to you. The good news is that this field, as well as many other fields and functions, can easily be added by you or by one of FrontRange's experienced dealers. One of the real advantages of becoming a GoldMine user is the extensive network of more than 1,000 dealers worldwide. These dealers are trained professionals who have focused on the product and can help with customization, support, and training.

All the Great Stuff You Can Do with GoldMine

GoldMine tracks all the names, addresses, phone numbers, and e-mail addresses you ever need. If you never use GoldMine as anything more than a glorified rotary card file, you're getting something from it. But you're missing out on most of the power for which your company paid good money.

Putting all your contacts into GoldMine

You can reap some excellent benefits if you religiously enter every lead and every account into GoldMine. And if you can convince everyone in your organization to do the same, not only do you have one organized location holding all your data, but

✔ Everyone with authorization in your organization can share data and schedules

✔ E-mail and other documents can be linked to appropriate records for historical purposes

✔ When a salesperson leaves your company, you can easily transfer her records to her replacement without losing a beat

✔ You can set up all sorts of imaginative, Automated Processes to help you with marketing, hunting, and farming

Keeping track of your life

You can use GoldMine to track your schedule and, in fact, your entire life. Just as importantly, GoldMine can keep schedules for everyone you work with and can help you coordinate your activities with theirs. This capability is one of the compelling reasons to use a business management system like GoldMine.

GoldMine lets you see what everyone else on your team is doing (although it also offers plenty of provisions for privacy); at the same time, it lets everyone else track what you're doing. GoldMine can even coordinate the data for remote salespeople (those people with a cell phone attached to an ear and a notebook computer or handheld device in hand, who dash from appointment to appointment and seldom venture into the office).

If your entire team uses GoldMine consistently to schedule both professional time and personal appointments, here are some results you may see:

✔ You can eliminate most instances of staff being over-booked.

✔ You can feel reasonably safe in scheduling meetings and appointments for others in your organization.

✔ You can let GoldMine automatically find a time when everyone on the team is free to meet.

✔ You have a record of team members' meetings, appointments, and activities.

Communicating with the outside world

You can use GoldMine to send a single letter to a customer, send batches of letters, or send broadcast faxes or e-mail messages. Twenty years ago, sending notices to your thousand best customers telling them about tomorrow's price increase would have been an almost impossible task. Now you can name that tune in three notes.

GoldMine communicates well with the World Wide Web. You can use it to collect all sorts of information from people surfing your Web site and then have GoldMine import that data directly into your database. GoldMine can also send acknowledgments automatically and schedule actions as a result of a Web inquiry. Very cool.

Intranet, schmintranet

The GoldMine InfoCenter lets you set up a central site, easily accessed by all users, for your company's rules, regulations, announcements, pricing information, and so on. Any file can easily be connected to the InfoCenter for instant retrieval, and you can set up GoldMine so that new announcements pop up automatically as users sign on.

You can even use the InfoCenter as a convenient place from which to disseminate information to clients and prospects. If you use this feature in conjunction with GoldMine's E-mail Center, you have an instant fulfillment center.

Keeping tabs on your projects

When it's a simple sale — say someone calls you out of the blue and orders $28 worth of white paper — you don't need much sales-tracking or forecasting capability. But when you have a six-week (or, as in one case at my company, a nine-year) sales cycle, having a system that keeps track of who should be doing what and when is a powerful thing. That's where the

Opportunity Manager comes into play. You use this tool to track a complex sale with a long sales cycle, along with the actions of the many people involved in the sale.

After the Opportunity Manager helps you win the deal, you may want to use the Project Manager to track all the phases of the job so you don't go off into left field with it. Nothing is worse than winning that million-dollar job and discovering too late that it cost you $3 million to get the job done.

Setting up Automated Processes

GoldMine allows you to program any number of Automated Processes, such as sending a follow-up thank-you letter immediately after a first sales call. In a sense, GoldMine with its Automated Processes is an entire marketing department in a box. Automated Processes are one of the most powerful and underutilized features of GoldMine. Just implementing a few good Automated Processes can pay for your entire investment in GoldMine.

Even a Great Piece of Software Can't Do Everything!

As good as GoldMine is, there are a few things it wasn't designed to do. But that's all right; no one piece of software was meant to do everything. The following sections explain a few of the things you shouldn't expect from GoldMine and offer solutions for getting the job done.

Use your own word processor

GoldMine has no built-in word processor; you don't want to use GoldMine to write a letter. Rather than reinvent the wheel, the designers decided that most users already have a good word processor, so GoldMine just integrates with some of the good ones already out there.

Over the past few years, the number of "good ones already out there" has dwindled basically to just one. So GoldMine integrates with Microsoft Word and (maybe) WordPerfect. Specific versions of GoldMine work with specific versions of each of these word processors. Turn to Chapter 13 to find out more about using GoldMine with your word processor.

Get some faxing software

Don't think of GoldMine as a replacement for your faxing software either. Output from GoldMine goes to your word processor and then to your faxing program. The better-integrated faxing systems then report back to GoldMine to show you that your document was actually sent, or that there was a problem.

First, make sure that you're using the appropriate version of GoldMine for your word-processing software. Then you can use any of the recommended faxing systems or even use a broadcast fax service bureau.

Get some accounting, quoting, and mapping software

Don't rely on GoldMine for help with accounting, quotations, proposals, expense reporting, or displaying maps. You can buy separate programs for each of these tasks, and they have interfaces specially designed to work with GoldMine. I discuss some of the more popular third-party products in Chapter 29.

Mining for Success

Although GoldMine was designed to coordinate a team, it works well for sole practitioners as well. If you are the whole team, in all likelihood you're in charge of sales, marketing, customer service, and administration. GoldMine can help you in every department; you just have to make a commitment to use it.

A discouraging number of Customer Relationship Management (CRM) projects (such as implementations of GoldMine) fail. Industry estimates show the failure rate at somewhere around two out of every three attempts. Defining failure isn't easy. But assume for now that failure implies that you have spent time and money on a system that isn't giving you what you need or isn't being used by your staff. Either way, it's not a pretty picture.

I'm sure that you would prefer not to be part of the majority in this failure statistic. Buying this book (and reading it, of course!) gives you an edge on the rest of the world. Here are some of the reasons for the astonishing failure rate for CRM projects and some suggestions on how to avoid failure when you're implementing a CRM project:

✔ Users buy the software in the morning and expect to use it that afternoon. The old adage, "Those who fail to plan, plan to fail," certainly applies to CRM systems in general, and to GoldMine in particular. Training is a key element in the success of the project.

✔ Users buy the software without planning out the design of their CRM system. Before implementing a CRM project, follow a couple of basic design rules:

  • Identify all the people or departments that interact with your prospects or clients. These are your potential users. For GoldMine in particular, your sales, marketing, and customer-service staff almost always need to be involved.

  • Gather input from as many people and departments as possible. A critical factor in your project's success is to involve users as early as possible in the design phase. That way, each of them has contributed to the project and has a vested interest in its success. Get their input early, and get it often.

✔ Users rush to implement GoldMine. Don't promise that the CRM system will be ready for the annual sales meeting next week. That's a recipe for discontent and failure. Remember the tortoise and the hare?

✔ Users don't customize their CRM to meet their individual or their company's needs. Take the time to customize GoldMine. Start with all the reports your staff currently uses, and then add some they aren't getting but would like to have. GoldMine lends itself to customization. And the more personal you make it, the greater chance the software will be accepted and used.

Don't Forget the Key Ingredient: Training

Don't shortchange yourself or your company when it comes to training. You can provide GoldMine training in several ways, and any one of them is certainly better than expecting the users to just figure out the program on their own. The following list shows some effective training methods, starting with the most effective and ending with the least effective:

1. Send every user to an authorized GoldMine Training Center.

2. Bring an authorized trainer to one of your regular company meetings and allocate a half-day or a full day to GoldMine training.

3. Bring an authorized trainer to your facility for training (and then confiscate all cellular phones and pagers).

4. Sign up for some Web-based training that several dealers offer.

5. Buy some computer-based training CD-ROMs and set aside time for each person to work through them.

6. Buy each staff member a copy of *GoldMine 6 For Dummies*. (Tell each person that he or she will get a one-week paid vacation upon finishing the book.)

7. Require each staff member to read the GoldMine manual. (This may require a two-week vacation.)

8. Tell your staff just to figure it out. This is how I do plumbing at home. Three hours into the project, I have a bigger leak than I started with. So I end up paying the plumber twice as much to fix my bathroom sink as he would have charged had I not messed it up in the first place. It took me 20 years to learn this, but now I just call the plumber at the beginning.

Chapter 2

Getting Around in GoldMine

- -

In This Chapter

▶ Examining the main menu

▶ Investigating the toolbars and the taskbar

▶ Understanding quadrants and tabs

▶ Using the right mouse button

▶ Finding information with browse windows

▶ Saving time by using F2 lookups

- -

Getting into and around GoldMine is simple. The initial sign-on dialog box asks you for your user name and possibly your password. After you enter that information, GoldMine's main screen appears with its menus, fields, icons, and functions. The main screen contains all the basic information about an account and is the central hub for everything you ever do in GoldMine.

Throughout GoldMine and, therefore, this book, the terms *account* and *record* are used interchangeably. An *account* is basically one customer or one prospect. If you do business with businesses, an *account* is the company, and the information on the main screen contains not only the primary person you deal with, but also other people involved within your customer's company.

In this chapter, I describe how to navigate the main screen. After you know your way around, you'll feel comfortable in later chapters as the book begins to get into more and more detailed activities.

The Main Screen

When you start GoldMine, you see the main screen, as shown in Figure 2-1. The main screen consists of the following parts:

Figure 2-1:
The main
GoldMine
screen.

✔ Pull-down menus

✔ Toolbars containing icons

✔ A taskbar containing functions

✔ Four quadrants containing fields

✔ File folder tabs

✔ Status line

Below the menus and toolbars, the window is divided into four sections, or *quadrants*. The fields within each quadrant are grouped logically. To find out what fields are available in each quadrant, see the "Putting information in four quadrants" section, later in this chapter.

The main menu

Like most Windows applications, GoldMine has a series of menu choices, as shown in Figure 2-2. These features are particularly useful to toolbar-challenged users. (See the next section for information about toolbars.)

Generally, the menu choices correspond to the toolbar icons. Using one approach or the other, you can begin a variety of activities, such as scheduling appointments, logging phone calls, or running reports. Whether you use the menu selections or the icons is really a matter of personal preference.

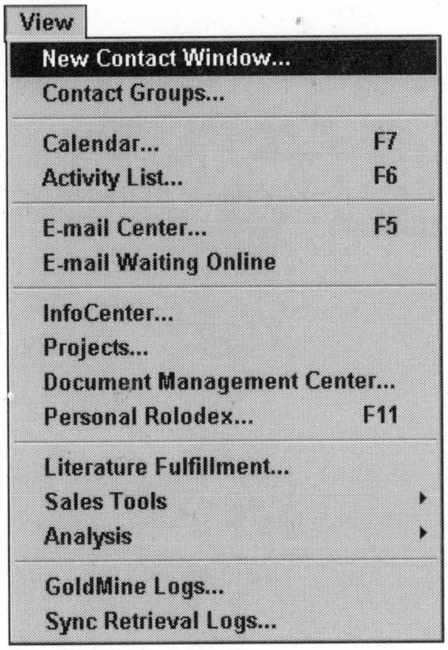

Figure 2-2:
A menu chosen from the main screen.

View
New Contact Window...
Contact Groups...
Calendar...   F7
Activity List...   F6
E-mail Center...   F5
E-mail Waiting Online
InfoCenter...
Projects...
Document Management Center...
Personal Rolodex...   F11
Literature Fulfillment...
Sales Tools   ▶
Analysis   ▶
GoldMine Logs...
Sync Retrieval Logs...

When you click a menu choice, the menu options are immediately displayed. Some of the selections contain a right-pointing arrow, indicating that you can make even more choices.

When you position your cursor over a menu item with a right-pointing arrow, another set of menu choices appears, as shown in Figure 2-3.

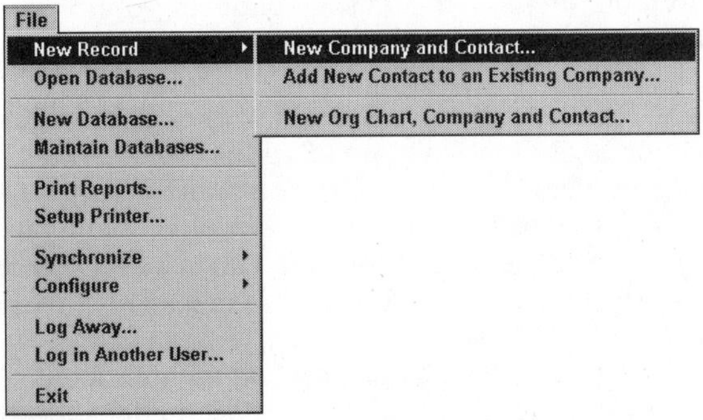

Figure 2-3:
An example of additional drop-down menu choices.

File	
New Record ▶	New Company and Contact...
Open Database...	Add New Contact to an Existing Company...
New Database...	New Org Chart, Company and Contact...
Maintain Databases...	
Print Reports...	
Setup Printer...	
Synchronize ▶	
Configure ▶	
Log Away...	
Log in Another User...	
Exit	

Choosing your GoldMine toolbars

GoldMine comes with as many as 160 toolbar icons that you can use. Way too many for me — 160 icons may be more than you'll ever need, too. But the good news is that GoldMine enables you to tailor your toolbars to your liking.

To choose which toolbars you want to display, position your cursor in the blank space to the right of the icons and right-click. (See the "Getting the hang of the right mouse button" section, later in this chapter, to find out what else you use the right mouse button for.) You then see a selection of toolbar choices, as shown in Figure 2-4. You can make one or more selections from this list. Feel free to play with the choices.

Figure 2-4:
Choosing
the toolbars
you want
to display
on-screen.

I like to display text with my icons. Button text consists of a one- or two-word message displayed within an icon. You can display button text by right-clicking a blank spot on the toolbar, and then choosing Options⇨Toolbar Options⇨Button Text from the shortcut menu, as shown in Figure 2-4.

Button text is useful for those people (like me) who can't remember what each icon does. Unfortunately, at lower resolutions (such as 800 x 600), you can't see all the icons nicely in one row. You could move some of the extras to a second row or off to the side by dragging groups of them, but you may not want to sacrifice the space on your screen. Life is full of compromises, so I choose to forgo the button text in favor of seeing all my favorite icons.

Whether or not you choose to display button text on your icons, you can see a phrase in the status bar telling you what the icon does. Each time you position your cursor over an icon, this phrase appears. (See Chapter 3 to find out how to set up your screen preferences to display phrases.)

Introducing the taskbar

The taskbar, new in version 5.7, is displayed on the left side of the main screen. It shows a series of icons, each of which performs a commonly used function. The taskbar is programmable, so you can create your own custom functions if you're so inclined.

Out of the box, GoldMine comes with the following taskbar icons:

- ✔ **QuickStart Lessons:** Selecting this icon leads you through a tutorial.

- ✔ **GoldMine Support Online:** Selecting this icon brings you to an interface allowing you to e-mail a question to the FrontRange tech support team, as well as to a section where FrontRange explains that it no longer offers telephone support for most of its products. FrontRange's official support policy has changed often in the past year, so it may be different by the time you read this book.

- ✔ **Solutions Partner Locator:** Selecting this icon brings you to the section of the FrontRange Web site that lists GoldMine dealers. If you're looking for help that is beyond the scope of this book, this is a good resource. FrontRange occasionally removes dealer listings entirely and has also had trouble keeping the listings current, so it's hard to tell what you might find.

- ✔ **Preferences:** Selecting this icon leads to the same window you find by choosing Edit➪Preferences from the main menu, where you can customize your settings.

- ✔ **Toolbars:** Selecting this icon enables you to customize all your toolbars.

- ✔ **Create a Company Contact:** Selecting this icon creates a new record; you can also select the Create New Record icon from the main toolbar to create a new record.

- ✔ **Contact:** Selecting this icon enables you to look up a record in the database. By default, the records are sorted by primary contact.

- ✔ **Calendar:** Selecting this icon takes you to your calendar window.

- ✔ **E-mail Center:** Selecting this icon brings you to the E-mail Center, where you can send or receive messages.

Putting information in four quadrants

The four quadrants of information, when taken together, comprise the main record, or the main account information. Most of the non-activity-related information is contained within these four areas. You should initially enter as much of this data as you can. You should fill in the rest as you gather the information, and you should make every effort to keep the information current. When addresses or phone numbers change, make sure you remember to change them here.

GoldMine is often referred to as *contact-centric,* meaning that everything revolves around individual contact records. To ensure that an activity is automatically linked to the appropriate contact record, you should make sure that you refer to the correct record whenever you schedule an activity.

Quadrant 1

Quadrant 1 contains basic company information, including the name of the company, the name of the main contact for the account, and the contact's department and title. The Last Name field normally is filled in automatically when you create a new record. You use the Dear (or salutation) field when you're corresponding with this account, the Source field to record how this account found you in the first place, and the Asst field to house the name of your main contact's assistant. I usually customize the Asst field and use it for some other purpose.

Some fields have lookup lists of predefined choices that you can choose from. GoldMine enables each user (as long as he or she has sufficient access rights to do so) to customize these lookup lists to make them really meaningful. An example might be in a field for Acct Mngr. You can enter all your codes for your account managers rather than using the predefined ones that come with GoldMine. Lookup lists are covered in more detail in Chapter 21.

Table 2-1 shows quadrant information in more detail than you find on the GoldMine main screen.

Table 2-1	Fields in Quadrant 1	
Field Labels	*Lookup List*	*Can Use to Locate Records?*
Company	Y	Y
Contact	Y	Y
Dept	Y	N
Last	Y	Y
Title	Y	N
Dear	Y	N
Source	Y	N
Asst	Y	N

Quadrant 2

Quadrant 2 contains standard address information and provides three lines for the street address. This space is usually enough for addresses in the United States, but you may have to do some serious abbreviating for addresses outside the U.S. This quadrant also contains City and State fields, and the Zip field can hold a full 10-character (nine digits plus the hyphen) zip code. The Country field should be left blank if the account is located in the same country as you are. Table 2-2 describes the quadrant fields in more detail.

Table 2-2	Fields in Quadrant 2	
Field Labels	*Lookup List*	*Can Use to Locate Records?*
Address	Y	N
City	Y	Y
State	Y	Y
Zip	Y	Y
Country	Y	Y
Merge	Y	N

Quadrant 3

Quadrant 3 contains fields for four separate phone numbers, each with space to include an extension number. You may want to change the field labels to something more specific, such as W Phone, H Phone, and O Phone, for Work, Home, and Other. See Chapter 20 to find out how to change field labels.

Many users requested that the E-mail address and the Web site address fields be placed on the main screen. These addresses, starting with version 5.0, now appear in Quadrant 3.

Notice that both the e-mail address and Web site labels appear differently than the other field labels. They're blue and underlined as most references to various Web addresses are. By clicking these labels, you can immediately send an e-mail message, or you can immediately launch this account's Web site.

You can have multiple e-mail addresses and multiple Web site addresses, but these are stored in the Details tab, as discussed in Chapter 6.

If you plan to have GoldMine automatically send faxes for you, do not change the label for the Fax field or use the field for another purpose. GoldMine can only retrieve the fax number from this field — you can't tell it to find the fax number somewhere else. See Chapter 15 for more details about faxing.

When you enter a phone number, you don't have to bother with typing punctuation. GoldMine automatically inserts parentheses and dashes for you. See Table 2-3 for a closer look at the fields in Quadrant 3.

Table 2-3	Fields in Quadrant 3	
Field Labels	*Lookup List*	*Can Use to Locate Records?*
Phone1	Y	Y
Ext	Y	N
Phone2	Y	N
Ext	Y	N
Phone3	Y	N
Ext	Y	N
Fax	Y	N
Ext	Y	N
E-mail	Y	Y
Web Site	Y	Y

Quadrant 4

Quadrant 4 contains the *key* (or *indexed*) fields. These key fields enable you to quickly sort to find particular records in the database. Out of the box, the key fields are labeled as shown in Table 2-4. But you may want to change the labels to better reflect the five most important pieces of information you want to collect on each account. I discuss changing field labels in Chapter 20.

Table 2-4	Fields in Quadrant 4	
Field Labels	*Lookup List*	*Can Use to Locate Records?*
Contact Type	Y	Y
Industry	Y	Y
Interest	Y	Y
Acct Mngr	Y	Y
Open	Y	Y

File folder tabs

Just beneath the main data section is a series of manila file folders, as shown in Figure 2-5. Each file folder tab contains an entire category of information. You can access any of the tabs by clicking the tab itself. I discuss these tabs in detail in Chapters 5 through 10.

In case you didn't see them, two more banks of tabs are hiding behind the first row and aren't quite so obvious. Just to the right of the Links tab is a small piece of another tab outlined in blue. This *tab-let* is a toggle switch you can use to move between the first and second bank of tabs. Click the tab-let to display the next bank of tabs. In the second bank, you find the Members, Tracks, Opptys, Projects, Partner, and PC tabs, as well as three blank tabs. The first two tabs are part of the Automated Processes feature; the next two tabs are from the Opportunity and Project Manager sections of GoldMine. (See Chapters 23 and 25 for more information about the Opportunity/Project Manager and Automated Processes.) The three blank tabs are reserved for use in future versions of GoldMine. (You can look, but you can't touch.)

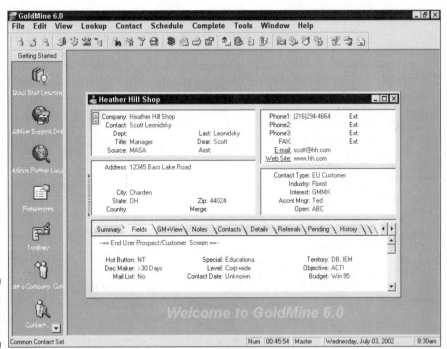

Figure 2-5:
The file
folder tabs.

Clicking the right-most tab, outlined in green on the main screen, brings you to a series of blank tabs. In fact, you see two banks of blank tabs here, which gives you a total of 18 additional areas that you can use for custom data. If you create custom field views or custom Detail views, they will be displayed in these two banks. See Chapters 20 through 22 for information about customizing GoldMine.

The right-most tab enables you to toggle between the third and fourth bank of tabs. Until you do some customizing, these two banks of tabs are completely empty.

GoldMine has an additional tool for navigating the banks of file folders. To the right of the tab-lets are left and right arrows. These arrows enable you to scroll sequentially through all the folders as if they were all in one bank.

The status line

The status line, shown in Figure 2-6, appears at the bottom of the GoldMine main screen and displays the following information:

- ✔ Name of the currently open database
- ✔ Status of the Caps Lock and Num Lock keys
- ✔ Name of logged-in user
- ✔ Date and time

Figure 2-6:
The status line provides useful information at a glance.

The status line also displays brief descriptions of the menu commands when a command is highlighted or, in the case of icons, when your cursor hovers over one.

Additional Navigational Tools

To be really comfortable with GoldMine, you need to strengthen whatever finger you use for the right mouse button, because you use it constantly in GoldMine. Browse windows, which are smaller informational windows or dialog boxes that pop up on demand, are another tool that must be in your arsenal. F2 lookups are an energy-saving device for those who hate to type, can't spell, or just want to do things consistently and efficiently. The following sections cover these tools in turn.

Getting the hang of the right mouse button

Back in the early days, when DOS was king, you used the F2 key to call for help or to get more information. In Windows, you use the right mouse button for this function. In GoldMine, you can use whichever method you prefer. Clicking the right mouse button (right-clicking) or pressing the F2 key gives you the same result.

It isn't always obvious in GoldMine, but in many situations (such as accessing a lookup list from a field, getting to a calendar, and so on) you can move deeper into your data by right-clicking. So when in doubt, try a right-click. It can't hurt, and it usually results in something good. For example, follow these steps to find additional information and choices:

1. **Click an existing tab to open it.**
2. **Right-click in the blank space.**
3. **Choose a selection from the menu that appears.**

Thanks, just window shopping

Many of the windows in GoldMine lead you to *browse windows,* which contain lists of data, such as names, activities, and reports. These lists are arranged in a columnar format. Figure 2-7 shows a typical browse window (or simply a dialog box with data) from the resource section of GoldMine. (The resource section allows you to keep a list of all your company resources, such as vehicles, projectors, training facilities, and so on that you may want to schedule, and you can see all these resources at a glance by using the browse window.)

Figure 2-7:
See your
resources at
a glance in
a browse
window.

Each browse window has a scroll bar on the right side that enables you to scroll though the data quickly. You can drag the scroll box up or down to reposition your view of the data, or you can scroll through the data at a more leisurely pace by clicking the up- and down-arrow buttons.

You can generally enter additional listings in a browse window by clicking the New button; you can delete entries with the Delete button; and you can edit entries by clicking Edit.

Using F2 lookups

Most of the standard fields in GoldMine, and all the custom fields you will ever build, have an F2 lookup list associated with them. This lookup list displays data selections that are preset and easily customizable. In GoldMine, the F2 lookup list is considered a special browser window that pops up from a data field when you press the F2 key. A typical F2 lookup list is shown in Figure 2-8. You can also click the arrow positioned just to the right of the field for yet another way to access the lookup list.

The F2 key is a holdover from the long-gone days of DOS, and you may find it more convenient to right-click instead of pressing the F2 key. Either way, you get the exact same lookup list. Lookup lists are time and energy savers, so try to use them whenever they're available. Here are some of the obvious reasons to use lookup lists:

✔ You type less.

✔ Information is always spelled the same way, providing consistency. This is especially important when you search for data or run reports that are sorted.

✔ Your staff can't make up unique responses that no one else knows about because you can restrict responses to only those official responses already in the lookup list.

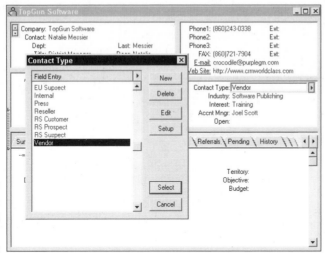

Figure 2-8:
A typical F2
lookup list.

You should restrict your users' ability to add, edit, or delete F2 lookup lists, or else you'll find that everyone in your company makes up his or her own favorite entries. I discuss the methods for restricting access to altering lookup lists in Chapter 3.

GoldMine features a special tool to enable you to know when a lookup list is available. Each field that contains a lookup list has a right arrow attached to the right side of the data area. In a nutshell, if it makes sense for a field to have a lookup list, it does. Sometimes, a field has a lookup list even when it doesn't make sense, like for the Address and Phone fields. You can also refer to Tables 2-1 through 2-4, earlier in this chapter, to see whether a particular field has a lookup list.

If you would like to see a lookup list in action, position your cursor in the Title field and right-click or click the right arrow adjacent to the field. You immediately see a lookup list with a variety of titles.

You can navigate the lookup list by

✔ Pressing the up- and down-arrow keys

✔ Pressing the Tab key

✔ Pointing at an entry with the mouse cursor

✔ Typing the first character (or two) of the choice you want

After you have highlighted your choice, click the Select button. Voilà! Your selection is automatically entered into the data field.

You (or whoever else is authorized to) can easily maintain lookup lists. Too many cooks stirring the pot here will definitely cause chaos. See Chapter 21 for details on customizing your lookup lists. For now, just be sure to use them whenever possible.

Chapter 3

Setting User Preferences

· ·

· ·

*T*he preferences settings in GoldMine enable you to put your own stamp on your copy of the software. If you're one of those eager beavers who just has to get right at it, you can probably skip this chapter. Read it later, or maybe never. Most of GoldMine works fine without your ever touching the settings.

On the other hand, if you're serious about making GoldMine work for you rather than the other way around, this is the chapter for you. In this chapter, you discover many interesting and powerful parameters you can set, and you don't need any programming knowledge to do so.

You can control hundreds of settings and options in GoldMine. Many of them deal with pretty technical stuff, however, so I skip over some of those in favor of the most commonly used and important settings.

You can access all user preferences through the toolbar by choosing Edit⇨Preferences, which gives you access to 14 separate tabs. You can also get to the Preferences dialog box by using the taskbar. Behind each door are some of the secret tricks that GoldMine dealers use to set things up.

Personal Preferences

If you click the Personal tab, you see a dialog box like the one shown in Figure 3-1. The Personal tab is one of the simplest of the preference tabs and enables you to see your user name and full name, and to change your title, department, phone number, and fax number. In addition, by clicking the Change Password button, you can create a new password for yourself, thus preventing the resident office snoop from checking out too much of your stuff.

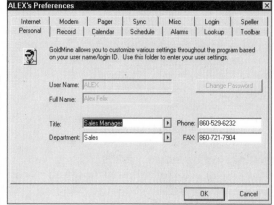

Figure 3-1:
Enter your
personal
information
on the
Personal
tab.

Be sure to use upper- and lowercase letters when entering your title and department, because you may want to use these later as part of your e-mail signature file.

You can move to another level of personal preferences and change your password by clicking the Change Password button from the Personal Preferences dialog box. In the dialog box that appears, type your current password in the Current Password text box. (Presumably, you know this password, or you wouldn't have been able to log on to GoldMine in the first place.) Then press the Tab key and type a new password in the New Password text box. GoldMine asks you to confirm your new password by retyping it in the New Password Again text box.

Keep your GoldMine password cryptic and short, or you may become annoyed if you have to enter something long and complicated every time you start GoldMine.

The whole point to password protecting GoldMine is that your data is safe because the password is secret, which means that no one else can access your data. The downside to passwords is that if you forget yours, you're going to be doing some reinstalling to get back to your data. You may want to write down your password and keep it in a safe place, such as in a locked cabinet in your office, or, like most people, on a sticky note stuck to your monitor.

Record Preferences

You can click the Record tab to customize the appearance of the main screen (see Figure 3-2). Two radio buttons enable you to set the shading of the screen background. You have two choices, either dark or light background, and the one you choose is purely a matter of your personal taste. Give each a try.

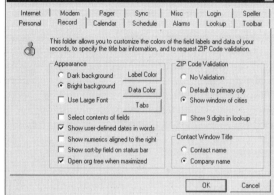

Figure 3-2:
Change
the main
screen's
appearance
on the
Record tab.

GoldMine also gives you a choice on the font size. Selecting the Use Large Font check box makes the characters larger on-screen. If your eyesight isn't quite what it used to be, using large fonts may be the best choice for you. You do pay a small price for this choice, however, because you can't see quite as many lines in your browse windows as you can see with small fonts.

You can also change the colors that labels and data appear in by clicking the Label Colors or Data Colors buttons on the Record Preferences dialog box. Be sure to use contrasting colors to distinguish the labels and data from the background. You can have some real fun by setting the labels and data to the exact same color as the background. Please don't actually do this because it renders everything invisible!

Following the Label Colors and Data Colors buttons, you see five check boxes that you can check to specify how data is entered or displayed:

✔ **Select Contents of Fields:** If this box is checked when you enter a data field, the existing data is highlighted, and whatever you type immediately overwrites the existing data. If this box is not checked, your new data is appended automatically to the existing data. Generally, you should leave this box checked.

✔ **Show User-defined Dates in Words:** This option applies only to user-defined fields, not to standard date fields such as those that appear in your Pending or History tabs. If you check this box, a typical date appears as Apr 1, 03. If this box is not checked, the same date appears as 4/1/03. Take your pick.

✔ **Show Numerics Aligned to the Right:** If you have a bunch of fields with numeric entries, sometimes the numbers are easier to read right-justified. Checking this box does just that for you.

✔ **Show Sort-by Field on the Status Bar:** If you check this box, the currently active index appears on the status bar.

✔ **Open Org Tree When Maximized:** Don't select this option unless you plan to make major and frequent use of the Org Tree system. The Org (Organizational) Tree is a system to connect or relate separate records in GoldMine to one another. For example, if you have separate records for each location of Burger King, you might use the Org Tree to show how they are each related. The Org Tree, which was revised in version 5.7 and enhanced again in version 6.0, is discussed in detail in Chapter 7.

The next section of the Record Preferences dialog box enables you to determine how the system deals with entering zip codes. If you select the No Validation radio button, you then have to type the city, state, and zip code. Don't do this.

Behind the scenes, GoldMine builds a zip code database for you as you enter records. GoldMine builds on its zip code file and continues figuring out what city goes with what zip code. This is a great feature; the second time you enter a record from the same zip code, GoldMine automatically fills in the city and state for you.

You can buy several ready-made zip code files that will save you considerable effort. Check either the FrontRange Web site or www.ccc24k.com.

Make sure you select the Show Window of Cities radio button. With this option selected, you can

✔ Enter the zip code, and then enter the city and state. GoldMine automatically fills in the city and state if the city and state are unique.

✔ If multiple choices are possible, GoldMine displays a browse window so that you can select the correct city and state.

Calendar Preferences

When you click the Calendar tab to display the Calendar Preferences dialog box, most of the choices are pretty self-explanatory. You can set up GoldMine to reflect your normal working hours and the days of the week you usually work. These choices affect how your calendar is displayed, as shown in Figure 3-3.

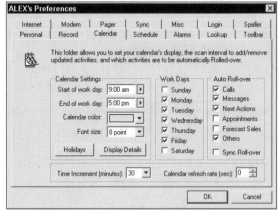

Figure 3-3:
Tell
GoldMine
what your
regular
work
schedule is
on the
Calendar
tab.

Click the Holidays button, and on the dialog box that appears, enter company holidays so that GoldMine won't schedule activities on those days. If you don't have Master access rights, ask your system administrator to take care of this task. The holidays are entered only once and are then in place in the schedule for everyone in the company.

You can actually schedule holidays based on the country in which you operate, as well as schedule personal holidays, such as your birthday or anniversary.

If you're like me, you may find that the Auto Roll-over options are some of the most significant ones available on the Calendar Preferences dialog box. Many are the days when I come into the office and have an overwhelming number of phone calls scheduled for me. Try as I might, I never seem to be able to make them all. If I do manage to make most of them, I want the remaining ones to be on my schedule for the next day. That's exactly what Auto Roll-over does. It takes activities that you have not completed by the end of a particular day and moves them to the next day's schedule. It works very well. Maybe *too* well — I now have 1,712 items on my activity list for tomorrow. I will be more diligent tomorrow, and I'm sure I'll get them finished.

You should select all the Auto Roll-over options except auto-forwarding of appointments. Just because you didn't make it to that appointment with the IRS yesterday at 2:00 p.m. doesn't mean that you should show up there today at 2:00 p.m. (Well, maybe you should, but then again, I'm not a qualified tax adviser.)

Schedule Preferences

When you click the Schedule tab, the Schedule Preferences dialog box appears, as shown in Figure 3-4. This dialog box is fairly simple and offers you the following five check boxes:

Figure 3-4:
Set up your preferences for scheduling activities on the Schedule tab.

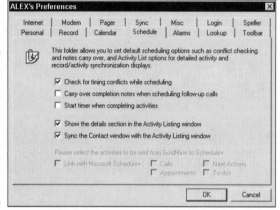

✔ **Check for Timing Conflicts While Scheduling:** As long as you have this check box selected, GoldMine warns you if you schedule yourself for two activities at the same time. Scheduling conflicts usually aren't an issue if you regularly schedule directly from the Calendar as I recommend, but selecting this option can't hurt.

✔ **Carry-over Completion Notes When Scheduling Follow-up Calls:** When you complete an activity and schedule a follow-up activity from the completion window, your notes are carried over to the follow-up activity if you have this option selected. I recommend that you select this one.

✔ **Start Timer When Completing Activities:** This option may be useful if you're tracking a telemarketing effort. In most cases, however, you don't need to select it.

✔ **Show the Details Section in the Activity Listing Window:** If you select this option, additional data fields appear at the bottom of the Activity Listing window. I recommend that you select this option.

✔ **Sync the Contact Window with the Activity Listing Window:** If you select this option and your monitor has an adequate resolution (greater than 640 x 480), you can see the related contact record when you highlight an item from the Activity List. I use this option also.

Alarms Preferences

When you click the Alarms tab, you see the Alarms Preferences dialog box, as shown in Figure 3-5. This dialog box contains the following options (as well as a few more esoteric ones that I intentionally leave out):

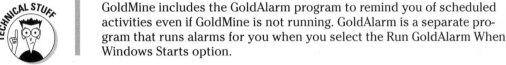

Figure 3-5:
Set up how GoldMine alerts you on the Alarms tab.

✔ **Disable Alarms:** Selecting this option turns off your alarms so that GoldMine doesn't remind you to keep your dentist appointment. Assuming that you use GoldMine to help keep you organized, selecting this option is counterproductive. My advice: Do not disable your alarms.

✔ **Pop-up Alarms:** By default, GoldMine displays alarms in a pop-up window on the right side of the screen. You can't miss one when it's triggered, and sometimes it becomes annoying when you get a barrage of alarms. You may want to consider a compromise solution, which is to have the alarm appear in the taskbar.

✔ **Alarms Default Lead Time:** The amount of time (in minutes) before a scheduled activity that the alarm window appears on-screen. To set the alarm to appear 15 minutes before each activity, type **15** in this field. Of course, 15 minutes is not always appropriate, so you can adjust this setting manually for every activity. Mine is set to 10 minutes, which usually works for me.

GoldMine includes the GoldAlarm program to remind you of scheduled activities even if GoldMine is not running. GoldAlarm is a separate program that runs alarms for you when you select the Run GoldAlarm When Windows Starts option.

✔ **When I Ignore Alarms, Snooze the Ignored Alarms for X Minutes:** This option works like the Snooze button on an alarm clock. If you ignore the alarms, they stop for a little while and then alert you again in a designated amount of time. The default snooze value is three minutes, but you can set it for whatever amount seems right to you.

✔ **Page Me with the Alarm When Not Acknowledged within X Minutes:** This option sets GoldMine to call your pager if you do not respond to an alarm within the specified number of minutes. Obviously, this option is valuable only if you have an alphanumeric pager set to work with GoldMine. The default value is 10 minutes. To disable this option, leave the check box blank.

✔ **Play Alarm Sound File:** This option sets GoldMine to play the .WAV sound file entered in the field to the right of the option. Windows comes with a number of .WAV files that you can use if you want your alarm to play something other than the standard alarm sound.

Lookup Preferences

If you click the Lookup tab, the Lookup Preferences dialog box appears, as shown in Figure 3-6. This dialog box deals with some of the parameters involved in helping you locate a particular record in GoldMine.

One option on this dialog box that you want to be sure is *not* checked is the Appear in 'Shrunken' Mode When Finding By option. If you select this option, it means that you have to click the Expand button every time you do a search for a record. That seems like extra work to me, so I recommend leaving this option unchecked.

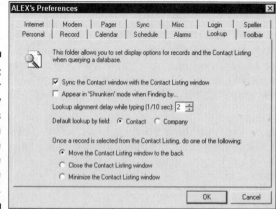

Figure 3-6:
Set up your
display
options
when
querying the
database
on the
Lookup tab.

Toolbar Preferences

The toolbar is near the top of the screen, where the GoldMine icons appear. If you choose the Toolbar tab, the Toolbar Preferences dialog box appears, as shown in Figure 3-7. You can regulate how the toolbar icons look on-screen by choosing various toolbar settings.

GoldMine provides lots of toolbar icons, and their uses are not always immediately obvious. Selecting the Basic, Standard, or Advanced radio buttons, respectively, provides you with an ever-increasing number of icons — probably more than you want or need. To start with a good selection of toolbar icons, choose the Basic option.

If you consider yourself to be toolbar-challenged, help is available. Choose the Show Button Text option, and GoldMine adds a one- or two-word explanation within each icon. Select this setting if you're uncomfortable with what some icons do. Sure, you sacrifice some screen space, but you also begin to figure out when to use a particular icon.

When you think that you know what most of the icons do (this may take a few days), deselect the Show Button Text option and select the Show Status Bar Help option. Then each time you hover your cursor over an icon, you see a short phrase displayed on the status bar to remind you what the icon is for. The icons are smaller without button text, which leaves more room on the screen for data.

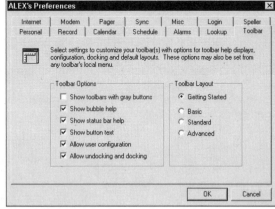

Figure 3-7:
Choose
how you
want the
toolbar to
appear
on the
Toolbar tab.

Internet Preferences

GoldMine plays very nicely with the Internet. In fact, working with the Internet is one of the most important aspects of using GoldMine.

If you click the Internet tab, the Internet Preferences dialog box appears. The options you can access on the Internet Preferences dialog box can be rather technical, but they are also critical.

Before you can use GoldMine with the Internet, you must sign up with an Internet Service Provider (ISP); you can choose a regional, national, or international provider. One important consideration when deciding on an ISP is how much, and where, you travel. If you want to avoid long-distance charges when you travel, hook up with a provider that has local coverage in the places you travel to most often.

Your ISP can provide you with most of the information you need to fill out your Internet Preferences. Figure 3-8 shows some sample entries for these fields.

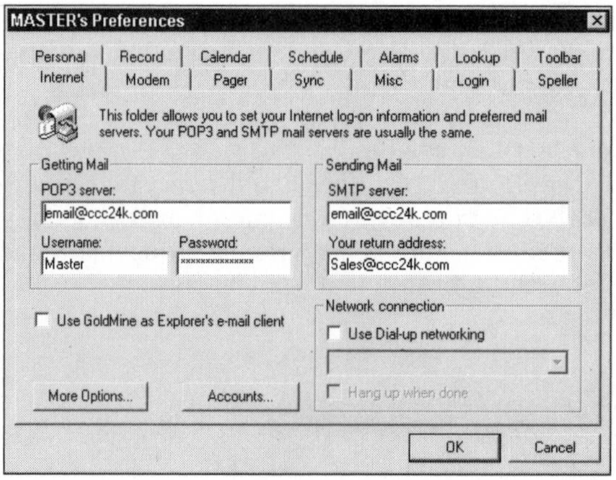

Figure 3-8:
Tell GoldMine where to find your e-mail servers on the Internet tab.

The Network Connection section determines how GoldMine connects to the Internet. If you use another program, such as Internet Explorer or Netscape Navigator for your Internet connection, you don't have to select the Use Dial-up Networking option; if you want GoldMine to dial in and make the connection, however, select this option.

Modem Preferences

If you click the Modem tab, the Modem Preferences dialog box appears, as shown in Figure 3-9. The options on the Modem Preferences dialog box are most significant for those users who want GoldMine to actually dial the telephone based on a phone number in a contact record. If you're sitting at home with a simple telephone and telephone line, or if you're in an office where you have your own line, this feature is simple and useful.

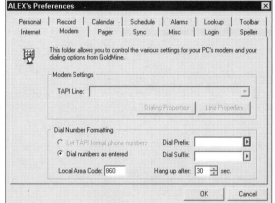

Figure 3-9:
Set up your
dialing
preferences
on the
Modem tab.

If your office has a central telephone system with multiple lines, however, you may need some technical help, along with additional hardware and software, to make GoldMine handle the dialing for you. I just dial my phone the old-fashioned way, by pushing the buttons myself.

If you're determined to implement this auto-dialing feature, and if you're running GoldMine under Windows 95 or beyond and have a modem installed in your computer, you shouldn't have to mess with the Dialing Properties, the Line Properties, or any other settings on this dialog box. The operating system sets these for you automatically.

Miscellaneous Preferences

If you click the Miscellaneous tab, the Miscellaneous Preferences dialog box appears, as shown in Figure 3-10. This dialog box starts with four check boxes. The first box, the Show 'What's New' in the InfoCenter When Logging In option, is the most important one. Be sure to select it. This option ensures that you're notified immediately when any issues, news, or policies are entered into your company's InfoCenter. (See Chapter 17 for more specifics on the InfoCenter.) You can leave the other three choices as they are.

The EPOCH Year field deals with the old Y2K issue. GoldMine handles this issue by using an *EPOCH year,* the year that determines what century GoldMine thinks a particular two-digit year belongs in. For example, with the EPOCH year set as 50, GoldMine places any two-digit year from 00–49 in the 21st century (2000–2049) and any two-digit year from 50–99 in the 20th century (1950–1999). Unless you have a compelling reason to change it, leave 50 in this field.

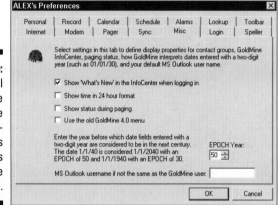

Figure 3-10:
Tell
GoldMine
your time
and miscel-
laneous
preferences
on the
Misc tab.

Login Preferences

If you click the Login tab, the Login Preferences dialog box appears.

The settings on the Login Preferences dialog box apply to everyone on your network, and your GoldMine administrator should establish the login settings. You probably shouldn't change any of the other Login Preferences options. The other parameters are meant to be used in a network environment and are set by the GoldMine administrator. (But if you're working alone with a single user license, *you* are the GoldMine administrator!)

You can elect to bypass the login banner only if you're not using a password. If you do select this option, GoldMine doesn't pause at the initial logon dialog box but goes directly to the main data screen. This is a small timesaver if you're not worried about security issues.

Speller Preferences

Finally, in version 6.0, GoldMine gave in to all those users who just can't spell or aren't the greatest typists. (Sorry, but GoldMine can't help you yet if you're grammatically challenged.) The most recent addition to preferences settings now includes a series of settings for controlling how you want GoldMine to spell check your various notepads and e-mails. Specifically, GoldMine now enables you to check the spelling in all the activity-related notepads.

Figure 3-11 illustrates the settings that I use and that I recommend for most users. The following list describes what the options do when the spell check runs:

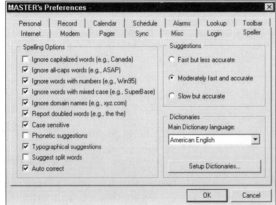

Figure 3-11:
Setting your
spelling
parameters
on the
Speller tab.

- ✔ **Ignore Capitalized Words:** Skips any words that begin with a capital letter. Use this option if your text typically contains many proper names.

- ✔ **Ignore All-Caps Words:** Ignores words containing all capital letters. Particularly in the high-tech and medical fields, it might be worthwhile to ignore things like HTML and EKG because roughly half the words people in these fields use are acronyms.

- ✔ **Ignore Words with Numbers:** Skips over words containing embedded numbers, such as Win98. Mixing numbers in with words is also a popular specialty of the high-tech industry.

- ✔ **Ignore Words with Mixed Case:** Skips any words containing an unusual mixture of upper- and lowercase letters, such as GoldMine.

- ✔ **Ignore Domain Names:** Ignores any words that appear to be Internet domain names (such as `www.ccc24k.com`).

    Generally, I have the spell checker ignore all kinds of words that have unusual capitalization or punctuation. There are just too many different kinds of words like this, particularly for those of us in the high-tech field. Simple capitalized words aren't so strange, so I allow the spell checker to do its thing on those words.

You can build your own dictionary of strange words you commonly use. If you do this religiously, it might then make sense to deselect some of the ignoring options.

✔ **Report Doubled Words:** Reports any word appearing twice in a row. I have a habit of typing "the the" often, so I select this option.

✔ **Case Sensitive:** Makes a distinction between capitalized and lowercase words. For example, "france" is considered different from "France," so "france" would be reported as a misspelling. When the option is disabled, "france" and "France" are considered identical. Selecting this option noticeably slows the spell checker.

✔ **Phonetic Suggestions:** Suggests alternative spellings based on phonetic (sounds-like) similarity to the misspelled word. This option tends to improve suggestions for badly misspelled words. Enabling this option increases the time required to locate suggestions.

Note that either Phonetic Suggestions or the Typographical Suggestions option must be selected, or GoldMine offers no spelling suggestions.

✔ **Typographical Suggestions:** Makes suggestions based on typographical (looks-like) similarity to the misspelled word. This option is appropriate for people who are generally good spellers — like me, of coarse.

✔ **Suggest Split Words:** Suggests two separate words as replacements for a misspelling containing two joined words. For example, the spell checker suggests "are you" to replace "areyou."

✔ **Auto Correct:** Changes words marked with "Auto Change" actions automatically are changed to their specified replacements. When this option is deselected, GoldMine prompts you before it changes the words.

✔ **Main Dictionary Language:** Allows you to set the language of the main dictionary used to check spelling. The list shows only languages for dictionaries installed on your system. To check spelling in a language other than English, select the language from the list.

✔ **Suggestions:** Determines the speed and accuracy of the initial search for suggested replacements for misspelled words. When a misspelled word is found, a search is automatically made for suggestions. Clicking the Suggest button in the Check-Spelling dialog box causes an increasingly more accurate (but slower) search for suggestions. My preference is faster *and* more accurate, but that one isn't offered yet.

Part II
Managing Contacts

The 5th Wave   By Rich Tennant

"Your database is beyond repair, but before I tell you our backup recommendation, let me ask you a question. How many index cards do you think will fit on the walls of your computer room?"

In this part . . .

The real point of GoldMine is the management of all your accounts. Assuming you have customers, clients, or accounts, this part of the book gives you a solid feel for entering and managing all the basic contact information in GoldMine.

How and when to enter free-form notes is an art form that may help keep you out of trouble later. Additional contacts that seem important enough to keep track of can be kept within the secondary contact system or managed within the newly enhanced Organization Chart. Random tidbits can be housed in the Details section. The Referral section allows you to relate one account to one or to many others.

Chapter 4

Creating and Viewing Client Records

In This Chapter

▶ Creating records

▶ Locating records

▶ Working with custom fields

▶ Grouping custom fields into views

*I*f you actively use GoldMine in your business, you probably need to create new records just about every day. And you may need to quickly locate existing records in the database many times each day. In this chapter, you find out how to do these tasks efficiently.

Out of the box, GoldMine is a terrific general contact-management system. But the developers don't know the details of your business, so they can't think of every field you may require. They're smart enough, however, to give you the ability to create these fields yourself. After you create fields, you can use your custom fields the same way you use all other fields. In this chapter, I show you how to enter a new record manually.

Creating a New Record

A sure sign of a growing, healthy business is a steady increase in the number of records in its database. You can add new records to your GoldMine database in the following ways:

 ✔ Manually type the information

 ✔ Import the information from various other databases (see Chapter 22)

 ✔ Synchronize the information from other GoldMine databases (see Chapter 24)

In most toolbar configurations, you can click the left-most icon, New Record, to produce the New Company and Contact dialog box that enables you to begin a new record, as shown in Figure 4-1.

Figure 4-1:
Create a
new record
in the New
Company
and Contact
dialog box.

The first two fields that you see in Figure 4-1 are the Company name and main contact person's full name (Contact). When you enter information into these fields, type them in upper- and lowercase letters. You may eventually want to send this data directly to your word processor to use the information in a letter, and your word processor will display them exactly as you typed them into the database. I discuss this topic in Chapter 13. Most people use a combination of capital letters and lowercase letters for contact and address information in a letter, so type your field names in GoldMine that way.

If you forget to use standard, consistent capitalization when you enter data, don't panic. The software police will not come looking for you, and you won't suddenly be assaulted by horrendous error messages. However, your letter will surely look less personal. Your client may recognize that the letter was computer-generated and figure that no human being even touched it. So spend a little time properly capitalizing your entries, and you may benefit from some warm, fuzzy feelings from your clients.

Dealing with Jr., Sr., and III

GoldMine tries to determine automatically the last name of a contact by looking at the name you enter in the Contact field. It takes the last full word you type, assumes that's the last name, and places it in the Last field on the main screen. This works fine if you type a simple name, such as **Jim Smith**. But if you type **Jim Smith, Jr.**, GoldMine mistakes **Jr.** for the last name and puts it in the Last field.

I often use the Last field to look up records in the database, and it's not helpful to have this field cluttered with hundreds of *Jr.*s rather than actual last names. The solution to this dilemma is to type the full name in the Contact field, including *Jr.* or *Sr.*; then when you return to the main screen, manually correct the Last field by changing *Jr.* or *Sr.* to the actual last name of the contact.

Entering U.S. telephone numbers

The Phone number field holds the primary telephone number for the client. Every telephone number can also include an associated extension of up to six characters. Six digits is the limit, even though it looks like more space than that is available.

Type the 10 digits of the area code and telephone number without parentheses, dashes, or any other punctuation. GoldMine automatically applies the format (909) 792-8636 to a U.S. telephone number.

You don't do any harm if you go ahead and type the punctuation; you're just working harder than you have to.

Entering telephone numbers for the rest of the world

Other countries use a variety of telephone number formats, so things get a little trickier when you're entering telephone numbers for clients outside the U.S.

To enter a telephone number in a format other than the standard U.S. format, select the International Format check box on this dialog box. After selecting International Format, you can type the phone number any way you want, and GoldMine applies no additional formatting. The field can hold up to 20 characters, not including the extension field.

The extension field has one of those right-arrow buttons next to it, indicating that it has a lookup list. The list is taken from the Extension field associated with Phone1 on the main screen. If you modify that lookup list on the main screen, those changes also appear on the Add a New Record dialog box.

Database terminology

The following are definitions of terms that relate to databases:

Bit: A single digit, either a 1 or a 0, and the basic building block for a byte.

Byte: A sequence of 8 bits making up one character (for example, a, D, 6, ?, or -).

Database: A group of files containing related information. A GoldMine database contains many files. For example, the database contains files for basic contact information (CONTACT1.DBF and CONTACT2.DBF) as well as files containing activity information (CAL.DBF and CONTSUPP.DBF). In fact, many files make up each database, and GoldMine can even manage multiple databases for you.

Field: A group of characters that means something, for example, a last name or an address. GoldMine gives fields names such as Contact, Phone1, Zip Code, and so on.

Record: A record is synonymous with an account in GoldMine. Sometimes, a record is also called a contact record. All the information relating to one person is stored in one account. Multiple secondary contacts can be linked to a record, or they can occupy their own records that may or may not be linked to the primary contact's record.

File: A group of logically connected fields stored together on a floppy drive or a hard drive. GoldMine stores all your pending activities together in one file.

E-mail addresses — you've got to collect 'em

Just like the fax machine, e-mail is here to stay. In fact, it's not hard to argue that, for many businesses, e-mail is rapidly overtaking the fax machine as the communication device of choice. Your clients likely have an e-mail address (or two or three). Making use of this technology is not just important, it's essential. Fortunately, GoldMine enables you to collect, store, and use e-mail addresses easily. E-mailing is discussed in Chapter 14.

If you religiously gather e-mail addresses for every new and existing account, you can send individual e-mails, broadcast e-mails, attached documents, photos, and almost anything else that is critical to business communication. But first you have to obtain the addresses and put them in the database.

Type the client's main e-mail address in the E-mail field on this dialog box; then leave the dialog box by clicking the OK button.

Entering Web site addresses

The bottom-most field on the Add a New Record dialog box enables you to enter your client's Web site. This address is clearly different from the client's e-mail address. The Web site defines the URL or address of the company's Web page.

If you enter the Web site address, GoldMine can easily direct you or any of your co-workers to this client's Web site. That is, you can pull up the client's Web page right from GoldMine.

You can enter only one Web site address on this dialog box. If a client has multiple Web sites, you can enter additional sites later within the Details tab of the main screen. See Chapter 6 for more information on using the Details tab.

Checking for duplicate records

As you enter new records into GoldMine, asking it to search for duplicate records is useful. GoldMine checks for you, based on up to four fields:

- ✔ Phone number
- ✔ E-mail address
- ✔ Contact name
- ✔ Company name

I suggest that you select both the Phone number and the E-mail address. If you enter either a phone number or an e-mail address that exactly matches one that already exists in your database, GoldMine notifies you before it adds your new record (but annoyingly only after you enter all the information into the Add a New Record dialog box), and then you have an opportunity to decide whether to proceed.

Contact name and Company name work a little differently. GoldMine checks to see whether what you just entered matches the beginning of any existing contact or company name. For example, if you enter **Computer**, the system warns you if it finds an existing record with Computer Control Corporation in the Company name field. This result may be desirable, or maybe not. The Contact name field works the same way. Try it; you can always turn off this feature if it aggravates you when you're really doing what you intended to do in the first place.

If you do create some duplicate records, you can combine them by using the merge/purge utility. You can find that utility on the Tools main menu. Selecting Merge/Purge Records brings you to the wizard that walks you through the entire procedure.

As soon as you click OK, you return to the GoldMine main screen. Your new record has now been created, and you can continue with all the additional fields on the main screen.

E-mail addresses never have spaces in them. When in doubt, leave out the space; it doesn't belong there. Some companies separate portions of their e-mail addresses with an underscore character (_). This is okay, although a bit confusing at times. Make sure that you have an @ sign somewhere in the middle of the address.

Finding a Record in Your Database

As you use GoldMine, the task you will probably find yourself doing most frequently is finding a record. Scheduling activities, writing notes, or checking a client's history requires you to look up the correct record. And every time the phone rings, you may want to quickly check the caller's record.

If you're like me, you get lots of calls every day. Some of these calls come from a person who clearly knows who I am, but for the life of me, I can't recall who he or she is. The last thing I want the mystery caller to know is that I don't remember him or her. So I sometimes need to quickly and quietly find a client's record while I'm saying hello and making small talk. With a little practice, you can find any record, no matter how many are in your database, in just a few seconds.

The official way to find a record

The official GoldMine User's Guide tells you to select the Find Contact icon from the main toolbar. From there, you can select the field you want to use to locate a record. Frankly, this method is just too slow for me. See the next section for my preferred method.

The secret and fast way to find a record

About half the fields on the main screen allow you to point your mouse at the *label* and double-click, which opens a browse window. For example, if you double-click the Last label, a browse window, like the one shown in Figure 4-2, appears. This browse window is actually called the Search Center, which is brand new in version 6.0. In the Search Center, you see a partial listing of your entire database sorted by last name.

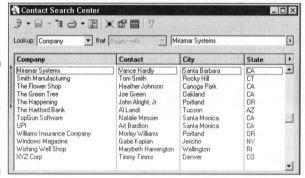

Figure 4-2:
Find records quickly by using the Search Center.

In order for the browse window to appear, be sure to point at and double-click the field label — not the text box where you enter data.

Refer to Tables 2-1 through 2-4 in Chapter 2 to see which fields display a browse window when you double-click the field label. In these tables, the fields with a Y in the "Can Use to Locate Records?" column are candidates for this trick. The fields I find most useful are Last, Company, and Contact.

The first field, Lookup, should be the same field you decided to Search on. You can change your search field here by selecting a different field from the Lookup drop-down list. In the blank space to the right type the first letter, the browse window positions itself at the first record in which the Last field begins with the letter you typed.

If a rectangular box is already drawn around the correct record, simply double-click it. If you aren't positioned on the record you're looking for, but you can see it nearby, move your cursor to it and double-click. If you can't even see the correct record on-screen, it means that lots of last names begin with the letter you just entered. Type another character or two of the last name. Keep typing until you see the record you want; then double-click it.

By using this method, you can grab any record you want within a few seconds, but you may have to practice a bit until you're comfortable and fast.

If you can't find the record, try using another field, such as Company or Contact. Remember that the Contact field begins with the person's first name, so that's what you have to search for. If all else fails, perhaps the record doesn't exist in your database. You may have to create it from scratch.

Using a Custom Field

Custom fields are fields that you, someone in your company, or your GoldMine dealer set up to meet your organization's specific needs. They don't come standard; they are developed because you need to track some particular data.

If you have more than a few custom fields, you can group them into *custom field views*. Each view is set up with a separate file folder tab and may have its own access rights. Consequently, certain people or groups of people may not be able to see or edit the data in a particular field view.

Who needs custom fields anyway?

Almost every business needs to track some unique information. GoldMine has all the common fields that most every business needs to use. Your business is probably a little different from mine, so you may need some fields that I don't need.

Each department in your organization probably tracks different information. The following lists show some examples of information particular departments may track:

✔ **Accounting department**
- Credit limit
- Credit terms

✔ **Marketing department**
- Related interests
- Will be a reference (Y/N)
- Wants newsletter (Y/N)

✔ **Sales department**
- Competition
- Purchases YTD
- Budget cycle

How custom fields get on-screen

Placing custom fields on-screen takes some design effort. Usually, an experienced GoldMine dealer handles this process, but nothing prevents you from doing it yourself.

Interview some people from the departments that use GoldMine to determine which custom fields you may need to add to your program. Review all the reports they currently use and any reports they plan to implement in the future. Reports always provide good clues as to what fields need to be available in the database. Ask as many questions as you can.

GoldMine provides three field types: numbers, text, and date. When you create a custom field, you must define the field type, field length, F2 lookup list, and access rights for the field.

Accessing field views

GoldMine is capable of holding hundreds of custom fields. More than ten or so, however, becomes unmanageable if they aren't segregated into logical groups. These groups are called *views,* and each view is associated with its own tab. Each tab resides in either Bank 3 or in Bank 4 of the File Folders. You can get there by toggling the right-most tab-let on the main screen.

While GoldMine 5.7 and beyond allow you to add up to about 400 custom fields, you could encounter a problem if you ever upgrade to GoldMine's FrontOffice Sales and Marketing System. This system is based on SQL and has a limit of about 255 custom fields. Quite a few people get tripped up by this issue, so consider limiting yourself to fewer than 255 extra fields if at all possible.

Particular access rights are often assigned to an entire view. For example, the Accounting view may have data that the marketing department doesn't need to see or change.

If your system has any custom field views, you access them by following these steps:

1. **Click the Fields tab.**

2. **Position the cursor anywhere in the area below the tab and right-click.**

   A selection window appears, listing all the additional field views.

3. **Select the appropriate field view from the first section of the selection window, as shown in Figure 4-3.**

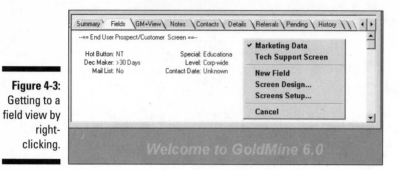

Figure 4-3:
Getting to a
field view by
right-
clicking.

Chapter 5

Entering Notes and Secondary Contacts

● ●

In This Chapter

▶ Adding notes to client records

▶ Entering secondary contacts

▶ Editing secondary contacts

● ●

*Y*ou can use GoldMine to maintain a complete audit trail of everything that has ever happened with each of your accounts. You use the notepad to record your notes about each of your accounts. Sometimes, this audit trail can get you out of trouble. Better yet, if you use it consistently, it can keep you from getting into trouble in the first place. The stark reality, however, is that you have to make it a habit to type in notes if you are to reap the benefits. That means you actually have to enter your notes every time you complete an activity. And remembering to enter your notes may be the hardest part.

In this chapter, you find a discussion of the main Notes and Contacts tabs. Every record in GoldMine contains a series of file folder tabs in the lower third of the main screen. In "The Main Notepad" section of this chapter, you discover how to view existing notes, how to enter new notes, and more importantly, what notes you should actually put there.

You find out how to find additional people listed in the Contacts tab and how to enter new or edit existing information in this chapter. You also discover how to determine when to use the Contacts section and when to create a separate record.

The Main Notepad

The fourth tab on the main menu is labeled Notes. When you click this tab for the first time in a particular record, the main notepad appears, completely blank. The main notepad, shown in Figure 5-1, is sitting there waiting for you to enter as much as 32K of text.

Figure 5-1:
The main
notepad.

What does 32K of space really mean? It's the equivalent of about eight single-spaced, typewritten pages. For most people, that's more than enough space to handle all the notes they ever need to take. And remember that you have eight pages for each and every record in your database. On the status bar, GoldMine keeps a running total of the number of characters that have been entered in the notepad for that particular record.

If you type lots of notes for a particular record, you won't be able to see them all on-screen at the same time. Use the scroll arrows on the right to scroll through the notepad.

What to put in the main notepad

So what notes go in the main notepad? GoldMine contains many different notepads. In fact, a similar notepad is associated with every activity that you schedule and/or complete. You should particularly understand the distinction between the main notepad and those in the scheduled and completed activities sections. See Chapters 8 through 10 for more details.

You should put general comments concerning the account into the main notepad. If you hear a rumor about a pending IPO, write it down here. If you have some concerns about your client's credit rating, something like that should go in the main notepad as well. If you had a problem with someone at the client site, put it here rather than in the Completed Activities notepad.

Designing a coherent report based on information in the main notepad is difficult. Finding key words or particular items that belong together can be hard. You may find it easier to create a report based on a particular user, a range of dates, or some kind of Result Code if those notes are in History rather than in the main notepad.

When you come back from an appointment and want to detail what went on, write those notes in the Completed Activity notepad. See Chapter 10 for more information on that.

Starting a new note

You may be tempted to click your mouse somewhere in the notepad and just start typing. With any version of GoldMine prior to June 1999, you will create trouble for yourself if you do.

Starting with version 5.0 of GoldMine, the program goes out of its way to correct your oversight if you absent-mindedly forget to date- and time-stamp your note. If you type directly into the Notes tab and then move on to another tab or record, and you then look back to the Notes tab, you see the date, time, and user stamp are there, automatically.

Find the toolbar icon that resembles a typewriter. Position your cursor over it, and you see a label that says Insert a Note. Remember to click this icon every time you want to enter a new note. When you click this icon, GoldMine automatically inserts your user name, your full name in parentheses, the date, and the time at the top of the notepad. You can see the results of clicking this icon in Figure 5-2.

Figure 5-2:
A note with
a date and
time stamp.

The user name is important as an attachment on each of your notes. GoldMine is a workgroup application, and the intent of a workgroup application is to coordinate a team of people working together. Therefore, you may not be the only person entering notes for this record. Later, when you review everything in the notepad, you will probably want to know who wrote each note. If you're the only user, having your name on every entry isn't critical, but the date and time stamp features still are.

The date and time stamp indicates when you started typing the note. GoldMine sorts the notes for each record chronologically, with the most recent note always at the top of the notepad.

In addition to these compelling reasons to always date- and time-stamp your notes, there is another. Many GoldMine users are part of a team in which at least some of the users are remote. By remote, I mean a staff member located in a separate office or someone in the field who is running GoldMine on a

Take notes — stay out of court

Several years ago, a local attorney called our office and asked us to send a computer technician to his office to repair a computer. The same request was made twice more in the following months. All three times, the technician was dispatched, the computer was repaired, and the attorney was billed. By this time, the attorney had run up bills totaling $830.

On December 31, this client sat down to pay his bills, apparently for the whole year. We received a check from him for $380. You might think that he mistakenly transposed the digits. But in two places on the check he had written, "Paid in Full." I knew that meant that if I cashed the check, I was accepting it as payment in full, and I would have no legal recourse toward collecting the money he owed us.

I called this client and convinced him to come over to our office. He initially refused to rewrite the check. In fact, he then claimed that he didn't owe us any money at all because I could not prove that any of our technicians had ever been to his office!

I showed him the GoldMine screens where we had three pages of date- and time-stamped notes detailing everything we had done in the past three months at his office. He asked if I could print it all out. I told him, "Yes, but only for the judge." He literally ran out to his car to get his checkbook, and he couldn't pay us fast enough.

I am certain that we never would have been paid had we not maintained the complete notes about all the work we had done for him.

The moral of the story is that you should write *everything* down. And be especially careful and thorough with your notes if your relationship with an account seems to be headed in an uncomfortable direction.

notebook computer. These people usually use GoldSync (an add-on to the Standard version; an integral part of the FrontOffice Sales and Marketing version) to synchronize their data automatically with the main database. Without a proper date and time stamp, GoldSync cannot synchronize data properly from the main notepad. This causes your notepad's information to become hopelessly jumbled. To avoid these problems, always click the Insert a Note icon before you begin typing a note.

The main notepad lets you type anything you want. But be careful: Everything you write can be read by everyone else on your team and possibly by others outside your team. Never type anything that you wouldn't put out for public view.

The Contacts Tab

In many, if not most, of your accounts, you deal with more than one person. When you need to keep track of more than one person for an account, you can add the information for each person you deal with by using the Contacts tab. GoldMine refers to these additional people as *secondary contacts*.

The Organization Chart was significantly enhanced in version 5.7. As a result, I now use the Contacts tab to house only those people I don't intend to directly correspond with. An example might be someone in the Accounts Payable department. I might need to call this person sometime, but I probably won't include him or her in my quarterly newsletter distribution list.

The Contacts section is the first section that is relational in nature. A *relational system* implies that you have a one-to-many situation. In this case, *relational* means there may be many secondary contacts for each account. In fact, you have an unlimited number of secondary contacts that you can attach to each account.

Entering a new secondary contact

To enter a new secondary contact, follow these steps:

1. **Click the Contacts tab.**

2. **Move the cursor anywhere in the area below the highlighted Contacts tab and right-click.**

   You see a shortcut menu (shown in Figure 5-3) that enables you to enter new contacts or edit existing contacts.

3. **Select New from the shortcut menu.**

Figure 5-3:
The shortcut
menu for
adding
secondary
contacts.

Look up...
Send E-mail...

Mail Merge...
E-mail Merge...

Options ▶

Find...
Output to ▶

New...

Delete...
Edit...

GoldMine then displays a data entry window in which you can enter a considerable amount of information about a new contact, as shown in Figure 5-4. The window contains four sections of information, just like the window for entering the primary contact's information.

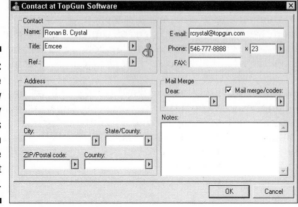

Figure 5-4:
Enter the
new
secondary
contact's
information
in the
Contact
dialog box.

In the first section, you see three fields:

- ✔ **Name:** Enter names just as you do on the main screen. Use upper- and lowercase letters, and first name followed by last name.

- ✔ **Title:** This field's purpose is obvious. You can make use of a lookup list with this field. The lookup list is the same as the Title lookup on the main screen.

- ✔ **Ref.:** The Reference field is really synonymous with the Department field on the main screen, and you should use it this way. See Chapter 4 for details on entering information on the main screen. The Reference field also has a lookup list.

The second section contains address information corresponding to the information in the second quadrant of the main screen. If this secondary person's address is the same as the address for the main record, then you can just leave it out. GoldMine assumes that if these fields are blank, the address is the same as the main record's address. Putting anything in the address fields, like a room number or PO Box, invalidates the address copy from the main record.

The third section contains fields for an e-mail address, a phone number, and a fax number. Each of these fields is specific to the secondary person you're entering. Again, you can leave out the phone numbers if they are the same as the primary contact's phone numbers, but remember to collect as many e-mail addresses as you can.

The fourth section contains the Dear field, mail merge codes, and another one of the ubiquitous notepads.

The Dear field, or Salutation field, is the same as the Dear field on the main GoldMine screen. Enter into this field the greeting you want to use when you write a letter to this person.

The mail merge codes enable you to regulate what correspondence this person receives. The mail merge field has a lookup list, and you can have multiple entries from the lookup list, of course. These mail merge codes work together with filters and groups that you can build. Filters and Groups are detailed in Chapter 12.

For example, you can build a filter to isolate which accounts, or which secondary contacts, should be receiving particular kinds of gifts for Christmas.

If you need multiple entries for mail merge codes, such as "XMAS, BD, ANN, NYD," keep your abbreviations short. You have a total of 20 characters, and the commas and spaces between entries count. The shorter your abbreviations, the more choices you can fit into one field. Please see Chapter 21 for more detail on using lookup lists.

Editing an existing secondary contact

Sometimes you create a secondary contact, but you don't have all the important information gathered at first. You may need to go back and enter the contact's address or e-mail address later. Or perhaps this person's phone number changed. You can add or edit information in a secondary contact's record by following these steps:

1. **Click the Contacts tab.**

2. **Right-click within the blank area below the tab.**

   A shortcut menu appears.

   Double-clicking the secondary contact you want to edit also enables you to edit a secondary contact's information.

3. **Select Edit from the shortcut menu.**

   You return to the original secondary contact window.

4. **Enter new information or edit existing information, and then click OK to save your changes when you're done.**

Swapping the secondary contact with the primary one

Occasionally, someone who was secondary becomes more important in the scheme of things, and you need to promote him or her to primary status. GoldMine enables you to do this easily:

1. **Click the Contacts tab.**

2. **Right-click the current secondary person you want to promote to primary status.**

3. **Click Options.**

4. **Click Swap with Primary, and then confirm that you really do want to do this.**

After you confirm, the person who was the main contact is dropped into the Contacts tab just like the rest of the commoners down there. The person who had been in the secondary section is promoted to the top. This swap can be temporary because you can reverse it very easily.

Converting a secondary record to a stand-alone record

Sometimes one of your secondary records deserves to become a separate record, either by itself or still somehow related to a main record. For example, a major change in the organization of an account may warrant a change to a stand-alone record.

To create a separate stand-alone record, follow these steps:

1. **Click the Contacts tab.**

2. **Right-click the current secondary person you want to deal with.**

3. **Click Options.**

4. **Select Convert to Record from the menu, and then confirm that you really do want to make the change.**

GoldMine removes the secondary contact from the initial record and creates a completely separate record for the contact. You can still maintain a relationship between the original secondary contact and the rest of the people at that account by using the Org Chart, which I discuss in detail in Chapter 7.

When you convert a record, there is an option to Include the Converted Contacts in the Organizational Tree. The default is that this option is checked. I usually only use the Org Chart for my most important accounts, so I suggest not creating an entry in an Org Chart if it is not a really significant account.

Chapter 6

Details and Referrals

The Details tab allows you to save random tidbits of information that relate to individual records. You can search for them and report on them as well. The Referrals tab enables you to relate one account in your database to another.

The Details and the Referrals tabs are two of the least understood and least used of the basic sections of GoldMine. But the truth is that they aren't that hard to understand, and they can both be very useful. In this chapter, you find out how to use them, and you find some recommendations on clever ways to make the most of them.

Taking Care of the Details

The Details tab replaced the tab that was called Profiles in GoldMine versions prior to 5.0. The functionality is still basically the same, but it has been enhanced a bit. Just as with profiles in previous versions, you can use the Details tab to store data that isn't necessarily needed for every record.

I like to think of the Details tab as containing random, relational information. By *relational,* I mean that one account in your GoldMine database may contain an unlimited number of detail entries. Another way to say this is to call it a "one-to-many relationship."

For example, suppose you want to keep track of a credit card number for each account. You could create a user-defined field for the credit card number. A *user-defined field* is a new field that you define and place into the

GoldMine database. It would be fine to use one of these fields until the first time a client tells you he has *two* credit cards you need to keep on file. You paint yourself into a corner by using a user-defined field for credit cards or for any other kind of data that might require multiple entries.

The Details tab solves this problem by enabling you to set up many different details and use each only when you need it. And you can use the same detail (such as the second credit card number) as many times as you need to for each account.

The Details tab also solves a problem sometimes involving the Fields tab. If you have any user-defined, custom fields, they are displayed in the Fields tab. For every record, whether or not you fill in any data in each of these fields, space is taken on your hard drive. So, if you developed 50 custom fields, but on average use only three of them, the other 47 take up space but don't really do anything for you.

When you enter your data into the Details tab, only then does GoldMine create the storage space it needs. If you don't have credit card information for an account, no space is taken up on your hard drive.

Using existing details

The Details tab includes 13 preset, separate details that you can use immediately, as shown in Figure 6-1. You may find some of these a bit far off the beaten path, and you may want to delete or ignore some of the more unusual ones, such as RS Expertise. By the way, this one stands for Reseller Expertise, and FrontRange uses it to track what each Dealer, like my company, is actually good at.

Without a doubt, the most important detail is the e-mail address. When you create a new record for a contact (see Chapter 4 for entering new records), one of the entries you make is in the E-mail Address field. When you do, GoldMine automatically puts this e-mail address directly into the Details tab for that record. The e-mail address is also displayed on the main GoldMine screen along with the phone numbers. You don't need to do anything special to put the e-mail address in either place, or even to use it later.

You're not limited to just this one initial e-mail address. You can enter as many more addresses as you need to, which is becoming increasingly common as more and more people have multiple e-mail addresses. GoldMine stores one e-mail address as the primary address, and the rest as secondary addresses.

Figure 6-1:
The preset details.

Aside from just storing data, the Details tab can also be actively used. For example, you can send an e-mail message to one of your accounts directly from its Details tab by following these steps:

1. **Click the Details tab.**

2. **Select the e-mail address you want to send the correspondence to.**

3. **Right-click and select Send E-mail from the shortcut menu.**

4. **Compose and send your e-mail message.**

Entering new details

If, for some reason, you didn't enter the e-mail address (or some other kind of detail) when the record was first created, it isn't too late. To enter an e-mail address after the record has been created:

1. **Click the Details tab.**

2. **Right-click in the area below the tab and choose New.**

   Immediately, the Detail Properties dialog box appears, shown in Figure 6-2, enabling you to enter a new detail.

The first field, Detail, stores the type of detail you're recording. This field wants to know, "What kind of information are you trying to set up here?"

Getting directions online

Another technique for getting assistance with directions is to make use of the GoldMine Web interface. Directly and automatically from the client record, you can have GoldMine dial into MapQuest or Yahoo! Maps on the Internet and provide you with a map and driving instructions.

To do so (assuming you have an Internet account and are connected), follow these steps:

1. From the main GoldMine menu, choose Lookup⇨Internet Search.

2. Select maps from MapQuest or Yahoo! Maps.

This Detail field has a lookup list that shows the preset details available to you. To access this list, right-click in the Detail field. Select E-mail Address and tab to the next field, labeled Reference. GoldMine stores the actual data for each detail in the Reference field. In this example, you enter the e-mail address into the Reference field. Remember that there should be no spaces, and an @ symbol should appear somewhere in the middle of the address.

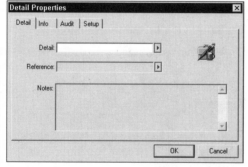

Figure 6-2:
Enter new information in the Detail Properties dialog box.

Modifying an existing detail

One of the details original to GoldMine is American Express Number. A detail also exists for American Express Card Holder. If you accept and collect credit cards, having a more general credit card detail that you can use for all your credit card information may be more useful. You can make the American Express Number detail more general by following these steps (this example applies equally well to any existing details):

1. **From the main GoldMine screen, click the Details tab.**

2. **Right-click in the area below the tab and select New from the shortcut menu.**

   The Detail Properties dialog box appears.

3. **In the Detail field, right-click so that you can see the Detail lookup list.**

4. **Highlight American Express Card Number and then click the Edit button.**

5. **Type** Credit Card Number **and click OK.**

   Credit Card Number immediately replaces American Express Number in the lookup list, and you can use it now.

You have now replaced an existing detail with one of your own. If you actually want to use it, use the Reference field to house the credit card number itself. Use the Notes field to record the expiration date, the exact name on the card, and any other information that you or your company needs to process credit cards. By the way, you probably don't need to specifically record what type of credit card it is because the first number of each major credit card designates the type it is. American Express starts with a 3, Visa with a 4, Master Card with a 5, and Discover with a 6. If you don't believe me, pull out your wallet and check — you have one of each, right?

Creating your own details

Creating your own, new detail isn't much different from modifying an existing detail.

Remember that using a detail for any field that either won't be used for every single record or when multiple entries may exist (as in the preceding credit card example) is appropriate.

One of my favorite details to add to the system is one for driving directions to the client's location. To create this detail, follow these steps:

1. **From the main GoldMine screen, click the Details tab.**

2. **Right-click in the area below the tab and choose New from the shortcut menu.**

3. **In the Detail field, right-click so that you can see the Detail lookup list.**

4. In the lookup list, click the New button.

5. Type Directions **and click OK.**

The list of details now includes an entry for directions, and you can use it any time. You may not need the Reference field, but you can use the Notes field to write down the specific driving directions to get to this client.

Using details for directions in this way is great. For example, if you go to see this client once every eight months, you don't need to keep asking how to get there. Or if someone else from your office is going, then he or she can check this detail and won't need to bother anyone else. Check out Figure 6-3 to see a typical directions detail.

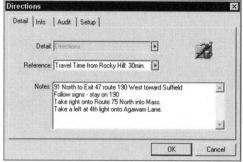

Figure 6-3:
Use a
custom
detail for
driving
directions.

To actually see the directions in a detail, you must double-click that detail entry. Including these directions in a custom-designed report is also possible. See Chapter 19 for more details on reporting.

More fields you can use with details

Sometimes the Reference and Notes tabs together do not allow for enough information. Recent versions of GoldMine have provided eight more fields in the Info tab that goes along with each detail.

You can even seek out a few more fields within the Details tab by using an add-on product called Details Plus. I discuss add-on products in Chapter 29.

You may want to try using the Info tab to keep track of one or more shipping addresses for each account. Or if you sell computers, you may want to track the details of each computer — the processor speed, the hard drive size, modem speed, amount of memory, and so on, as shown in Figure 6-4.

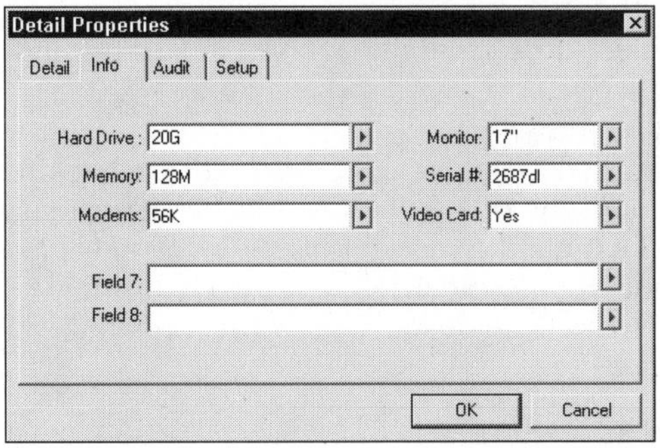

Figure 6-4 illustration: Detail Properties dialog box showing the Info tab with fields Hard Drive: 20G, Memory: 128M, Modems: 56K, Monitor: 17", Serial #: 2687dl, Video Card: Yes, Field 7, Field 8, and OK / Cancel buttons.

Figure 6-4:
The Info tab
stores more
details.

You may want to consult the GoldMine Reference Manual for further explanation of this advanced topic, and/or have an Authorized GoldMine Dealer actually set this up, and then you can access this data.

Finding specific detail records

GoldMine provides you with a way to easily look up particular records within the Details tab. For example, if an e-mail message comes to you with an address you don't recognize, you can manually check your database to find out who the mystery sender might be by following these steps:

1. **From the main menu, choose Lookup⇨Detail Records.**

2. **Choose the appropriate Detail Record type from the lookup list.**

   For this example, choose E-mail Address.

3. **Type the first couple of letters of the e-mail address you are trying to find.**

   GoldMine brings you to its main contact window sorted by e-mail address and positioned at the first e-mail starting with the letters you just specified.

Making Use of Referrals

The Referrals tab on GoldMine's main screen enables you to link one record to another or, perhaps, one record to many other records. The Referrals tab is *relational,* meaning that one piece of data links to multiple pieces of other data. By linking one record to another, you can quickly see what the relationship between two or more records might be. Suppose for example, that your accountant referred 17 other clients to you. You thank her and record each of the referrals in your accountant's GoldMine record. Makes her look a lot more important, doesn't it?

An important note is that the Referrals tab is bi-directional, so after you link A to B, B is linked back to A. The relationship works like a toggle switch. By double-clicking a referral listing, the record that the referral is linked to appears. You can get right back to the original record by double-clicking the referral listing again. In Figure 6-5, you can see two records linked to each other in the Referrals tab.

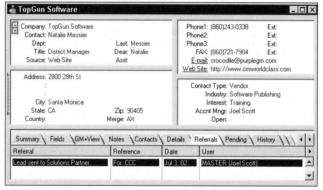

Figure 6-5:
Record
leads from
a client
on the
Referrals
tab.

Even if you don't have to track leads you have given out to your dealers, you may want to use the Referrals tab for some kind of related activity. Working with an account that uses a consultant (or an accountant, or an attorney) presents an opportunity to employ the Referrals tab. A referral is especially useful if this same consultant pops up in other accounts of yours, and it's also relevant if you're part of a multi-level distribution system.

How FrontRange uses the Referrals tab

The staff at FrontRange uses the Referrals tab to track which leads have gone to which dealer.

When you call FrontRange to request a dealer's name, you are connected with an account manager. One of the first things she does is to check whether a record already exists in the database for your company. If not, she creates one. After she does that, she may decide to refer you to a dealer. If she does, she then uses the Referrals tab to link your record to the record of that dealer.

To create a referral link, follow these steps:

1. **From the main GoldMine screen, click the Referrals tab.**

2. **Right-click in the area below the tab and choose New from the shortcut menu.**

   A window displaying all the records in your database appears.

3. **Double-click the record you want to link to.**

   The Referral Properties dialog box appears, enabling you to enter the referral information. On the left side of the dialog box, you see the original record and an empty Reference field below it. On the right side of the dialog box is the listing for the record to which the referral is being placed. You use the two reference fields (one for each record) to indicate what the relationship is between the two records.

Each of these two Reference fields can have a lookup list. If you plan to make extensive use of referrals, you should set up these lookup lists to ensure some consistency in the relationships you use. Refer to Chapter 21 for more details on using lookup lists.

For example, if you were referring CRMworldclass to *The Wall Street Journal,* you might set up the referral as shown in Figure 6-6.

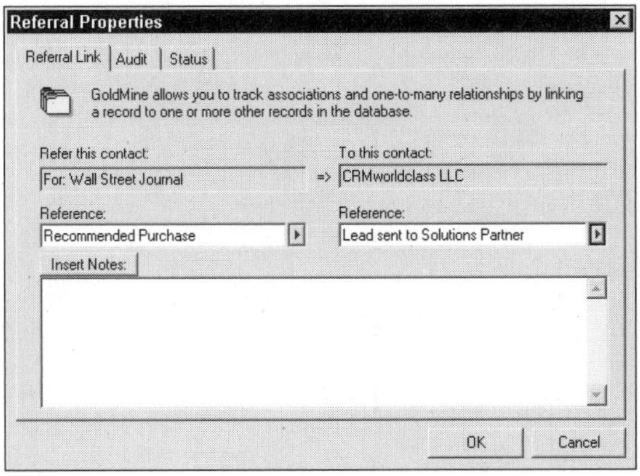

Figure 6-6:
A typical referral.

At my company, we prioritize our clients and prospects, usually based on projected or actual revenue. However, the Referrals tab can influence our priorities because an account that may never generate any revenue for us itself may refer so much business to us that we give it preferred status.

Chapter 7

Using the Organizational Chart

*T*raditionally, GoldMine keeps each of its records (your accounts) separate. GoldMine allows you to associate an unlimited number of secondary contacts with each record, but when you enter a secondary contact, you are somewhat limited by the fields that GoldMine provides.

If you need to track more information about secondary contacts than GoldMine allows, you can make each of them a separate record and relate them all via the Org Chart (also called the Org Tree). For example, if you do business with all the Major League Baseball teams, each team would have a separate record in GoldMine. You could use the Org Chart to group them all together, so you can more easily send them coordinated correspondence.

If the secondary contact information is sufficient, you may still want to make use of the Org Chart to actually display a simple version of each account's departmental structure, so you can see who reports to whom and how each person relates to the other people in the company or department.

GoldMine also has a global replace function that can be accessed nicely via the Org Chart. And, finally, the Org Chart is an easy way to simulate filters, which are discussed more fully in Chapter 12.

How and When to Use the Org Chart

Knowing when to use secondary contacts and when to use the Org Chart is not always clear. I have developed some general rules about when to use the Org Chart, as follows (if the person or people you need to enter information for don't match these criteria, make them secondary contacts):

✔ If a very important account (I call them Focus Accounts) has multiple people associated with it, it's a candidate for the Org Chart.

✔ If you have more than a few people in your own company, you should have an Org Chart for yourselves, and it should be organized either by geography or by function.

✔ If you need more information than the secondary contacts area allows, separate those contacts into their own records and make an Org Chart.

✔ If you need to relate otherwise separate accounts, use the Org Chart.

Use the Org Chart sparingly. In all likelihood, not every record needs one.

Displaying the Org Chart

You have several ways to get to the Org Chart. Whichever way you choose, you get to the exact same place, so it is really just personal preference. The Org Chart is always displayed to the left of the main GoldMine screen.

The Org Chart icon

The basic, standard set of icons contains one icon that brings up the Org Chart. That icon is shown in Figure 7-1. If the Org Chart is not currently displayed, clicking this icon automatically pops it up on the left side of the GoldMine screen. This icon works like a toggle switch, because clicking it while the Org Chart is displayed makes the Org Chart disappear.

Clicking the border/divider bar

Within the left-most vertical bar of the main GoldMine screen is a series of blue hash marks, called the border/divider. When you place your cursor over these hash marks, the cursor changes to a pointing hand. The border/divider also works like a toggle switch, alternately displaying and hiding the Org Chart. You can use either the Org Chart icon or the border/divider to bring up the Org Chart.

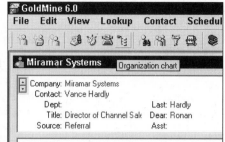

Figure 7-1:
Accessing
the Org
Chart.

Setting preferences to automatically display the Org Chart

Within the preferences settings (discussed in Chapter 3), you have another way to make the Org Chart visible. To change your preferences settings, follow these steps:

1. **From the main menu, choose Edit➪Preferences.**

   The Preferences dialog box appears.

2. **Click the Record tab and select the Open Org Tree When Maximized option.**

   Selecting this option (shown in Figure 3-2 in Chapter 3) causes the Org Chart to be automatically displayed whenever you maximize the GoldMine window.

3. **Click OK.**

You should only select this option if the majority of your GoldMine records actually have an associated Org Chart. If you do have this option selected and the Org Chart is visible, you can make it disappear by clicking either the Org Chart icon or the border/divider.

Org Chart Structure

Basically, the Org Chart is divided into three types of entries: organizations, sections, and contacts. The most general entry is the organization, indicated by a small book icon beside the organization's name. In the simplest case, you can think of the organization as one company with multiple people and/or multiple branches listed underneath. Keep in mind, though, that you can actually have multiple organizations within one Org Chart.

Beneath the organization entry, you can have one or more section entries, indicated by a folder icon beside the section's name. You can think of a section as a department or, perhaps, separate locations within a company. You can also have sections within sections, and these can be nested four or five deep.

Each section can have multiple contacts, indicated by the page icon beside the contact's name. Contacts are individual records for people you deal with. You can have a particular record associated with more than one section. For example, someone might be in both the sales and in the marketing departments. Keep in mind that if you have the same contact in more than one section and later use the Org Chart as the basis for sending e-mails, you could end up sending multiple messages to the same person.

Figure 7-2 shows a typical Org Chart with entries in each category.

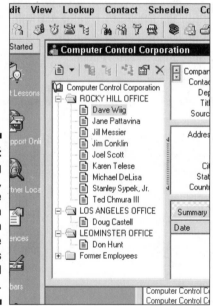

Figure 7-2:
An Org
Chart,
complete
with an
organization
and multiple
sections
and
contacts.

After you have displayed the Org Chart, you see six icons above the Org Chart and either a large blank area (if you have not yet created an Org Chart for this particular record) or the current Org Chart structure. You can also access the same Org Chart functions by right-clicking while the cursor is positioned within the Org Chart itself. In fact, you can access more functions by right-clicking than via the icons, so I focus on Org Chart functionality via the right mouse button.

Starting a Brand New Org Chart

If a record does not yet have an Org Chart, then the Org Chart window is blank. You can start a new Org Chart as follows:

1. **Position the cursor within the blank Org Chart window, right-click, and choose Create a New Organization.**

2. **Select the Look Up Another Contact and Create an Org Chart option.**

   Use this option if you want to start the Org Chart with some other record from your database.

3. **Alternatively, select the Create an Org Chart Based On option.**

   Choose this option if you are already positioned on the correct record.

After you create your first entry in the Org Chart, several other functions become available by right-clicking in the Org Chart window, as shown in Figure 7-3.

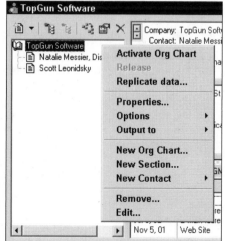

Figure 7-3:
Options
within the
Org Chart.

Starting a new section

You probably want a separate or new section for each department or, perhaps, for each location within an organization. To create a new section

1. **Highlight the section nearest where you want the new section placed.**

2. **Right-click the highlighted section and choose New Section.**

   The Section Properties dialog box appears, as shown in Figure 7-4.

3. **Type a name for your new section heading in the Section Heading field.**

   Make sure the name differs from your other headings, of course.

4. **Choose where you want the new section to fall in the Org Chart by choosing from the Insert New Section drop-down list; then click OK.**

You have the option of placing this new heading under, above, or below the highlighted section. *Under* means to add a new section nested within the highlighted section; *below* means to add a new section so it's on the same level and falls beneath the highlighted section in the Org Chart; and *above* means to add a new section so it's on the same level and on top of the highlighted section in the Org Chart. Figure 7-5 shows the results of adding new sections under, below, and above the Leominster Office section. Although the terminology is certainly confusing, you can see in the figure how adding a new section under, below, and above works.

Adding new contacts

You add a new contact record to an Org Chart by right-clicking in the Org Chart and choosing New Contact from the shortcut menu (refer to Figure 7-3). From the dialog box that pops up, you select an existing contact and add it to the section you are in, or you can enter a brand new record into the database and have it automatically placed in the Org Chart.

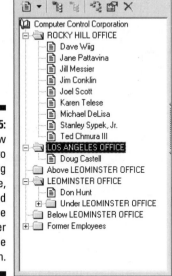

Figure 7-5:
Adding new
sections to
the Org
Chart above,
under, and
below the
Leominster
Office
section.

Activating a Filter from the Org Chart

The first choice in the Org Chart shortcut menu, Activate Org Chart, allows
you to set up a filter associating related records (refer to Figure 7-3). Actually,
the Org Chart can simulate either filters or groups, which are discussed in
detail in Chapter 12. After you have selected an existing filter, you can do a
broadcast fax or e-mail to just those records, or you can use the replicate
function (discussed in the following section). You can simulate a filter by
using the Org Chart as follows:

1. **Click the book icon (to indicate the whole organization) or click the
   folder for the section that you want to use as a filter.**

2. **Right-click and choose Activate Section from the shortcut menu.**

   Examine the title bar at the very top of the screen to confirm that the
   proper section has been selected. Note that even if you pick the entire
   organization, the title bar still indicates a section.

3. **When you're done with this filter, right-click the section or organization icon and choose Release from the shortcut menu.**

Replication

The third choice on the Org Chart shortcut menu handles replication. *Replication* is another term for copying data from one place to another. This is a powerful tool, which is similar to the Global Replace function that can be accessed by choosing Tools➪Global Replace Wizard from the main toolbar. Using replication is a little simpler than using the Global Replace function, however.

An example of a great way to use replication is to make a global change or update to related contact records. If you have set up an Org Chart to represent your own company, it might look something like the Org Chart shown in Figure 7-2. Suppose the area code for your company's phone number just changed. You can update everyone's record in one fell swoop with replication:

1. **Go to any record within your organization and correct the phone number in that record.**

2. **Bring up the Org Chart attached to this record.**

3. **Position your cursor over either the entire organization or just the appropriate section.**

4. **Right-click and choose Activate from the shortcut menu.**

5. **Without moving the mouse, right-click again and choose Replicate Data.**

   The Replicate Data dialog box appears, as shown in Figure 7-6.

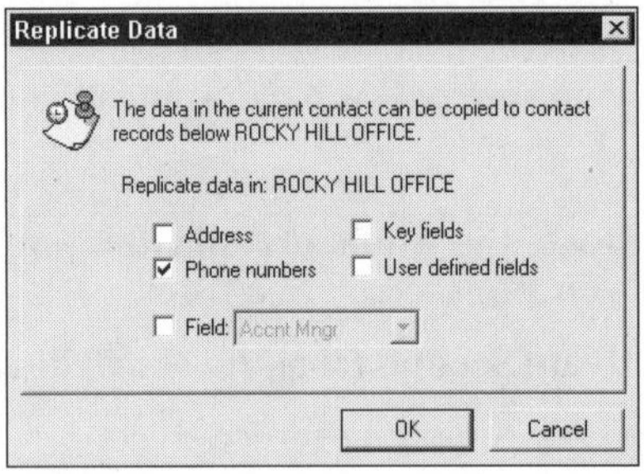

Figure 7-6:
Replicating
phone
numbers.

6. **Select the Phone numbers option and click OK.**

7. **Click Yes.**

GoldMine proceeds to change all phone numbers and phone extension fields in each of the records that are part of the selected organization or section.

A Little Security for Your Org Chart

The fourth choice in the Org Chart shortcut menu regulates the properties of this Org Chart. Properties are similar to record ownership and determine who can access and modify records. By default, the Org Chart defers to the record ownership of the first record entered into the Org Chart. Under most conditions, you don't need to deal with this function, but an example of a typical application can't hurt.

In the financial services arena, a special type of security called a Chinese Wall is used. Particularly in brokerage firms, it's important for the brokers not to know what deals their investment bankers are working on. So the investment bankers need to apply record ownership and curtaining properties to these kinds of records to prevent the brokers from illegally using inside information.

To set up Org Chart security, follow these steps:

1. **Right-click in a blank space in the Org Chart and choose Properties from the shortcut menu.**

   The Org Chart Properties dialog box appears.

2. **Click the Access tab on the Org Chart Properties dialog box.**

3. **Use the lookup lists to select the appropriate group or user who should have either read rights and/or updating rights.**

4. **Click OK when you're done setting up access rights.**

Part III
Managing Activities

The 5th Wave — By Rich Tennant

"WELL, SHOOT! THIS EGGPLANT CHART IS JUST AS CONFUSING AS THE BUTTERNUT SQUASH CHART AND THE GOURD CHART. CAN'T YOU JUST MAKE A PIE CHART LIKE EVERYONE ELSE?"

In this part . . .

*H*aving thousands of accounts is great, but you won't keep them for long if you never do anything with them. The real purpose of GoldMine is to enable you to schedule and track everything that's supposed to happen and everything that has already happened. This part of the book shows you how GoldMine can effectively nag everyone to make sure nothing falls through the cracks, and how all the history gets recorded for every account.

If you've ever tried to fool yourself or your manager with your exciting sales forecast, you'll see how to accomplish that very same thing within the confines of GoldMine. And if you've ever tried to focus on a particular set of accounts (like just the ones in Toledo, or just your best sources of revenue), this part shows you how to do just that by using filters and groups.

Chapter 8

Scheduling Activities

. . . .

In This Chapter

▶ Defining activities

▶ Viewing the Calendar

▶ Scheduling and changing appointments from the Calendar window

▶ Scheduling activities for other people

▶ Using the iCal feature

▶ Making recurring appointments

. . . .

Keeping track of names, addresses, and phone numbers is the heart of GoldMine; recording pending activities in the Calendar is the soul. If you don't enter pending activities, you won't have a record of completed activities, and then you'll waste most of the power of GoldMine.

Plan on putting your entire life in the Calendar. Sure, you're using GoldMine for all your business appointments, but you can put the Little League games and the dentist appointments in there, too. That way, GoldMine reminds you about all the things you don't want to forget (and nags you about the things you'd like to forget).

This chapter shows you how to harness the organizational power of GoldMine's Calendar to track the activities in your busy life. I also show you how to share your Calendar with other members of your team, a feature that my co-workers and I find really powerful and efficient. I also discuss how to share appointment information with people who don't yet use GoldMine. Don't worry — GoldMine has plenty of safeguards built in, and enough privacy so that no one will ever know about those weekly tee times or shopping trips. Trust me.

Defining Activities

GoldMine features nine types of activities, all accessible on the main menu by choosing Schedule (see Figure 8-1). Most of these activities also have their own icons in the main toolbar. In the following list, I explain the different types of activities:

Figure 8-1:
Activities within the Schedule menu.

✔ **Call:** Generally, outgoing phone calls are scheduled with this coding, although incoming conference calls may also come under this scheduling regime.

✔ **Next Action:** Often, when you complete an activity with a client, you need to schedule a follow-up. For example, after a fact-finding meeting, you might schedule a "Review of Proposal" meeting as your Next Action.

✔ **Appointment:** An appointment can be a meeting that is scheduled either inside your office or at some other location. Meetings are usually person-to-person affairs, but more and more, meetings occur through the Internet with Microsoft's NetMeeting, Webex, or PlaceWare.

✔ **Literature Request:** This type of activity is used to schedule orders for your shipping or fulfillment department to send out. These could be marketing materials or actual products.

✔ **Forecasted Sale:** GoldMine has a simple sales forecasting system, and you actually schedule the closing of a sale in the same way you schedule anything else. I discuss sales forecasting in Chapter 11.

✔ **Other Action:** This is a catch-all category for activities that just don't fit nicely anywhere else. In my office, non-billable, R&D projects are scheduled as Other activities.

✔ **Event:** You use the event category to schedule daylong or multi-day activities. For example, a trade show that requires you to be out of the office for an entire day would be scheduled as an event. I don't like using Events too much, because they don't show up as obviously on your Calendar as other types of activities.

✔ **To-do:** To-dos don't have a time of day associated with them, so they never show up on the main Calendar. You see them listed below as special items. For example, a reminder to pick up milk and bread on the way home or to do some research at your competitor's store would fit in this category.

✔ **GoldMine E-mail:** From this selection you can create and/or schedule an outgoing e-mail to other users on your team.

Whatever type of activity you're scheduling, as soon as you click OK to actually schedule it, GoldMine automatically puts a record of the activity into the Pending tab of the appropriate record. You can always see it or edit the activity from the Pending tab. In addition, it shows up on your Activity List and on the Calendar itself.

Viewing the Calendar

To schedule an activity, open the Calendar by clicking the Calendar icon (the blue icon that looks like one of those old-fashioned, single-day flip calendars) on the main menu. The main Calendar window appears, as shown in Figure 8-2.

Those options include seeing a daily, weekly, monthly, or yearly view of the Calendar. I find the daily and weekly Calendar views to be the most useful. These views show enough detail for me to understand exactly what I have scheduled. As you progress to the monthly and yearly views, you see less and less detail about specific activities. You can select any of these views using the tabs on the Calendar View window.

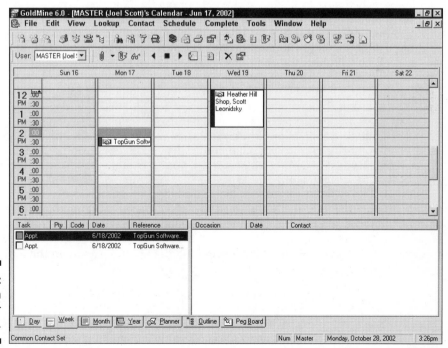

Figure 8-2: The main Calendar window.

In addition to these presentations, you have a choice of several other types of views. These options are all additional tabs on the local scheduling window:

- **Planner:** Displays a Calendar for multiple GoldMine users. To display this Calendar, click the Planner tab.

- **Outline:** Displays a Calendar in an outline, or hierarchical, format. To display this Calendar, click the Outline tab.

- **Peg Board:** Displays a status chart of other GoldMine users. To access this display, click the Peg Board tab. This feature allows users to log in or log out and post a message regarding their whereabouts. It also checks for inactivity as measured by the existence or absence of keystrokes on the keyboard.

Entering Activities on the Calendar

You can schedule an activity either from the Calendar or by using the main GoldMine menu. Both of these methods land you at the same place — the Scheduling dialog box. Scheduling from the Calendar, however, saves you the effort of manually entering the date, time, and duration of each activity; these items are automatically filled in. Using the main menu allows you to schedule activities that shouldn't really occupy a significant block of time, such as quick phone calls or short in-house meetings.

Make sure that the active record is the one you want to schedule an activity for. But if you need to schedule an activity for another record, you can temporarily switch records in the scheduling window by selecting the right arrow adjacent to the Contact Person. After you finish scheduling, GoldMine takes you back to your original record. This clever new option is useful if you're in the midst of writing a summary of your recent meeting with Client A and suddenly remember that you need to schedule an appointment with Client B.

Scheduling activities directly from the Calendar is generally best for appointments or for any activity with a significant duration. Follow these steps:

1. **Open the Calendar by clicking the Calendar icon on the toolbar.**

   The Calendar's main window appears.

2. **Select either the daily or weekly view by clicking the appropriate tab.**

3. **Click and drag the mouse over the desired time for your activity.**

   When you release the mouse, the main Schedule an Appointment dialog box appears, shown in Figure 8-3, where you fill in additional details. (See the next section for more information about the Scheduling dialog box.)

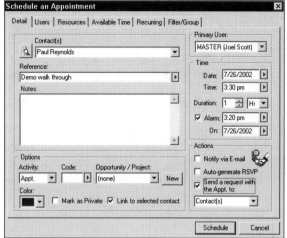

Figure 8-3:
Enter an
appointment
on your
Calendar
with the
Scheduling
dialog box.

To schedule an activity from the main menu without opening the Calendar, follow these steps:

1. **Choose Schedule from the main GoldMine menu.**

2. **Choose the appropriate type of activity from the Schedule menu.**

   See the "Defining Activities" section, earlier in this chapter, to find out about the different types of activities.

Creating a personal record for yourself is a good idea. When scheduling an activity for yourself, such as a dentist appointment, you can then attach that appointment to your own record in the database.

Always link pending and completed activities with an existing record in GoldMine. GoldMine, by default, links each activity you schedule with the record that's currently active. For personal appointments, you should have a record for yourself (complete with home address and phone numbers) and link your own personal appointments to that record.

Filling in the Scheduling Dialog Box

After you use one of the two methods for getting to the Scheduling dialog box, you see a series of fields you must fill out. I discuss each of these fields in the following sections.

The Contact field

The first field you see on the Scheduling dialog box (refer to Figure 8-3) is the Contact field. By default, this field contains the primary contact from the record you were just using. Click the icon to the left of the primary contact field to temporarily activate a different record in your database. You can also select multiple contacts or even multiple GoldMine users for the same appointment.

Always select the main person you're meeting with. If you're meeting with a whole group of people, select the one person who should be contacted if someone needs to find you while you're at this meeting.

The Code field

The next field is labeled Code, which GoldMine uses to describe the nature of the appointment. Typical examples of activity codes are

- ✔ SLS — Sales
- ✔ ADM — Administrative work
- ✔ PER — Personal

Colors, colors, everywhere

Colors are a great way to specify types of activities. When you use different colors for different kinds of appointments, these colors show up very clearly on your Calendar. Then, whenever you look at your Calendar, you can very easily see what kind of day you're going to have.

My colleagues and I developed the following color-coding scheme at our company that works very well for us:

✔ **Gray:** A tentative appointment that still needs to be confirmed

✔ **Yellow:** An assignment requiring us to be in the office, like tech support

✔ **Red:** An appointment away from the office

✔ **Blue:** An appointment in the office

✔ **Green:** Personal time

Feel free to develop your own scheme for your company. Any consistent color scheme that makes sense to everyone in your company is better than no color scheme at all.

You can see and use these choices by right-clicking in the field or by clicking the drop-down arrow to the right of the field. In the Code field, you should make up a short series of codes that cover pretty much every reason you may ever deal with an account. You can use these codes later to develop reports that select and sort based on your activity codes. See Chapter 21 for further information on adding codes to lookup lists.

The Primary User field

The next field you see on the Scheduling dialog box is the Primary User field. GoldMine assumes that you're scheduling this appointment for yourself; therefore, you generally see your own user name showing up here. If you are indeed scheduling for yourself, you can just skip this field entirely.

If you right-click in the Primary User field, the names of all the other users on your system appear. You can schedule for someone other than yourself by simply selecting his or her name. This feature is called *delegating* and is one of my favorite tools in GoldMine. See the sidebar, "The art of delegating," later in this chapter, for tips on delegating.

The Reference field

Use this field for a short description of the activity. Sometimes you may schedule activities many months in advance. When an activity suddenly pops up on your activity list, the Reference field reminds you what the activity is all about. For example, you may use "Initial Sales Call," "Project Review Meeting," "Technical Support," or my personal favorite, "Close Deal." Make up your own list, and put it into the lookup list for this field. Again, you can refer to Chapter 21 for details on adding items to a lookup list.

The Notes field

You can use the Notes field as a reminder of specific information pertinent to this meeting, such as, "Remember to bring three copies of the proposal and a slide projector." Some people also use this field for directions to the account, but I prefer to put that information into the Detail section.

This Notes field does not require date- or time-stamping, so you need only click in the field and start typing.

Just to the right of the Contact field is an innocent-looking right arrow. You no longer need to activate the appropriate record before going to the scheduling window. You can click this right arrow, select the record for which you are scheduling an activity, and then actually be returned to the original record that you were working on. Very cool.

The Date field

On the right side of the Scheduling dialog box is the Time section. Every appointment, of course, has a date and a time associated with it. If you don't enter a date and time, then the appointment won't show up properly on your Calendar, and you may not realize that you need to be doing something. If you began your scheduling directly from the Calendar, then the Date and Time fields are already filled in for you.

You can enter a date into the Date field by retyping the date, or you can use the toggle buttons to the right of the Date field to increase or decrease the date, one day at a time. Both of these methods are a little clunky and are reserved for those who don't appreciate the subtleties of life.

The best way to change the date is to position the cursor in the Date field, and then right-click the mouse button. Voilà — a month's worth of the Calendar instantly appears, as shown in Figure 8-4. You can move ahead (or backwards) if necessary by clicking the Month or the Year scroll buttons. When you see the date you want, just double-click. GoldMine automatically fills in this date on the Scheduling dialog box.

Figure 8-4:
Select a date for your appointment.

The Time field

The Time field works the same way as the Date field. Right-click in the Time field, and a clock divided into 15-minute intervals appears, as shown in Figure 8-5. You can see the tic marks on the rim of the clock corresponding to the 15-minute intervals.

Figure 8-5:
Set the time for your appointment.

If you were ever a fighter pilot, the use of this clock is obvious. If not, this is how it works: The *only* way to manipulate this clock is by positioning the cursor on the rim and clicking the time you want to start your activity. To set an appointment for 3:30 p.m., for example, click halfway between the 3 and 4 on the clock's rim.

Every appointment has an expected duration. Make sure you enter a duration either in minutes or in hours. If you don't, you end up with conflicting appointments and a generally messed-up schedule.

Come up with a company-wide standard for dealing with travel time. Failing to account for travel time on your Calendar may result in someone putting another appointment in your schedule right when you're driving back from the first appointment. Color codes work well for this kind of situation. (See the sidebar, "Colors, colors, everywhere.")

If you select the Alarm, GoldMine automatically reminds you of an activity by putting a notice on your screen ten minutes (you can adjust this interval in User Preferences) before the scheduled activity time. This reminder is excellent for out-of-the-office appointments, but if you overuse this function, you may find it a bit annoying. When I schedule an appointment for someone else in my office that tends to run late, I always make use of the Alarm feature.

Using the Options

You generally use most of the Options fields only if you're part of a team. I explain these Options and their purposes in the following list (refer to Figure 8-3 for the location of each of these options on the main Scheduling dialog box):

- **Mark as Private:** If you label an activity as Mark as Private, other GoldMine users can see that some amount of time is blocked out of your Calendar, but they won't be able to see exactly what you're doing or where you're going.

  Use this option too much and your boss and co-workers are bound to be a little suspicious. And, because the boss probably has Master access rights, he or she can find a way to see what you're doing anyway.

- **Link:** This button, which is on by default, links the activity to the account that's active. It's hard to imagine a reason to ever turn this off. Suggestion — just leave it alone.

- **Notify:** This button can be an extremely important tool to use whenever you schedule for someone else. If you click this button, GoldMine immediately notifies the person for whom you're scheduling the activity. This notification isn't the same thing as an alarm, which goes off shortly before the activity.

  For example, if you schedule Harry to make a presentation to the Board of Directors next Thursday, you can be fairly sure that he would like to know about it more than ten minutes beforehand. Click the Notify button, and GoldMine immediately sends Harry an e-mail message with the information about the activity you entered into his Calendar. Forget to use this button once or twice, and you're guaranteed to hear about it.

- **RSVP:** You can select the RSVP button when you schedule an activity for someone else. It allows you to keep track of when, and if, activities that you have scheduled for other users are completed. This field is particularly useful when activities are delegated to other network or remote users. GoldMine creates an RSVP message on your Calendar as soon as an activity you scheduled for another user is completed or deleted.

Rescheduling an Activity

In real life, most people usually look at a calendar before scheduling anything. GoldMine is no different. You can go directly to the Calendar by clicking the

Calendar icon. This brings you immediately to your Calendar, so you can see what is already scheduled. Most people think it is important to look before they leap.

The easiest way to reschedule an appointment is directly from the Calendar by using the drag-and-drop method (just like dragging cards when you're playing the Solitaire in Windows). Click to select the appointment, hold down the left mouse button, and drag the appointment to the new date or time, and then release the mouse button. You can also make the appointment longer or shorter by dragging the top or bottom of the appointment to extend or reduce the time allotted to it.

Scheduling Activities for Other People

GoldMine enables you to schedule activities for other users by accessing their Calendars. This works very well in my office, and I highly recommend it. But you must consider several key elements when you schedule an activity for someone else:

- ✔ **Make sure that the other person is okay with this arrangement.** Also make sure up front that everyone on the team agrees to the efficiency of the idea.

- ✔ **Make sure to schedule directly from the other person's Calendar.** You do so by changing the User to the person for whom you're scheduling. When you change the User, you immediately see that other user's Calendar. (See the section, "The Primary User field," earlier in this chapter, for more information.) Because you're probably less familiar with someone else's Calendar than you are with your own, *check it first* to make sure you're not creating a conflict.

- ✔ **Make sure that you *always* use the Notify button.** Doing so is courteous and professional. Using a color-coding scheme, such as gray for an appointment that the user needs to confirm, is a good idea too.

Using the New iCal Features

The iCal feature is a hottie, and it comes under the heading, "If you can't beat 'em, join 'em." The developers at FrontRange realized that many people use tools other than GoldMine for their scheduling and their e-mail. The most common tool, of course, is Microsoft Outlook. The relatively new iCal feature allows you to use GoldMine to schedule meetings with anyone using a scheduling program that makes use of the iCal standards. You can translate that into Microsoft Outlook and Lotus Organizer. If you haven't convinced the Outlook stalwarts in your company to convert to GoldMine, you can use this new feature to coordinate your schedule with theirs. If some of your clients or vendors use Outlook, you can use GoldMine to formally request a meeting with these people.

This feature works both ways. Anyone using Outlook can send a meeting request to you. You can accept, reject, or suggest an alternative. After you agree, that meeting appears in both the GoldMine Calendar and in the Outlook calendar.

iCal standards still vary a bit from system to system, so not every function works properly with every iCal-based program. For example, recurring appointments in GoldMine may not translate perfectly to other programs. But for regular, simple stuff, iCal is great.

Scheduling a meeting with an Outlook user

The key to scheduling a meeting with someone using an iCal-based system is the little check box in the lower left side of the Scheduling dialog box. You can see this check box in Figure 8-3. Selecting this option sends an e-mail message to the recipient. The message is formatted in such a way that should the recipient accept your invitation, the meeting automatically posts itself in his or her Calendar.

The best way to test out all this iCal stuff is to schedule a meeting with yourself as the recipient. That way, you won't annoy all your friends as you experiment. When you're confident, you can try it with a real Outlook user.

Responding to a meeting request

You may receive a meeting request from an Outlook or Lotus user. The fifth option on the window, shown in Figure 8-6, allows you to check your own Calendar before deciding to accept, decline, or revise the meeting schedule.

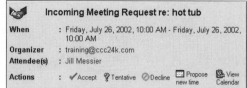

Figure 8-6:
An incoming
meeting
request.

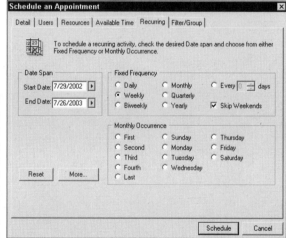

Scheduling Recurring Activities

Many times, you have a regularly scheduled activity. For example, if you have a team meeting every Monday morning at 8:00 a.m., you don't have to painstakingly enter it on your Calendar for every week of the year. You can go into the Scheduling dialog box and click the Recurring tab, as shown in Figure 8-7. This tab enables you to automatically schedule a daily, weekly, or monthly activity from now until the cows come home.

Figure 8-7:
Use the
Recurring
tab to
schedule
regularly
occurring
activities.

The recurring appointment system is a great way to make sure you always remember to make the phone, rent, and tax payments on time. This applies to company and to personal activities. (Remember, the personal ones should be scheduled against your own personal record.) A color code for payments may also be helpful.

The art of delegating

Delegating is an absolutely great way to avoid ever having to actually do any work yourself. On the other hand, a few rules of professional courtesy exist that you should probably be aware of before you start delegating activities:

✔ **Don't ever schedule anything for a co-worker without properly alerting him or her.** Properly alerting someone requires setting an alarm and clicking the Notify button. Although you may think that hollering across the hall is adequate, always cover yourself with an electronic notification.

✔ **Don't schedule appointments for people who will be upset that you're messing with their schedules.** You must understand and respect the pecking order in your organization.

✔ **Don't tell your client that the person you're scheduling for will absolutely be there.** Whenever you schedule for someone else, clarify to your client that you do so tentatively; the appointment still requires final approval by the user. Use the appropriate Calendar color (in the color scheme at my work, it's gray) for a tentative appointment.

✔ **Don't delegate all the nasty or boring stuff.** If people get the idea that you're doing that — well, remember that they can delegate things to you, too.

Chapter 9

Viewing Scheduled Activities

*W*hat good is scheduling activities unless you can easily view them? You can see scheduled activities in GoldMine by using either the Calendar or the Activity list. The Calendar displays the same basic information as the Activity list in a graphical format. The Activity list displays all your open activities, or selected categories of open activities, in a list format for any user. (*Open activities* are any scheduled activities that have not yet been completed.)

In this chapter, you find out how to view your scheduled activities as well as those of your co-workers. You also discover the different ways you can view activities. By viewing scheduled activities, you can determine what you and everyone else in your organization will be doing today, tomorrow, or any time in the future, and you can plan your time accordingly.

Viewing Activities Using the Calendar

Almost anything you can see from the Activity list you can also see from the Calendar view. The advantage of looking at the Calendar is that it provides a more graphical presentation, which, if you use color coding for your activities, can be a very clear way to look at your day's or week's action. (See Chapter 8 for more about color-coding your activities.)

You can get to the Calendar by clicking the Calendar icon on the toolbar.

Viewing open activities with the Calendar

The first thing I do when I arrive at work each morning is check my Calendar. I look at all my scheduled activities, and then I review the schedules for everyone else in my office. (See the "Viewing Groups of Users on the Calendar" section, later in this chapter.) That way, I immediately know who is on vacation, who is in the office, and who is scheduled to be out at some other location.

By consistently using the color-coding scheme, such as the one suggested in Chapter 8, your view of the Calendar gives you a quick and easy way to see what's going on for that day or week.

When you open the Calendar, the basic User's Calendar window appears, as shown in Figure 9-1. The default view is Day. You can change the view on the Calendar by clicking the following tabs:

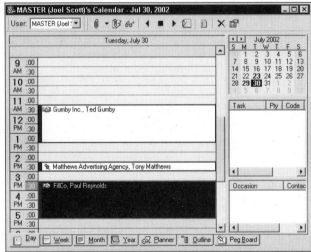

Figure 9-1:
You can see scheduled activities on the Calendar window.

✔ **Week:** You see seven days of activities, Sunday through Saturday, even if you don't work weekends. I select this Calendar view most often.

✔ **Month:** From this view, you can get an overall perspective of how busy a month you have, but few details are visible. You can see what each activity is by hovering the cursor over the activity and looking at the Status bar. You see the contact's name and reference of the activity. This is true on the Year view, also.

Depending on your selection in the Options⇨Show Work Days Only option from the local menu, each month either displays all calendar dates or only your working days for the month. All specified dates appear regardless of whether or not activities are scheduled.

✔ **Year:** As the highest level in the hierarchy, a year contains all activities grouped by months.

✔ **Planner:** You can check the schedule of one or more GoldMine users by clicking the Planner tab in the Calendar. Your settings in the Calendar tab of the Preferences window determine the period of days that the Planner tab displays. (See Chapter 3 to find out how to set preferences.) By default, the Planner shows 18 days of activities for the current user. Each activity is represented by a colored bar that shows the amount of time reserved for the activity, as shown in Figure 9-2.

✔ **Outline:** You can display your scheduled activities in a hierarchical structure by clicking the Outline tab. Each Calendar level is graphically represented by an icon. This view, shown in Figure 9-3, is a concession to those who are devoted to Day-Timers. The Outline view displays a tree with branches that correspond to the Year, Month, and Day tabs:

✔ **Date:** Each date lists all scheduled activities.

✔ **Peg Board:** In the Calendar, the Peg Board tab displays the login status and activity of individual users and system availability. For individual users, GoldMine tracks login/logout times, total logged time, and activity as determined by keystrokes and mouse use. When you need to leave your desk, you can *log away*, posting your location and expected time of return. See Figure 9-4.

Figure 9-2: Check other users' schedules on the Planner tab.

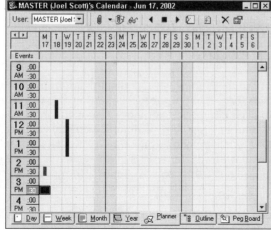

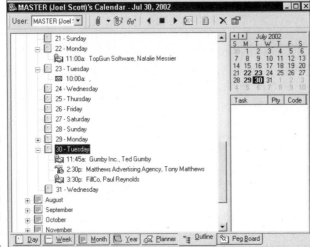

Figure 9-3:
Display
activities in
a hierarchy
on the
Outline tab.

Figure 9-4:
Track users
on the Peg
Board tab.

Viewing completed activities from the Calendar

By default, when an activity is completed, it disappears from the Calendar. I discuss completing activities in Chapter 10. A setting also exists within the Calendar that allows even completed activities to remain on the daily or weekly view of the Calendar. I highly recommend using this setting. By using this preference setting, you can look at past days or weeks on your Calendar to see what you (or others) have done. This is often useful, for example, when compiling your long overdue expense report. To retain completed activities on your Calendar, complete the following steps:

1. **Display the weekly view of your Calendar.**

2. **Right-click anywhere within the Calendar, and choose Activities from the shortcut menu.**

The Select Activities to View dialog box appears, as shown in Figure 9-5.

3. **In the right-hand column labeled Completed Activities, check all the activities you want to remain on your Calendar, and then click OK.**

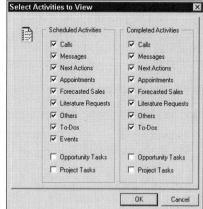

Figure 9-5:
Selecting past activities to keep on your Calendar.

From this point on, your completed activities are displayed with a gray background and a horizontal line through the listing. That way, you can look at last week's Calendar to remind yourself what you actually did. An example is shown in Figure 9-6.

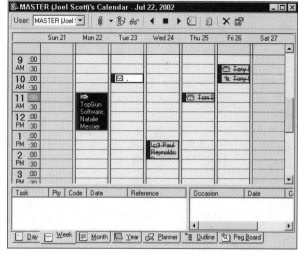

Figure 9-6:
Completed activities displayed on the Calendar.

Modifying the listing within each Calendar activity

You can use an option setting within the Calendar to determine exactly which fields display on the Calendar. Space is limited within each Calendar listing, so you don't want to view more than one or two fields at a time. The most important fields are probably the Contact Person and the Company fields, although you can elect to display any field or fields in the database. The following steps show you how to modify the display options on your Calendar:

1. **Display the weekly view of your Calendar.**

2. **Right-click anywhere within the Calendar and choose Options from the shortcut menu.**

   The Calendar Display Reference Properties dialog box appears, as shown in Figure 9-7.

3. **Select the fields you want to display and then click OK.**

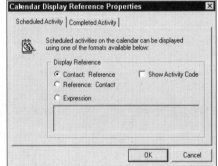

Figure 9-7:
Calendar
display
options.

Using the normally available selections, you can have the Calendar display either the company name or the contact name related to an activity. If you would like a little more information, you can arrange it by entering an expression in the dialog box, as shown in Figure 9-8. These expressions need to be written in dBASE, which is a little too technical for this book. But a good example will go a long way toward enabling you to create your own expressions in this case.

If you would like to see both the company name and the contact name on your Calendar, you can have GoldMine display exactly that by entering the following dBASE expression:

```
Trim (contact1->company)+", "+trim(contact1->contact)
```

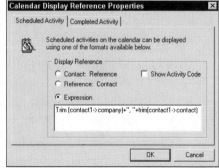

Figure 9-8:
Using an
expression
to specify
data to
display
on the
Calendar.

The `Trim` function removes all the unnecessary spaces surrounding the data.
The expression within the parentheses specifies the name of the data file followed by the data field itself. The two fields are separated by a comma and a
space.

Checking the Activity List

In addition to using the Calendar to view scheduled activities, another way to
find out what your coming attractions are is to use the Activity list. By using
the Activity list, you can see a little more information, such as the Reference
field related to each activity. To access the Activity list, click the View Activity
List icon on the Basic toolbar. A browse window appears, shown in Figure 9-9,
categorizing all the activity information into 11 categories, arranged as the
following tabs:

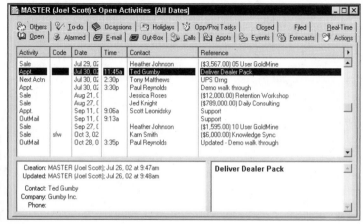

Figure 9-9:
View your
activities
as a list.

✔ **Open:** Displays all pending activities, regardless of category, for a particular user.

✔ **Alarmed:** Shows all pending activities with an alarm.

✔ **E-mail:** Lists pending GoldMine and pending Internet e-mail with information about the sender and the subject matter.

✔ **Out-Box:** Lists Internet e-mail messages that have been created but not yet sent. This situation happens if you choose to queue your outgoing e-mails rather than send them immediately. See Chapter 14 to find out how to send e-mail and use the Out-Box. When you're ready to actually send your outgoing e-mails, go to this tab, right-click, and choose Send to send all the previously queued messages.

✔ **Calls:** Lists pending phone calls. If you select auto-forwarding for calls (see Chapter 3), you may see pending phone calls that you were supposed to make but haven't gotten to yet.

✔ **Appts:** Lists pending appointments along with information about the date, time, duration, the primary contact, and reference.

✔ **Events:** Shows all scheduled events.

✔ **Forecasts:** Lists pending sales with data on projected close date, probability, amount of sale, product, and primary contact.

✔ **Actions:** Lists pending Next Actions.

✔ **Others:** Lists pending Other Activities.

✔ **To-do:** Lists pending to-do activities.

✔ **Occasions:** Shows personal holidays that you set up, such as birthdays and anniversaries.

✔ **Holidays:** Lists company holidays, such as New Year's Day and Christmas.

✔ **Opp/Proj Tasks:** Shows scheduled tasks that are associated with either an Opportunity or an on-going project.

✔ **Closed:** Lists all completed activities for a specified date range.

✔ **Filed:** Lists all available information about GoldMine and Internet e-mails that have been sent. This tab is similar to the Closed tab, but is specific to closed e-mails.

✔ **Real-Time:** Lists all *completed* activities for all dates and all users.

Getting back to the account

If you double-click any activity within the Activity list, GoldMine brings you directly to the proper account. From there, you can check either the Pending tab or the History tab. These tabs are often useful if you want to see more details, such as Notes, or if you want to make some modification to that activity.

Changing the focus of the Activity list

By default, the Activity list shows you the activities that are assigned to you (your user name) and the activities that are scheduled for the current date. You can change either of these settings so that you can see activities assigned to others and activities scheduled for a future date. By positioning the cursor anywhere within the data section of the Activity list and right-clicking, you get a menu list of choices, as shown in Figure 9-10. From this list, you can choose a variety of options.

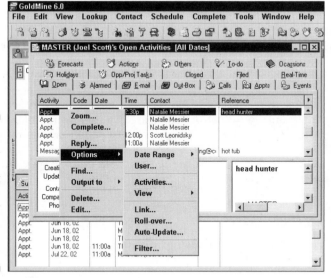

Figure 9-10: Right-click an appointment to change the user or date shown in the Activity list.

The two most obvious choices are Date Range and User. Select Date Range to reset the default date(s) of the display. Select User to view someone else's Activity list.

Forwarding activities

By right-clicking within the Activity list, you can also forward activities either to yourself (to complete at a later date) or to another user. This option is called *Roll-over* and is potentially dangerous. More than one GoldMiner has come to grief using it. With one click of the mouse, you send all your scheduled activities to someone else, and no easy way exists for you to get them back, even if you really didn't mean to do it. *Auto-forwarding* is a good substitute for forwarding things to yourself, and *territory realignment* works well to reassign activities to another user. My recommendation: Leave Roll-over alone; it has bitten more than one user in the past. Instead, use Territory Realignment, which is an option under Tools in the main menu. The Territory Realignment Wizard walks you through the entire procedure.

You can now transfer all your scheduled activities to an (yours or someone else's) iCalendar (iCal) file. This is useful if you have to use Outlook instead of GoldMine, say if you're going on vacation and will only have access to Outlook on your laptop. You can transfer your scheduled activities to an iCalendar file by right-clicking in the Activity Window, selecting Output, and then selecting iCalendar file.

Viewing Groups of Users on the Calendar

You can actually view up to 16 users' schedules simultaneously, which is useful if, for example, you want to see whether anyone from your Boston office is available to go to Halifax, Nova Scotia, next week. This is made particularly simple if all your Boston people are in a user group that you have already created. To see a list of all registered users, follow these steps:

1. **Click the drop-down arrow in the User field in the upper-left corner of the Calendar window.**

   A shortcut menu appears.

2. **Select Multiple Users.**

   This choice leads you to a dialog box listing all the registered users, as shown in Figure 9-11.

3. **Select as many users as you would like and then click OK.**

   You are limited to displaying a total of 16 separate users.

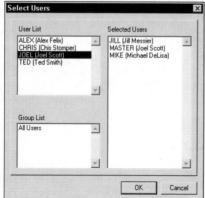

Figure 9-11:
Select
multiple
users to
view their
Calendars.

Another approach to viewing multiple users is to select a group. See Chapter 12 for more information on groups. A typical group may be the "Sales" group, or those people who work in one of your regional offices. Then, instead of selecting those individuals, you can select the group of which they are members.

Chapter 10

Dealing with and Completing Scheduled Activities

· ·

In This Chapter

▶ Delegating activities to other people

▶ Rescheduling activities

▶ Deleting activities

▶ Ignoring activities

▶ Completing activities

· ·

*T*he whole point of using the GoldMine Calendar system is for you to schedule all sorts of activities and then dispose of each of them in some logical fashion. In this chapter, you find out how to get all scheduled activities off your Calendar and get home for dinner on time. I promise.

You have three ways to view previously scheduled activities:

✔ **Directly from the Pending tab of an individual record.** Use this method when you want to focus on a particular account and have easy access to the Pending folder. See Chapters 8 and 9 for more details on how scheduled activities are related to records.

✔ **From the Activity list.** Use this method when you want to view all your different types of scheduled activities for some time period.

✔ **From the Calendar.** Using this method is often the best, particularly when you deal with activities that have a specific duration that you need to reschedule.

Regardless of the method you use to access your scheduled activities, you have five and only five things you can do with an activity: delegate, reschedule, delete, ignore, and complete. In this chapter, I explain these five actions and how to accomplish completing your activities by using these actions.

Four Ways to Complete Your Activities

In this section, I describe four of the five ways to complete an activity. Each of these methods is valid and gets the job done; however, these methods are temporary or weak solutions. To discover the fifth and best way to complete an activity, see the upcoming section, "The Best Way to Complete an Activity."

Delegating activities to other people

Remember, the fundamental design goal of GoldMine is to allow a team of people to coordinate themselves. In this fashion, one way to complete an activity is to delegate it to someone else, which is my personal favorite. To delegate an activity, follow these steps:

1. **On the Schedule dialog box, look for the User field in the upper-right corner and click the down arrow next to the field.**

   A lookup list appears, and you immediately see all the registered Users on your team. If you don't see a list, then no other Users exist, and there just isn't anyone to delegate anything to. Too bad.

2. **From the list of registered users, select the person to whom you want to delegate the task.**

3. **Click the OK button and GoldMine immediately places this task on your "delegee's" Calendar.**

You won't be very popular in the office, however, if you don't let people know you've just delegated some task. Even setting the Alarm to go off 20 minutes before the task is scheduled may not be enough time. No one wants just 20 minutes' notice before giving a presentation to the Board of Directors. Refer to Chapter 8 for delegating etiquette.

Always click the Notify button when delegating tasks to someone else. When you do so, GoldMine immediately sends an e-mail message to that person, letting her know that you have scheduled her for this activity.

Rescheduling activities

One of the most common actions you'll take with an appointment is to reschedule it. The easiest way to reschedule an appointment is to do it directly from the Calendar. Not only is the Calendar the best way to see what alternate times are available, but physically changing the time of the appointment from the Calendar is simple.

I like to use the drag-and-drop method for rescheduling. From either the daily or weekly Calendar view, simply highlight an existing activity and drag it to some other available time slot on either that day or another day. GoldMine automatically changes the time and date on the Pending tab and on the Activity list. If you need to make more than a minor adjustment to a scheduled activity, you can double-click the specific activity in the Pending tab. This brings you right back to the original Schedule dialog box, and you can defer the appointment for a year or more, or turn a one-hour sales call into a three-day presentation.

Deleting activities

The only time you should ever consider deleting an activity from your schedule is when you inadvertently schedule it for the wrong account. To delete an activity, follow these steps:

1. **Right-click the activity within the Pending tab.**

2. **From the menu that appears, choose Delete and confirm by clicking the Yes button.**

3. **Find the correct account.**

4. **Schedule it all over again.**

You're probably inclined to delete an appointment when your client calls you and cancels your appointment. Resist the urge. Instead, complete the appointment and make a notation in the activity notepad that your client canceled, or alternatively, use a Result Code to indicate that the client cancelled the appointment. That way, you create a historical trail of events that documents every appointment you've made and the action taken. The following story is a perfect example of the importance of completing an activity rather than deleting it.

An insurance agent (I'll call him Moe) was having a hard time with a troublesome customer. Moe had scheduled an appointment at 2:00 p.m. with the customer to renew a policy, but the customer called Moe and told him not to come . . . ever.

So Moe deleted the appointment in GoldMine. At 2:30 p.m. on the appointment day, the client called Moe's boss and complained that Moe had once again not shown up for an appointment. Moe's boss checked the account's Pending and History tabs and found no evidence that Moe had ever scheduled the appointment because Moe had deleted the appointment. Assuming that Moe had just blown another appointment, the boss fired him.

Ignoring activities

You don't have to do anything to ignore an activity. But if you choose to ignore an activity, it stays on your Calendar until you act on it. If you set the preferences to auto-forward uncompleted activities (see Chapter 8) to the next day, soon you'll have hundreds of activities scheduled for yourself. Coming into the office and finding a few thousand tasks on your schedule is pretty discouraging. And if you've set an Alarm for an activity, the Alarm annoyingly continues to nag at you until you have no choice but to do something constructive, like completing it.

The Best Way to Complete an Activity

When you run out of all the other options and can no longer delegate or reschedule an activity, it's time to actually complete it. After all, you were really supposed to do that in the first place. While I use the word "complete" in different ways, let there be no mistake here: *Completing an activity* means accomplishing the intended task (like going to the meeting or making the phone call) and then taking it off your schedule.

You can complete an activity from the Calendar, the Activity list, or the Pending tab. In this section, I explain the time and the place to use each method. The first two methods allow you to review all of your daily activities and dispose of them. The Pending tab method forces you to go from one account to another. I like to use the Calendar method for completing most of my activities, but it's all just a matter of personal preference.

Completing from the Calendar

To complete an activity from the Calendar, you must have the Calendar window in front of you. (Open the Calendar by clicking the Calendar icon on the Basic toolbar.) I prefer to complete activities from the weekly Calendar view (click the Week tab on the main Calendar window), but the daily view also works well for this exercise.

To complete an activity from the Calendar, follow these steps:

1. **Right-click the activity on the Calendar and select Complete.**

   The Complete an Activity dialog box appears.

2. **Fill in all the appropriate fields on this dialog box.**

   The most important fields to fill in are

   - **Result Code:** Usually, you use the COM code to indicate the activity is complete.

   - **The Activity notepad:** Enter notes about the appointment or the call here.

   - **The Time field:** Use this field if you want GoldMine to track how much time you spend on particular activities or with a particular client.

3. **If you want to follow up on this activity with another activity for this client, select the Schedule a Follow-up option at the lower left of the dialog box.**

4. **When you're finished, click OK.**

   You may want to use the Follow-up option if you have just come back from an initial sales call, for example, and you promised your prospect that you would come back in a week with a proposal. If you select the Schedule a Follow-up option, you then select from the lookup list what type of action is next. When you have done this, GoldMine brings you to yet another scheduling dialog box so you can start all over again scheduling another activity for this account.

As soon as you complete a scheduled activity, GoldMine automatically moves it from the Pending tab (on the main screen) to the History tab, where all the completed activities for each account are stored.

Completing from the Activity list

If you're more list-oriented than graphically inclined, you may prefer to complete your activities from the Activity list. You can access the Activity list by clicking the Activity List icon from the main toolbar.

You can display the Activity list with many different options:

- ✔ **The type of activities to be displayed.** For example, you may only be interested in seeing appointments, or perhaps just phone calls. Just select the appropriate tab on the Activity List window.

✔ **The range of dates to be displayed.** Right-click within the browse area to show a shortcut menu, as shown in Figure 10-1. When you select Options, a submenu appears, allowing you to change the range of dates for the Activity list display.

Within the Activity list options is the Roll-over option. If you use this option improperly, you can easily transfer all your pending activities to another user. Because no way exists to get these activities back without also getting all of that user's regular activities, you could come to grief with this option.

Completing from the Pending tab

Complete an activity from the Pending tab if you want to focus on one particular account, and if you're trying to dispose of some of the scheduled activities for that account.

After you highlight the Pending tab, you immediately see all the scheduled activities associated with that account. To complete any particular activity, you need only right-click the activity. As you can see in Figure 10-2, you get a shortcut menu. One of the choices is Complete, and you should choose that one.

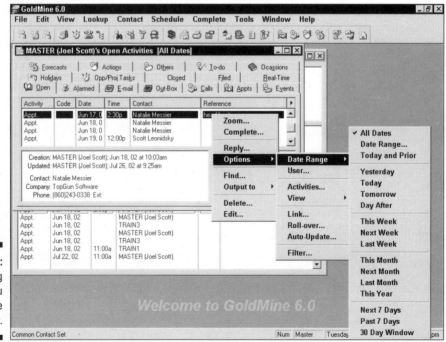

Figure 10-1: Changing what you see in the Activity list.

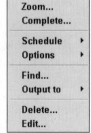

Figure 10-2:
Completing
activities
right
from the
Pending tab.

Zoom...
Complete...

Schedule ▶
Options ▶

Find...
Output to ▶

Delete...
Edit...

Selecting the Complete choice leads you directly to the same Complete an Activity dialog box that the other two methods also arrive at. From there, you can fill in a Result Code, add some notes, and can immediately go into Follow-up mode.

Completing your activities, no matter which of the three methods you employ, transfers that pending activity directly to the History tab.

Chapter 11

Sales Forecasting

In This Chapter

▶ Entering your forecast

▶ Viewing your sales pipeline

▶ Viewing and completing a forecast

Sales forecasting is a basic tool that has been used by salespeople and teams since the Precambrian Period (before 1982). The basic idea is to enter quotas, forecasts, and completed sales and to analyze each of these at every stage. By entering your expectations, you can then compare your forecast against reality as time marches on. Within GoldMine, you can also view statistical graphs and print reports to see how you and your team are progressing.

A forecasted sale is really just a special case of a scheduled activity. Basically, you assign a sale to a user (usually yourself) and schedule when you think you will close it. If you consistently perform this routine for every realistic opportunity, you can use GoldMine to compile all sorts of sales forecasting graphs and reports. These graphs and reports can relate to one salesperson or to an entire group of them.

If you have a sales manager, she no doubt always asks for your forecast. A good sales manager who has access to her people's forecasts will change her end-of-the-month question from, "When are you gonna close that thing, already?" to "What can I do to help you with this opportunity?" Forecasting becomes a whole new and nicer way of working together.

Entering Quotas and Forecasts

Setting challenging but realistic goals for yourself and your team is a basic ingredient of success. It applies to all facets of life and is what the monthly and annual quotas are all about.

Setting up a quota

Around the Thanksgiving holiday every year, I sit down and assign myself and my team goals for the coming year. I break our goals down into bite-size monthly sales numbers, trying to make each month a little better than the one before and trying to set the goals to be challenging enough to be exciting, but realistic enough so no one gets frustrated. Goals and quotas are also an important part of business planning: Someone else's annual budget is based on your quota.

You assign quotas for individual users from the Quote Analysis dialog box. To assign a quota, follow these steps:

1. **From the main menu, choose View⇨Analysis⇨Quota Analysis.**

   The Quota Analysis dialog box appears.

2. **Click the New button at the bottom of the dialog box.**

   The Quota Profile dialog box appears (see Figure 11-1).

Figure 11-1:
A typical
sales quota.

3. **In the User field, select the intended User from the lookup list.**

   Remember that quotas are specific to individual users.

4. **Enter the date for the beginning of the particular quota period.**

   You can do so by scrolling, by right-clicking to get to the Calendar, or by simply typing a date.

5. **Enter the date for the end of the quota period.**

   By default, dates are set for monthly quota periods.

6. **Type the dollar amount of expected sales in the Quota field.**

7. **When you're finished, click OK.**

GoldMine automatically generates numbers for the Forecast field, Closed Sales field, and Lost Sales field as you schedule and complete forecasted sales activities, but only if you use the proper Result Codes (COM and LST for Closed and for Lost respectively).

You can always adjust your quotas if they become unrealistic. You can do this on the same Quota Analysis dialog box. By highlighting an individual quota entry and then clicking the Edit button, you can revise numbers up or down, or change date ranges.

You can always look at your ratio of closed sales to quota or forecasted sales to completed sales with the radio buttons at the bottom of the Quota Analysis dialog box. By selecting the radio button for percentage of Quota, GoldMine compares your actual closed sales to your current quota. The radio button for percentage of forecast compares closed sales to what you have forecasted for a particular date range.

Entering a forecast

To enter a forecast for an account, follow these steps:

1. **Locate the account to which you intend to sell your product.**

2. **From the main GoldMine screen, choose Schedule⇨Forecasted Sale.**

    The Schedule a Forecasted Sale dialog box appears, as shown in Figure 11-2.

Figure 11-2:
Enter a sales forecast in the Schedule a Forecasted Sale dialog box.

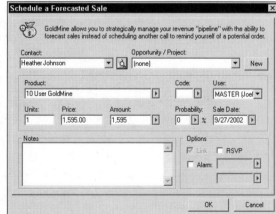

3. **Fill in the Contact field.**

This field defaults to the primary contact for the account. You can change this entry by either typing another name or, better yet, selecting another contact from the lookup list. This lookup list displays every additional contact that has been entered as a secondary contact. If you didn't select the proper account before beginning your forecast, click the right arrow to the right of the Contact field to temporarily select the proper account. Assigning a sale to an Opportunity can be done in the Opportunity / Project field. Opportunities and Projects are discussed in detail in Chapter 23.

4. **In the Product field, enter the product line you intend to sell to this account.**

The Product field has a lookup list that you should be sure to set up correctly and use consistently. Chapter 21 discusses lookup lists. If you randomly enter all sorts of different product names, you'll be disappointed when you try to run a sales report grouped by product. I discuss sales reports in Chapter 19.

5. **In the Units field, enter how many of these products you expect to sell.**

You can use decimals here to indicate fractional quantities.

6. **Enter the price of the product into the Price field.**

As soon as you fill in the Price field, GoldMine automatically calculates the total amount of your projected sale. Items such as sales tax and shipping are usually not included here.

7. **In the Probability field, enter the probability that you will complete the sale.**

This field is always interesting. Your choices are integers ranging from 0 to 100. Neither of those two numbers is actually appropriate. If your sale has a zero probability, then you probably shouldn't waste your time predicting it. In fact, just go on to the next opportunity. A probability of 100 percent indicates that you already have at least a signed deal. If that's the case, this sale is complete and shouldn't be in your forecast anymore.

I usually don't bother forecasting a sale unless I think at least a 30 percent chance exists of closing it. Develop your own guidelines for determining when and if a sale should be in your forecast. Consistency in this area is good not only for yourself but throughout your entire team.

8. **In the Anticipated Sale Date field, enter what you feel is a likely date for the completion of the sale.**

This field is also a fun item. Most of the time, this date is the result of a guessing game. If you enter a date that's not too far away, your forecast report looks good for the short term. Your sales manager will be pleased.

At least, she'll be pleased until that date comes and goes, and the deal isn't done. I assume you've been doing this kind of forecasting one way or another for a long time now. Pick a date in whatever way seems to work for you. I enter the most realistic dates I can.

The products, projected sale amounts, probability, and forecasted closing dates can all be modified as your sale progresses. You should make it a habit to modify these things as needed to keep your overall forecast on target.

9. Select the Alarm check box if you want to be reminded of this sale.

I usually don't use the alarm. Instead, I suggest using the Notes section to remind you, or the sales manager, of details such as special pricing or unique payment terms.

10. When you finish entering your data, click OK to register this sales forecast.

That's basically all there is to entering a new sales forecast. You can now see it, access it, and edit it from the Pending tab on the account's main screen.

Sales forecasting is easy, requiring only six or seven entries and, as a result, you may never need to compile another forecast report again.

Click the Recurring tab on the Schedule a Forecasted Sale dialog box to enter multiple sales at once. For example, if you sell an insurance policy that requires 36 monthly payments for the next 3 years, you can describe this payment, as shown in Figure 11-3. In this way, you need only enter the sale once, not 36 separate times.

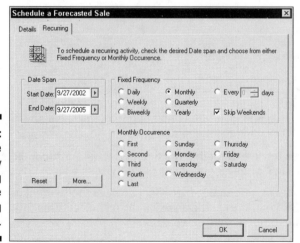

Figure 11-3: Schedule regularly occurring sales on the Recurring tab.

Viewing Your Sales Pipeline

If you or a manager previously entered a quota, you can readily compare your current situation with this guideline. You can see the sales projections in tabular format or in graphical format. Neither of these allows you to see individual sales, but you can see those from the Forecasts tab of the Activity list, which is discussed in the "Viewing individual items in the forecast" section, later in this chapter.

Analyzing sales in tabular format

Tabular format is the simplest way of looking at your sales projections. In this format, you can see weekly and monthly subtotals and totals. Start with this method before going on to the graphical format that requires a few more specifications before you actually see any results:

1. **From the main menu, choose View➪Analysis➪Forecast Analysis.**

   The Forecasted Sales Analysis dialog box appears, as shown in Figure 11-4.

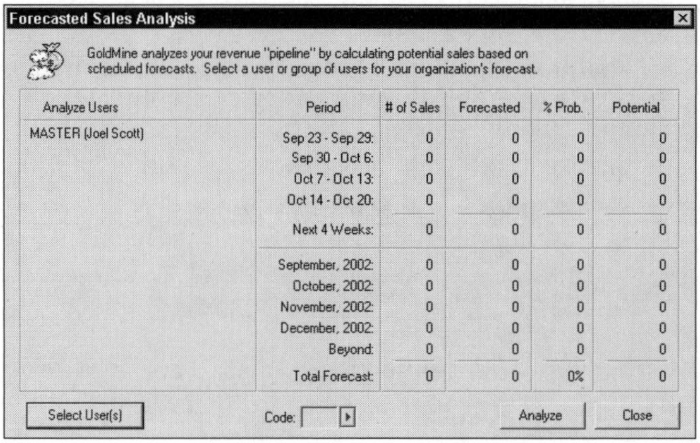
Forecasted Sales Analysis
GoldMine analyzes your revenue "pipeline" by calculating potential sales based on scheduled forecasts. Select a user or group of users for your organization's forecast.
Analyze Users
Period
# of Sales
Forecasted
% Prob.
Potential
MASTER (Joel Scott)
Sep 23 - Sep 29: 0 0 0 0
Sep 30 - Oct 6: 0 0 0 0
Oct 7 - Oct 13: 0 0 0 0
Oct 14 - Oct 20: 0 0 0 0
Next 4 Weeks: 0 0 0 0
September, 2002: 0 0 0 0
October, 2002: 0 0 0 0
November, 2002: 0 0 0 0
December, 2002: 0 0 0 0
Beyond: 0 0 0 0
Total Forecast: 0 0 0% 0
Select User(s)
Code:
Analyze
Close

Figure 11-4: The Forecasted Sales Analysis dialog box.

2. **In the lower-left corner, click the Select User(s) button to select whichever user or users you want to analyze.**

   From the Select Users dialog box, you can select individual users or groups. After you do this, the analysis dialog box returns, but you won't see anything different yet.

3. **Click the Analyze button at the bottom of the dialog box to see some totals.**

   You should almost immediately see statistics for the current four-week period, for the next four months, and everything beyond, too, as shown in Figure 11-5.

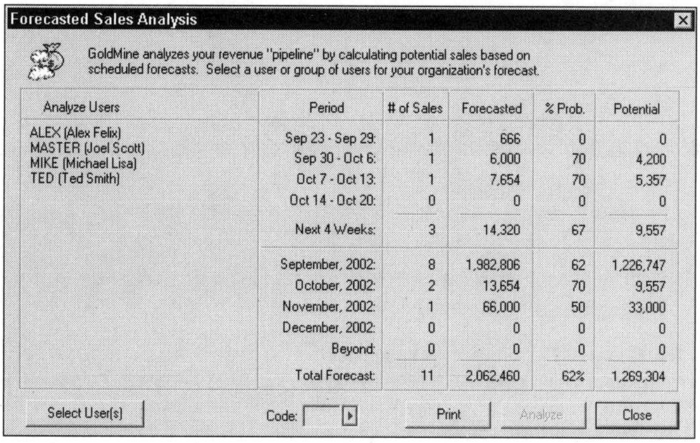

Figure 11-5:
Click the
Analyze
button to
see sales
forecast
statistics.

Most of these numbers are obvious, except for the column labeled Potential. Potential is a computed number and is the product of the total forecasted amount and the average probability. In other words, the potential sale amount is the amount you will probably sell in each time period.

Analyzing sales in graphical format

Sometimes a graph is worth a thousand tables. You can view your sales using graphs by following these steps:

1. **From the main menu, choose View➪Analysis➪Graphical Analysis.**

   The Graphical Analysis Options dialog box appears, as shown in Figure 11-6. The dialog box is divided into five sections:

   • Graph Type

   • Users

   • Activities

   • Time Span

   • Options

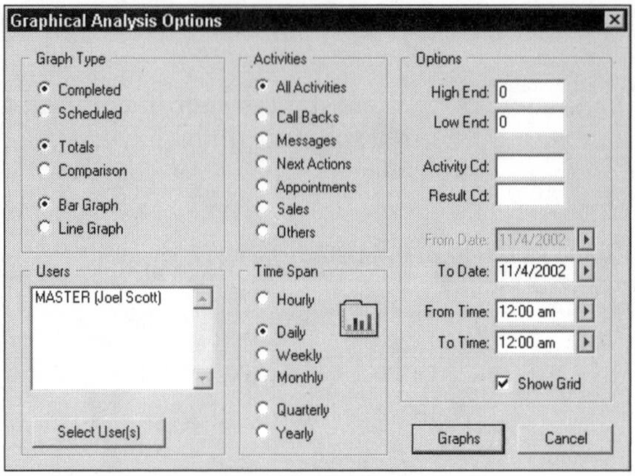

Figure 11-6:
The
Graphical
Analysis
Options
dialog box.

This dialog box has a lot more options than the tabular analysis dialog box; however, it's not really hard to get through.

2. **In the Graph Type section, select Scheduled and choose whether you want to see the data as bars or lines — feel free to experiment.**

3. **In the Activities section, select Sales.**

4. **Make the Time Span either weekly or monthly.**

5. **Select the appropriate user(s) or group(s).**

6. **Click the Graphs button to see a graphical analysis of your sales.**

   It may take GoldMine a few seconds to cook up your graph, but you should shortly see a neat graph of your future.

7. **Click the Close button at the top right to exit this dialog box.**

Viewing individual items in the forecast

Both the tabular and the graphical methods of examining your forecast give you summary information only. To see each pending sale, follow these steps:

1. **From the main menu, choose View⇨Activity List and then click the Forecasts tab.**

   Immediately, you see the browse window detailing the individual forecasted sales for the selected user, as shown in Figure 11-7. You can change the user if you want.

2. **To see further details on each sale, double-click a sale.**

The particular account for that sale appears. The forecasted sale itself is in the Pending tab for that account. You can examine the sale in the Pending tab by double-clicking the sale. Or easier still, right-click the highlighted sale (while still in the Activity listing) to zoom in on it, but then you can't edit it.

Figure 11-7:
The Activity list shows individual forecasted sales.

Forecast reports

GoldMine comes with an extensive series of standard reports, some of which relate to sales forecasting. You can review these reports by first accessing the report section. Clicking the Reports icon on the main screen takes you directly to the Reports dialog box. You can also access the reporting section by selecting File⇨Print Reports.

Refer to Chapter 19 for more details on reporting, but for now, select the category of reports called Analysis, as shown in Figure 11-8. On the left side of the dialog box are the predefined sales forecasting reports. One typical example is shown in Figure 11-8.

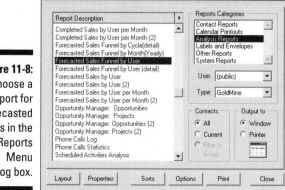

Figure 11-8:
Choose a report for forecasted sales in the Reports Menu dialog box.

Viewing a group forecast

In the Forecasted Sales Analysis dialog box, notice a button in the lower-left corner that allows you to select users. Click this button, and another dialog box appears that allows you to select either individual users or groups of users.

Selecting a group of users is particularly useful if, for example, you're a sales manager and you want to see how all your people are doing versus their quotas or forecasts. As long as you have defined each of these salespeople as belonging to a specific group, you can easily do this analysis in a moment.

Double-clicking any User or any group of Users listed just below will automatically move those people into the list of selected Users. After you have done this, click OK, and then click the Analyze button on the Forecasted Sales Analysis dialog box.

Completing Your Forecasts

One way or another, win, lose, or draw, you eventually need to complete your forecasted sales. You attack this from either the individual account's Pending tab, from your Calendar, or from the Activity list. I usually start at the individual account's Pending tab. Highlighting the particular forecasted sale and right-clicking brings you to an option to complete the sale, as shown in Figure 11-9.

Figure 11-9:
Completing
a sale.

Several key elements are available for you to consider as you complete the sale. The first is the Private option on the upper-right part of the Complete a Sale dialog box. You can select this if you never want anyone to know what you sold. The Privacy button is particularly useful *(not)* if you expect a commission for the sale. To be truthful, I can't think of too many reasons to ever select this.

Further down the Complete a Sale dialog box are the Code and Result fields. I use the Code field to further describe the type of sale. For example, I might want to separate software and hardware sales for reporting purposes. The Result field allows the exact status of the deal to be further categorized. For example, you may lose a sale for many different reasons. Perhaps the client abandoned the project (ABA), or you lost it to a competitor because your management wouldn't budge on the price (PRI). Make up your own lookup lists for these two fields. Refer to Chapter 21 for help with lookup lists.

On the right side of the dialog box in Figure 11-9 is the Success field. You have two choices for this field: You either Closed the sale or you Lost it. Your selection governs how this sale is reported on the Statistical Analysis and Quota Analysis dialog boxes discussed earlier in this chapter.

Chapter 12

Using Filters and Groups

In This Chapter

▶ Getting familiar with filters

▶ Creating and using filters

▶ Building and using groups

As your contacts increase and your database grows, you'll quickly find a need to isolate certain kinds of records. For example, you may want to see all your accounts in Albany. Another time, perhaps just those accounts in Colorado. Yet another time, perhaps you want to see only Moe's accounts that have fax numbers. You can organize your records using filters and groups.

Filters perform much like spaghetti colanders. You can use a filter to drain away all the records you don't need, leaving just the ones you want.

Groups are like filters on steroids. Using groups allows for faster access to sets of records, and groups allow you to generate sets of records where no logical method exists to select them other than pointing at individual records. This method is called *tagging*. See the "Building groups from manually tagged records" section for more information about tagging records.

After you create either a filter or a group, you can use either tool to regulate exactly what data shows up on a report, or which accounts receive correspondence, or who to schedule for a phone call via Automated Processes. These components of GoldMine are extremely powerful.

Understanding Filters

Using GoldMine, you can build simple or sophisticated filters. A simple filter may depend upon just one field — for example, all the accounts in one city. A more sophisticated filter may be a function of several fields and requires some understanding of Boolean logic. (*Boolean logic* deals with the evaluation of mathematical expressions that contain one or more ANDs, ORs, NOTs, and parentheses.)

But don't worry. Even if Boolean logic isn't your cup of tea, the next few sections show you how to create almost any filter you ever need.

Accessing the filter system

To access the GoldMine filter system, choose Lookup⇨Filters from the main menu, or click the Filters icon at the top of the screen. The Filters and Groups window appears, as shown in Figure 12-1.

Figure 12-1:
The Filters
and Groups
window.

The View Filters field displays either a specific user or Public. You can assign filters to particular users. In Figure 12-1, you can see the existing filters belonging to MASTER. You can assign more general filters as Public filters. This assignment process is really more a way of separating filters into manageable sections than anything else.

The window shown in Figure 12-1 displays all the existing filters that belong to MASTER. To really explore how to set up your filters, you need to create a new filter.

Creating and using a new filter

To create a filter, follow these steps:

1. **On the Filters and Groups window (refer to Figure 12-1), click the New button.**

   The New Filter dialog box appears, as shown in Figure 12-2.

2. **Enter a name for and assign an owner to your new filter.**

   GoldMine accepts almost anything as a filter name, but you should name your filters logically and specifically. When you come back in six months looking for some filter you're sure you have already created, you don't want to see a list of filters called Filter#1, Filter#2, and Filter#3. For example, if you want to create a filter to isolate accounts in Connecticut, name that filter something like "Accounts in Connecticut" or "Connecticut records."

To assign an owner, either select yourself, Public, or another user who hasn't read this chapter and needs your help. Assigning an owner to a filter allows you to group your most commonly used filters together. Also, when setting user preferences (see Chapter 3), you can prohibit a particular user from accessing someone else's filters. That way, one salesperson would be unable to see another salesperson's accounts.

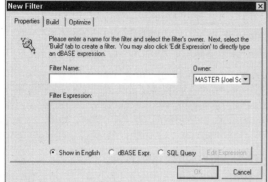

Figure 12-2: Starting a new filter.

3. **Click the Build tab to move on to the real action of building your filter.**

   The Build tab is shown in Figure 12-3. On this tab, you select the field you want to base your new filter on, the operator, and a value.

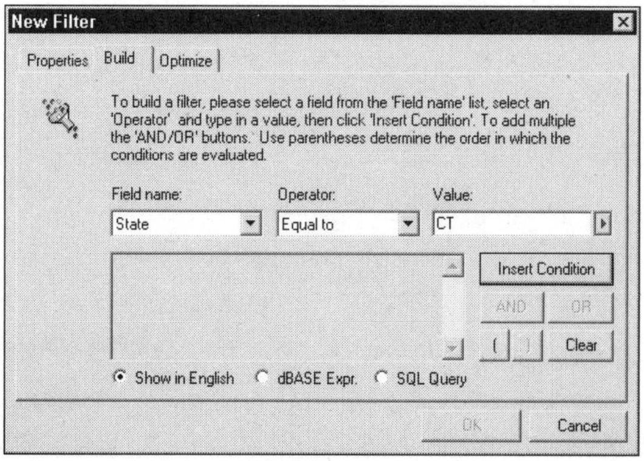

Figure 12-3: Specifying a new filter's parameters.

A. Select the field you want to base your new filter on.

Click the down arrow to the right of the Field name (refer to Figure 12-3) to display all the available fields, and then select a field. If you want to isolate all your records for the state of Connecticut, you would select the State field here, and then go on to Operator and Value.

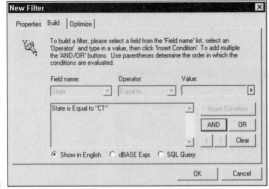

Only GoldMine's standard fields and user-defined fields are available for use in Filters. Supplementary fields, such as e-mail address and those others in the Details tab, can only be accessed by using Groups.

B. Select an operator from the lookup list.

For example, if you choose Equal to (the simplest of all the operators), you're asking GoldMine to locate all the records where the field exactly matches the value you supply.

C. Enter a value in the Value field.

The value you enter must match entries in your records. For example, if you use State as your field name, then your value must be the abbreviation of the particular state you chose. In other words, use "CT" as your value rather than "Connecticut" because the State field itself uses abbreviations rather than the full state name.

D. Click the Insert Condition button.

Your growing filter now displays in the rectangular area below the Field name field. Your filter is practically built, and your dialog box should look similar to Figure 12-4.

Figure 12-4:
A
completed
filter.

E. Click OK.

The dialog box that lists all available filters appears. You should see your filter listed alphabetically. Your new filter won't do anything yet because you haven't *activated* it. Activating a filter causes

GoldMine to focus on just those records that meet the conditions of the filter.

4. Activate your filter by clicking the Activate button.

The main GoldMine screen appears. In the title bar, you see a statement that your filter is active, and the last record you were dealing with is on the screen. That old record may be in front of you even if it isn't part of your filter. This is curious but not harmful.

When your filter is active, as soon as you press Page Up or Page Down or scroll to another record, you begin seeing the effect of your filter. GoldMine ignores all the records in the database that don't match the filer, so you only see the records that match the criteria in your filter.

At this point, you can use your filter with

- ✔ **Any of the reports you want to run:** As long as your filter is active, any report you run will have only those records that the filter has found. See Chapter 19 for details on reports.

- ✔ **Mail, fax, and e-mail merges:** You can send correspondence to just a subset of your entire database by using a filter. See Chapters 13 through 15 for details.

- ✔ **Automated Processes:** These processes are a great way to regulate your marketing efforts. Chapter 25 discusses the details of Automated Processes.

When you get the hang of filters, you'll discover that they're critical to your daily work and that they can help you with such things as

- ✔ Replacing fields globally

- ✔ Deleting unwanted records

- ✔ Merging/purging of records

- ✔ Creating transfer sets for synchronization

- ✔ Exporting

- ✔ Scheduling

- ✔ Running reports

Releasing a filter

As long as a filter is active, you won't be able to easily use records outside the scope of that filter. You can get your entire database back by releasing the active filter. You can release a filter by

> ✔ Clicking the Filters icon from the main screen
>
> ✔ Clicking the Release button on the Filters and Groups window

After you release your filter, the main screen returns, and the title bar shows nothing but the name of the current record.

Counting records in a filter

When you completely finish entering a filter, the Filters and Groups window appears. Every time you finish developing a filter, ask GoldMine for a count of the records that the filter finds. You can do so by highlighting the specific filter, right-clicking, and selecting Count from the menu that appears, as shown in Figure 12-5. You could alternatively use the Preview tab instead of Count. The Preview option shows you the specific records that are included in your filter.

Figure 12-5:
Counting
records
in a filter.

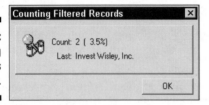

GoldMine immediately begins counting how many records in the entire database fall within the scope of this filter. Many times when you develop a filter, you don't know ahead of time exactly how many records you will find. That's okay, but you may want to know approximately how many are within a filter.

What you don't want is a filter that finds either no records at all or one that decides every record in the database is part of the filter. In either of these cases, something is likely wrong with your filter expression. If you encounter this situation, go back and review your filter expression and adjust it.

Generally, you get a record count somewhere between none and all records in the database and the percentage of the database included in the filter. You can use this number to help you manage the use of the filter. If your filter finds only three records, you may not consider that enough people to invite to a seminar. If the filter finds thousands of records, you may consider that too many for the mailing you had in mind. Adjust the filter until it finds a number of accounts you're more comfortable with.

Sometimes patience is a virtue

One of the advantages of filters is that no matter when you want to use one, it finds all the records it's designed to find. Your filter can find records that didn't even exist when the filter was initially created. It does so by searching the entire database for records every time you activate the filter.

Sometimes, that strength also can be a weakness. If you have a large database (many thousands of records), it may take a considerable time to find those records. A 10,000-record database may require several minutes for a filter to find all of its records. You could view this as a good time to get a cup of coffee or to investigate the Optimize button on the Build Filter dialog box. Optimizing allows you to restrict the filter's search to speed things up a bit. Groups were developed, in part, to reduce your number of trips to the coffee machine and to speed things up a little.

Reviewing Boolean logic

You may need to examine logical operators if you want to prepare for more sophisticated filters. If this section brings back bad memories of eighth-grade math class, I apologize in advance.

If two or more fields need to be involved in the development of a filter, they must be connected to one another with logical operators. The operators are

- ( )
- AND
- OR

The *order of precedence* specifies which of the preceding operators GoldMine evaluates first. Another way to look at it is, "Which of these is the most important?" It turns out that the order shown in the preceding list is the exact sequence that GoldMine uses to evaluate an expression.

This sequence corresponds with algebra. Everything within the parentheses is calculated first, then the expressions separated by AND are evaluated, and the OR connections are done last. This order is very critical to the proper development of sophisticated filters.

Looking at a more sophisticated filter

An instructive example of a sophisticated filter comes from real life at my company. We plan to host a User Group meeting and want to invite all our clients from Connecticut and Massachusetts. I decide to fax the invitations rather than mail them. I need to develop a filter that isolates just the right accounts.

Whenever you want to develop a filter that's even moderately complicated, write it out on paper first, and then copy it character by character into the GoldMine filter system. Editing a filter that isn't quite right is relatively difficult, so you may just as well plan a little up-front to avoid frustration later.

In the User Group meeting example, three statements need to be coordinated:

✔ The State field contains CT.

✔ The State field contains MA.

✔ The Fax field contains a fax number.

The filtering system gives only the three previously mentioned operators — the parentheses, ANDs, and ORs. Each of the three statements needs to be connected with an AND or an OR. As I set up the filter, my first few attempts don't work correctly — so you don't make similar mistakes, I show you where I go wrong and how I fix the mistakes.

Just take one piece of the projected filter and connect the first two expressions. I first try

```
State equals CT AND State equals MA
```

No matter what else follows in this filter expression, no records can be part of this filter. Using the AND conjunction effectively asks GoldMine to find accounts in both states. But no account can be in both states at the same time — only one State field exists per record, and you can enter only one state there. What I'm really looking for are any accounts either in CT *OR* in MA. Thus, the OR conjunction is the correct one here. So the correct expression for this part of the filter is

```
State equals CT OR State equals MA
```

Next, I need to make sure that each record the filter finds contains a fax number in the Fax field. I don't need to check for any specific value; I'm only concerned that something is actually in the field. I make the assumption that if anything at all is there, it's a valid fax number:

```
State equals CT OR State equals MA AND Fax Exists
```

Because the order of preference requires that expressions separated by AND be evaluated before expressions containing an OR, I still have a problem.

The computer first looks for accounts in MA that also have fax numbers. And that's fine. But the next thing it does is look for any accounts in CT regardless of the existence of any fax number. The way the preceding expression is con-figured, no connection exists between the account being in CT and it also having a fax number. A set of parentheses fixes this problem:

```
(State equals CT OR State equals MA) AND Fax Exists
```

By enclosing the first two expressions within parentheses, you take advantage of the order of precedence again. First, the computer checks each account to determine whether it's in CT or MA. If it finds a record that complies, it then immediately checks whether it has a fax number. Any record that complies with all three expressions is counted as part of the filter. So the last expression is actually correct and produces the desired results.

Building and Using Groups

The basic concept of groups is the same as that for filters. A _group_ is a fixed set of records that meets a set of conditions you have defined. Using a group, you can isolate a subset of the data whenever you want. You can use groups with reports, mail-merge forms, and Automated Processes. Groups can be created based on scheduled and historical activities and on other supple-mental fields, which filters can't handle. Each GoldMine user can create an unlimited number of groups, and each group can have an unlimited number of records.

The number one advantage of groups is their speed. When you create a group, GoldMine automatically creates an index file that points to each record within the group. This index file allows you to access each record within the group almost instantaneously. Unlike filters, you don't have to wait for records to be found when you activate a group.

The index file is created automatically only once — when the group is first created. As you add records to your database, those new records that belong within a group are _not_ automatically put into the group. You must add them manually. That's the price you pay for the speed you get with groups.

GoldMine has a Group Building Wizard to assist in the creation of groups. A _wizard_ is an intelligent system that walks you through a procedure, giving you your options and helping with questions. The Group Building Wizard allows you eight different bases for building a group:

✔ Filtered records

✔ Previewed records

✔ SQL queries

✔ Tagged records

✔ Search results

✔ Scheduled Calendar activities

✔ Completed History activities

✔ Supplemental contact data

Of these, filtered records and tagged records are the most commonly used bases. I explain how to create groups by basing them on a filter and by manually tagging individual records in the following sections. You may someday also want to create a group based on Calendar or History activities, or even on supplemental contact data.

Usually, the best candidates for groups are sets of records that don't change much over time. If a small percentage of your accounts are major accounts, according to whatever your definition of major is, then these accounts constitute a good set of records to turn into a group.

Building groups from filtered records

If you already have a filter, its population is fairly stable, and you want to speed your access to those records, you can create a group from that filter. To create a group based on a filter or expression, go to the Filters and Groups window and follow these steps:

1. **Select New from the Groups window.**

   A Group Profile window appears, requesting that you provide a name for your new group. After you've named your group, click OK. The Group Building Wizard begins.

2. **Select the Filtered Records option.**

   With this option, you can use any predefined filter to add records to a group. When a group is built based on a filter, all contact records that match the selected filter become permanent members of the group. The wizard also gives you the opportunity to create a brand new filter upon which your group will be built.

3. **Select a specific filter.**

   The Build a Group Based on a Filter dialog box appears, containing the following options:

   • **Build on a Filter:** Lists all the defined filters for the group's owner. Click the drop-down arrow and then select the desired filter.

   • **Owner:** A GoldMine user who "owns" the filter. Selecting a different user from the drop-down list associated with this field changes the display of defined filters in the Build on a Filter field. To display a list of available user names, click the arrow to the right of the field. If you don't have access to other people's filters, don't get too involved with changing users here. Your access rights are determined in User Preferences, which I discuss in Chapter 3.

- **Build on an Expression:** Displays the expression corresponding to the filter displayed at the top of the list of predefined filters in the Build on a Filter option. To type a new filter expression, select the radio button corresponding to this option.

- **Build Filter:** Enables you to build a filter as opposed to picking one from the list of predefined filters.

Building groups from manually tagged records

Sometimes no logical way exists to select the records you want in a group. An example might be when you want to send a mailing to your ten best friends, but no field exists in GoldMine defining friends.

Instead of struggling with a filter to make your group, you can *tag*, or manually select, multiple contact records from the Contact Listing or the Activity list or the new Search Center. As you select records, GoldMine indicates the total number of tagged records in the title bar.

To tag a record, you can either

✔ Press and hold the Ctrl key and then click each record you want to include in the group

or

✔ Press and hold the Shift key and press the down-arrow or up-arrow key to move to the record that you want to select, and then press the spacebar

You can remove the tag from any record selected in the Contact Listing by repeating the same steps by which you tagged the record. This method works like a toggle switch.

Records remain tagged as long as you don't close the Contact Listing window. You can minimize the window, but if you actually close it, all tagged records lose their tags. To actually create the group, after records are individually tagged, use the Group Building Wizard to create the group.

After a group is created, you can perform any standard merge operation on those records, including printing, sending e-mail and fax messages, and scheduling. Groups, just like filters, need to be activated before you use them, and they need to be released when you're finished with them.

Part IV
Managing Documents

The 5th Wave   By Rich Tennant

"The new technology has really helped me get organized. I keep my project reports under the PC, budgets under my laptop, and memos under my pager."

In this part . . .

There's just no substitute for good communications. In this part of the book, you find out how to properly link your word processor to GoldMine. After you have accomplished this, you can directly manage not only Microsoft Word-based communications, but also individual faxes and broadcast faxes.

My favorite, and perhaps the most efficient means of communication today, is e-mail. In this part, you figure out how to manage your GoldMine-based e-mail within the Document Management Center.

Chapter 13

Connecting to Word Processing

· ·

In This Chapter

▶ Setting up Word to work with GoldMine

▶ Inserting GoldMine fields into Word documents

▶ Using GoldMine Forms

▶ Linking documents with GoldMine

· ·

GoldMine 6.0 comes with links to almost any current flavor of Microsoft Word you happen to be using. In the old days, GoldMine supported a couple of other word processors, namely WordPerfect and AmiPro. Support for AmiPro died some time ago, and official support for WordPerfect has been withering away.

If you want to use a word processor in conjunction with GoldMine (and you certainly should), plan on teaming up with Microsoft Word. If you prefer a less expensive approach, you can integrate GoldMine with either Notepad or its big brother WordPad.

In addition, GoldMine now supports a link to Adobe Acrobat. The links to both Word and Acrobat are created via the QuickStart Wizard. In this chapter, you get a few tips on using the QuickStart Wizard and a few tips on the integration itself.

Setting Up Word with the QuickStart Wizard

Obviously, if you don't already have a copy of Microsoft Word, you aren't going to have much success with this section. Specifically, you need Word 97 or later. That means GoldMine 6.0 integrates with Word 97, Word 2000, or Word 2002.

The QuickStart Wizard begins automatically when you first install GoldMine from the CD. You can manually start the wizard by choosing Tools⇨Quick Start Wizard from GoldMine's main menu. (Figure 13-1 shows the QuickStart Wizard.) Click the right-most icon to reveal the word processor integration — the Integrated Solutions Wizard. Select either Adobe Acrobat or Word, as shown in Figure 13-2.

Figure 13-1:
The
QuickStart
Wizard.

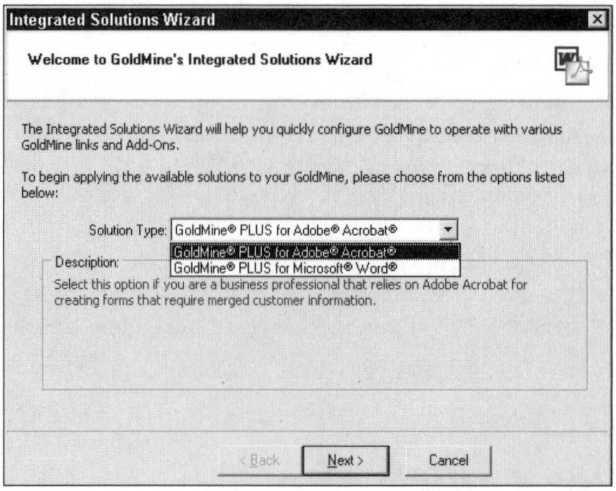

Figure 13-2:
Choosing to
integrate
Acrobat or
Word with
GoldMine.

The Integrated Solutions Wizard guides you through the integration quite painlessly. You're best off if you're connected to the Internet, as the wizard downloads the GoldMine/Word link directly from the FrontRange Web site. Make sure that Word is not running at this time because the installation process adds your GoldMine integration options directly to your main menu and toolbar in Word. After this is complete, your version of Word resembles what is shown in Figure 13-3, with an additional menu item for managing document merging from GoldMine.

Figure 13-3:
Your
integrated
Word
toolbar.

Inserting GoldMine Fields

You can insert two kinds of GoldMine fields (shown in Figure 13-4) into your Word documents. The first type of field is more like an expression or a combination of several fields that can be inserted directly from GoldMine. These expression fields are preceded by an ampersand (&) sign. An example of a useful expression field is &FullAddress. You can insert this into the header of a letter you are writing, for example. The advantage of using this kind of expression is that some intelligence is built in. This expression is clever enough to eliminate blank lines and trim trailing spaces. If the street address is only two lines, a blank third line won't be inserted into your letter.

If you select &FirstName, GoldMine parses out the main contact's first name and inserts that wherever your cursor is located within your Word document.

The second type of field you can enter into a Word document is a simple GoldMine field, such as Title or Phone1.

The actual insertion of GoldMine fields into a Word document is done by following these steps:

1. **Position your cursor in the document precisely where you want the inserted field to begin.**

2. **From Word's main menu, select GoldMine⇨Insert GoldMine Field(s).**

3. **Pick one or more expressions or fields successively from the drop-down list that appears.**

Figure 13-4:
A partial
listing of the
GoldMine
fields
available for
insertion in
Word.

GoldMine Forms

After you create text and insert GoldMine fields, save the Word document as a GoldMine Form by choosing GoldMine⇨Save as GoldMine Form. That creates a template with insertion instructions. You can then access the document with the Mail Merge function within the Document Management Center window. When you do a merge from one or more GoldMine records, the information in each GoldMine record automatically replaces the insertion instructions you put into the document.

GoldMine Linked Documents

After you perform a mail merge with one or more records, GoldMine automatically links that document to the appropriate record so you have an entry in the History tab and, possibly, an entry in the Links tab. Linking documents is discussed in further detail in Chapter 16.

The word "possibly" is important: It's completely up to you whether you want a copy of each document filed with each GoldMine record. Generally, if you are doing an occasional letter or are customizing each one, you will want to retain a copy.

If you send a blast of hundreds or thousands of identical documents (such as a form letter), you don't want to keep a thousand copies of the same document. Usually, having a single master copy of the document and having an entry in each record's History tab showing when the document was sent is sufficient.

Figure 13-5 shows the Document Template Properties dialog box, which allows you to control what information gets stored and/or linked after a document is sent. You get to this dialog box by right-clicking any of your template forms that appear in the left pane of the Document Management Center window.

Linking hundreds or thousands of documents is not recommended because it is unnecessary, takes up extra storage space on your hard drive, and creates enormous sync session that may cause your remote users unnecessary pain via lengthy sync times or worse, unsuccessful syncs.

Setting up at least a few standard templates that include your usual headings and signature section will save you more than enough time to justify your investment in the whole system. Do this and use it well, and you will be a happy camper.

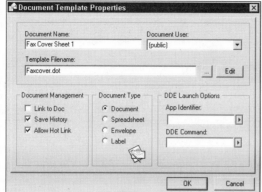

Figure 13-5:
The
Document
Template
Properties
dialog box.

The simplest way to set up a template letter is to copy (or clone) an existing one. GoldMine 6.0 comes with a simple letter template you can use for this purpose. To find a template and clone it, perform the following steps:

1. **Click the Print Documents icon on the GoldMine main menu.**

   The Document Management Center window appears.

2. **From the left panel of the Document Management Center window, highlight Letter: Blank Letter.**

3. **Right-click the template form and select Clone from the shortcut menu that appears.**

4. **In the next window, select either Public, if you want everyone to have access to this template, or select a particular user, such as yourself.**

   Your cloned document is now listed in the left panel of the Document Management Center and is ready for you to make any necessary revisions.

5. **Highlight the new template name in the left panel and give it a new and appropriate name.**

Chapter 14

Sending and Receiving E-Mail

· ·

In This Chapter

▶ Configuring your e-mail system

▶ Sending and receiving e-mail

· ·

*I*f you are one of those people who thinks e-mail is now just the current fad, then you can skip this chapter entirely. Papyrus, quills, and the abacus could make a comeback, and then you'll be in seventh heaven. (I still have one of my slide rules just in case.)

Despite the plague of spam, e-mail is one of the best communications tools ever developed. It's fast, easy, and basically free. All these things appeal to me, and apparently to many others as well.

The entire Document Management System, of which e-mail is a part, was completely revised for version 5.0 of GoldMine and further enhanced in version 6.0. In particular, FrontRange recognizes that many, many people use Outlook as their e-mail client. Rather than fight that trend, the GoldMine/ Outlook interface continues to become more and more robust. If you or others at your company are dedicated to using Outlook for e-mail, you can find a detailed, free download about this at www.ccc24k.com.

In addition, e-mail in GoldMine 6.0 now features full HTML capability, so you can read and create rich content e-mails.

In this chapter, you find out how to set up your GoldMine system to handle all your e-mail requirements, how to send an individual e-mail, how to send broadcast e-mails, and how to receive and catalog incoming e-mails.

Configuring Your E-Mail System

Before you can use GoldMine's e-mail system, you must first set up an Internet account, and you must configure GoldMine to use that account. To access the Internet, you must have an account with an Internet Service Provider (ISP). This ISP must provide true Internet mail access. AOL, for example, does not provide true Internet mail access. There are many regional, national, and international providers with good, competitive service. For more information on finding an ISP and getting started on the Internet, pick up a copy of *The Internet For Dummies*, 8th Edition, by John Levine, Carol Baroudi, and Margaret Levine-Young (published by Wiley Publishing, Inc.).

Entering your ISP's account information

When you sign up with an ISP, you are given account information that you need to configure your GoldMine interface. This is done within GoldMine's User Preferences dialog box. Please refer to Chapter 3 for more information on setting up user preferences.

The new QuickStart Wizard guides you through the set up of your e-mail account in GoldMine. If you are already beyond the initial installation and still need to configure your e-mail, follow these instructions:

1. **Choose Edit⇨Preferences from the main menu.**

    The User Preferences dialog box appears.

2. **Click the Internet tab, as shown in Figure 14-1.**

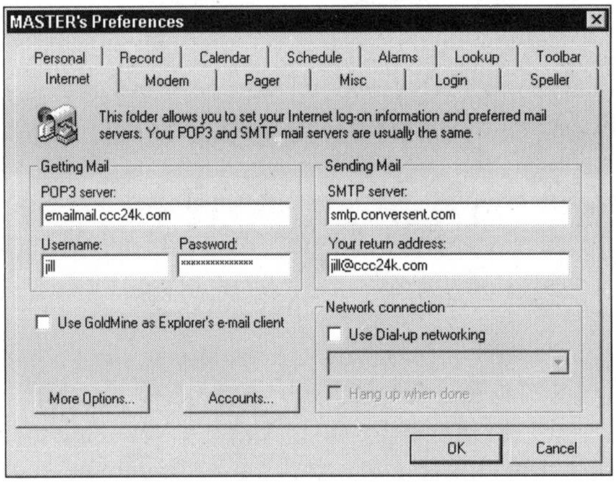

MASTER's Preferences

| Personal | Record | Calendar | Schedule | Alarms | Lookup | Toolbar |

| Internet | Modem | Pager | Misc | Login | Speller |

This folder allows you to set your Internet log-on information and preferred mail servers. Your POP3 and SMTP mail servers are usually the same.

Getting Mail

POP3 server:
`emailmail.ccc24k.com`

Username: `jill`   Password: `*************`

Sending Mail

SMTP server:
`smtp.conversent.com`

Your return address:
`jill@ccc24k.com`

☐ Use GoldMine as Explorer's e-mail client

Network connection
☐ Use Dial-up networking
☐ Hang up when done

[More Options...] [Accounts...]

[OK] [Cancel]

Figure 14-1:
Set up your Internet preferences.

---

3. **Enter the appropriate information, using the following explanations as a guide:**

    • **POP3 Server:** The name of the server that holds your incoming e-mail, and can be entered either as something like `mail.something.com` or as the actual IP address, which might be something like 207.187.163.57. In either case, your ISP provides this information.

- **Username:** You set up your user name with your ISP.

- **Password:** You also set this up with your ISP, and when you type it in, it appears on the User Preferences dialog box as a series of asterisks for security purposes.

- **SMTP Server:** The name of the server that processes your outgoing e-mail. It may or may not be the same as your POP3 server address. I use my actual IP address for both these fields.

- **Your Return Address:** Your actual e-mail address that probably appears on your business cards or that you tell people.

- **Network Connection:** The last field on the Internet tab of the User Preferences dialog box is for your network connection. If you do not have a dedicated connection through a router, or something like that, you do not need to select this option. If, on the other hand, you want GoldMine to dial in and make the connection for you each time you start the program, select the Use Dial-up Networking option. If you do select this option, you may also want to have GoldMine hang up for you when you are done. If so, then select the Hang Up When Done option.

4. **To set more options, such as composing, retrieval, and additional account information, click the More Options button in the lower-left portion of the Internet tab.**

   Clicking this brings you to the dialog box shown in Figure 14-2. This dialog box allows you to tailor how you compose, retrieve, view, and customize your e-mail messages.

5. **Click OK when you're finished.**

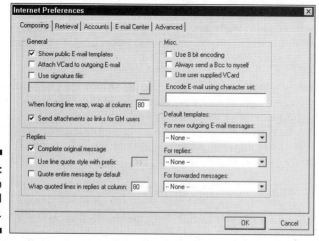

Figure 14-2:
Setting up
more e-mail
options.

Setting options for composing your messages

This section deals with the most significant settings within the Internet Preferences dialog box in GoldMine. Each of these settings is discussed in the following sections. The new rules and wizards are set up within the E-mail Center itself and are discussed in the "Sending E-Mail Messages" section, later in this chapter.

Attaching a VCard to outgoing messages

You can have GoldMine attach your *VCard* (a .VCF file) to each of your outgoing e-mail messages. A VCard contains information similar to that of a contact record, such as the entries you made in your Personal tab, or other information that you enter outside of GoldMine. If the receiving system has VCard capabilities, the system will decipher the .VCF file to import this information. If the e-mail recipients use GoldMine to retrieve e-mail, they can use your VCard information to create a contact record in GoldMine, if a record does not already exist for you in their databases.

I don't use this option myself because many of my non-GoldMine using recipients can't make use of it and virtually all my GoldMine-using e-mail buddies already have a record for me in their databases. I don't really care to receive .VCF files from anyone, either, because I don't want to store them on my hard drive anyway.

Adding your signature to Internet e-mail

You can configure GoldMine to attach a signature file to all Internet e-mail messages. The word *signature* is here just to fool you. A *signature file* is a text file that contains special information about you and your organization, telephone number, quotations, or any other text. You can use a signature to close each of your e-mails with your name, contact information, and even a little advertising.

I get far too many e-mail requests from people who don't even bother to tell me who they are. All I get is an e-mail message saying, "Please send me pricing," or "Send literature on Client Retention." I am happy to do this, but only if I know with whom I am corresponding. Proper etiquette dictates that you provide this information; using a good signature file is the easiest, most consistent way to do so.

To create and use a signature file, follow these steps:

1. **Open Notepad and type in the text you would like to serve as your e-mail signature.**

2. **Save the file to the folder where GoldMine is installed.**

   Typically, GoldMine is installed in your root directory or a subfolder under Program Files. Name the signature file whatever is sensible for you. (I use a convention that takes the user name followed by the letters *sig* to tell me it's a signature file.)

3. **From the main GoldMine screen, choose Edit⇨Preferences and on the dialog box that appears, click the Internet tab.**

4. **Click the More Options button, and click the Composing tab.**

5. **Select the Use Signature File option; click the Browse button and browse to the file you created in Step 1.**

6. **Click OK when you're finished.**

You can be a little cleverer, however, and create a general-purpose signature file. You do this by putting variables into the signature file that you create in Step 1 in the previous step list; follow the rest of the steps as written to use the signature file. These variables are automatically filled in every time any user on your system sends an e-mail message. The information is taken from each user's own .INI file that is created during the initial setup. Figure 14-3 shows an example of a more general signature file that ensures each user on your system has a consistent message at the bottom of each e-mail message.

Figure 14-3:
A general
signature
file using
variables.

```
<<&UserFullName>>
<<&User_Var.Title>>

<<&User_Var.Company>>

phone: <<&User_Var.Phone>>
email : <<&User_Var.E-Mail>>
web   :<<&User_Var.URL>>
```

Now that GoldMine 6.0 can handle HTML, signature files can be built using WordPad (Notepad's bigger brother) and can include some fancier stuff, such as fancy fonts and graphics. A company logo comes to mind as a nice touch.

Additional options for composing e-mails

Within the Composing tab of the Internet Preferences dialog box (refer to Figure 14-2), you can make some additional choices, as explained in the following list:

✔ **When Forcing Line Wrap, Wrap at Column X:** Specifies the character at which GoldMine wraps the text to the next line. By default, GoldMine wraps to the next line at the 80th character in a line.

✔ **Complete Original Message:** Places the original message in the History tab when you either reply to or forward a message. If you do not want to designate the original message as a completed activity when you respond, leave the check box corresponding to this option blank.

✔ **Use Line Quote Style with Prefix:** Specifies the characters that GoldMine uses to identify lines quoted from the original message when you copy those lines into your reply. By default, GoldMine uses >>.

✔ **Quote Entire Message by Default:** Specifies that GoldMine copies the entire text of the original message in your reply, using the characters entered in the Use Line Quote Style with Prefix option. This is a good option to select if you want each e-mail you send to contain a thread of the previous messages from a correspondent.

✔ **Wrap Quoted Lines in Replies at Column X:** Specifies the character at which GoldMine wraps to the next line of quoted text. You can use this option to create an indented block for text quoted from the original message. By default, GoldMine wraps to the next line at the 80th character in a quoted line.

✔ **Default Templates:** Select an existing e-mail template from the corresponding drop-down list that appears when you work with one or more of the following message types:

- New outgoing e-mail messages

- Replies

- Forwarded messages

To apply no default template to any or all of the messages, select None.

When you finish defining settings, either click another tab to continue defining options, or click OK to close the Internet Preferences dialog box.

Retrieving e-mail from the Internet

You can define a variety of options for retrieving Internet e-mail messages. These options, as shown in Figure 14-4, can specify the location of attachments, scan intervals, and the criteria that GoldMine uses to select messages for retrieval.

To define criteria for e-mail retrieval, follow these steps:

1. **Choose Edit⇨Preferences, click the Internet tab on the dialog box that appears, and then click the More Options button.**

2. **Click the Retrieval tab, and choose from the following options:**

   - **Delete Retrieved Mail from Server:** Removes messages from the Internet mail server upon retrieval.

   - **Open 'Read E-mail' Dialog on Retrieval:** Retrieves e-mail and opens the Read E-mail dialog box, displaying the first retrieved message.

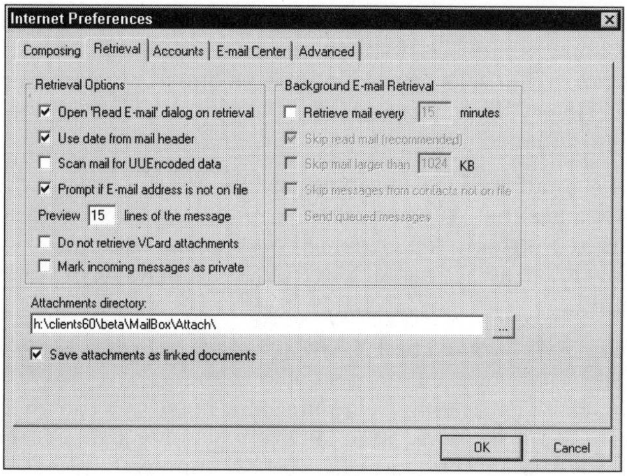

Figure 14-4:
Choosing
your e-mail
retrieval
options.

- **Use Date from Mail Header:** Sets the date of incoming mail to the date sent, as indicated in the header information of the message. Selecting this option ensures that your e-mail is posted in true chronological order on your calendar.

  If you don't retrieve e-mail frequently, however, you may want to leave the check box corresponding to this option blank. For example, with this option selected, a mail message sent four days prior to retrieval is posted in the calendar with the 4-day-old date.

- **Scan Mail for UUEncoded Data:** Sets GoldMine to scan the Internet mail server for any e-mail messages that contain UUEncoded attachments. Selecting this option does not affect retrieval of MIME-encoded files.

- **Prompt If E-mail Address Is Not on File:** Sets GoldMine to display the Attach E-mail to Contact dialog box upon retrieving an unlinked e-mail message, from which you can select options for linking the message.

- **Preview X Lines of the Message:** Specifies the number of lines of text that GoldMine retrieves with the message for display in the lower pane of the E-mail Center window. By default, GoldMine retrieves the first 15 lines.

- **Retrieve Mail Every X Minutes:** GoldMine automatically connects with your POP3 mail server to check for new mail at the interval as specified in minutes. For example, if you want to retrieve waiting Internet e-mail every two hours, type 120 in this field. The default value of 15 sets GoldMine to scan for and retrieve waiting e-mail every 15 minutes. You must select this option to define any options listed in the Rules section.

To retrieve e-mail for the account, you must select the Auto-retrieve option from the Account tab of the Internet Preferences dialog box. If you do not select the Auto-retrieve option but select the Retrieve Mail Every X Minutes and Send Queued Messages options, GoldMine sends queued mail only.

- **Skip Read Mail (Recommended):** Bypasses displaying any e-mail messages that you have already read if you have not selected the Delete Retrieved Mail from Server option. This option is available only if you select the Retrieve Mail Automatically Every X Minutes option.

- **Skip Mail Larger Than X KB:** Retrieves only Internet E-mail messages that are equal to or smaller than the kilobyte (KB) value in this field. By default, GoldMine skips messages that are 1,024 kilobytes or larger. This option is available only if you select the Retrieve Mail Automatically Every X Minutes option.

- **Skip Messages from Contacts Not on File:** Retrieves e-mail only from those contacts who have Internet e-mail address entries in their detail records. This option is available only if you select the Retrieve Mail Automatically Every X Minutes option. This might help reduce incoming spam, but you might also miss something important from some new prospect.

- **Send Queued Messages:** Sends all queued messages when automatically retrieving mail — see the description previously in this list for the Retrieve Mail Automatically Every X Minutes option. The Send Queued Messages option is available only if you select the Retrieve Mail Automatically Every X Minutes option.

- **Attachments Directory:** Designates the destination for retrieved e-mail attachments. Type the entire path information. To search for the destination, select the Browse button, which displays the Browse for Folder dialog box.

3. **When you're done defining retrieval settings, either click another tab to continue defining options or click OK to close the Internet Preferences dialog box.**

Sending E-Mail Messages

GoldMine 6.0 has a unified e-mail system, enabling you to use the same E-mail Center for both internal (other users on your GoldMine system) and external (Internet mail) correspondence. In addition, you can send an e-mail message to an outsider who uses, say, AOL, and send a copy to your sales manager, another GoldMine user on your team. I refer to this type of e-mail as "dual e-mail."

To create an e-mail message to a primary contact, you can simply position your cursor on the E-mail field label on the main screen. In GoldMine 6.0, this field label is similar to a hyperlink. Clicking it brings you immediately to the Create E-mail window, as shown in Figure 14-5.

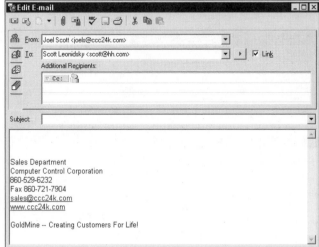

Figure 14-5:
Starting an
e-mail
message.

Addressing a message

GoldMine assumes you intend to send an external e-mail to the primary contact of the record that is currently active. You can easily redirect this, however, if you want to send this e-mail to one of the secondary contacts at this account. Click the down arrow to the right of the recipient in the To field. You then get a list of all the other contacts at this account for which you have an e-mail address. Selecting another contact replaces the default recipient, as shown in Figure 14-6.

You can expand the scope of your recipient list by clicking the right arrow button. You have a total of five options, as follows:

- ✔ **To: Contact:** You can use this option to redirect your e-mail to any person at any account in your GoldMine database.

- ✔ **To: Manual Recipient:** You can use this option to redirect your e-mail to someone who may not even be in your database, as long as you know his or her e-mail address and are willing to type it in.

- ✔ **To: GoldMine User or Group:** This choice allows you to send the message to another GoldMine user on your team, or even to an entire group of users, for example, everyone in your Minneapolis office. (See the "Sending messages to a group" section, later in this chapter.)

✔ **To: Distribution List:** You can build a distribution list of recipients. This is similar to a group and allows you include an almost random list of people who should get regular messages from you.

✔ **To: Outlook (MAPI) Recipient:** This is part of the interface to Microsoft Outlook, and allows you to redirect your e-mail output to someone in your Outlook address book.

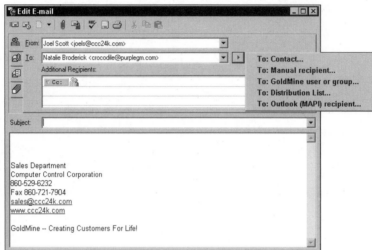

Figure 14-6:
Choose
additional
recipients to
e-mail.

You can further expand the recipient list by clicking the CC (carbon copy) symbol just below the primary recipient's name. The menu that appears (shown in Figure 14-7) allows you several more options:

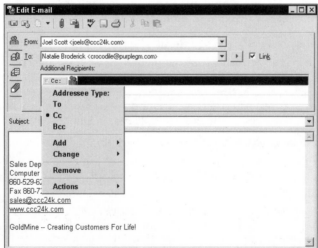

Figure 14-7:
Expanding
your
recipient
list.

✔ **To:** You can manually enter an e-mail address that may not exist in your database.

✔ **CC** *(carbon copy):* You can select one or more additional primary or secondary contacts to receive this message.

✔ **BCC** *(blind carbon copy):* You can select one or more people to send this message to, but the primary recipient will not know you have sent it to anyone else. For example, you might use this to notify someone of a problem and to simultaneously inform his or her supervisor.

Composing the subject and body of a message

The subject appears as a header so your recipient has some idea what this message is about. Below that, of course, is the area in which you compose your actual message. Simply type your message in there.

Many people, aware of viruses and other suspicious things, won't read or even download messages that don't have a recognizable Subject field. If you want your messages properly dealt with, make the subject succinct.

Completing a message

After you address and compose your message, you can check your spelling, attach a file or files, or print your message before you send or save it. You select these options by clicking the icons on the Create E-mail window's local toolbar, as shown in Figure 14-8. The icons are as follows:

Figure 14-8:
Click an
icon for
more tasks.

✔ **Send:** Immediately sends your e-mail message.

✔ **Queue:** Puts the message into a queue with other messages for later transmission. This might be useful, for example, if you are composing e-mails in an airplane and intend to send a batch of them later.

✔ **Save as Draft:** Saves the message if you need to work on it later, before you send it.

- ✔ **Attach Files:** Attaches one or more files of any type to your e-mail.

- ✔ **Encrypt:** Puts a password on your message and enables you to add 32- or 128-bit encryption. If you use GoldMine's encryption, only another user with GoldMine (and only in the United States, believe it or not) can read it.

- ✔ **Check Spelling:** Runs the spell checker on your message. This is good if you can't spell and your recipient can. While you're composing, or when you're done composing a message, you can click the Check Spelling icon to avoid embarrassing yourself.

- ✔ **Save as File:** Saves the message as a file on your system in addition to sending it.

- ✔ **Print:** Prints the message.

- ✔ **Cut, Copy, and Paste:** The standard tools to manipulate your data within your document or from/to another document.

Also notice the Link check box, which is already selected by default. This selection automatically creates a link between this e-mail and the active account. In this way, a record of this e-mail appears in the History and in the Links tabs of the main record.

Sending messages to a group

One of the more powerful features of the e-mail system is its ability to automatically send an e-mail message to each member of an active group of accounts. This should be one of the cornerstones of your marketing program. Not only can you use this to send an initial blast to prospects, but more importantly, you can use this as part of a client retention system. You should be regularly corresponding with all your clients, making sure your name gets in front of them as often as possible. This applies equally well to simple e-mail messages and to e-mail templates.

The first step in sending e-mails to a select set of accounts is to activate either a filter or a group. See Chapter 12 for details on this. After you have activated your filter or group, you can send the e-mail message to each of them quite easily. The following is a step-by-step outline for sending a boiler-plate e-mail to a group of people after you activate a filter or group:

1. **Click the Print Documents icon on the GoldMine main toolbar.**

2. **Right-click on an e-mail template such as the Hello template that comes with GoldMine 6.0 and select Merge from the shortcut menu, as shown in Figure 14-9.**

   The Mail Merge Properties dialog box, shown in Figure 14-10, appears.

You can now decide to send your e-mail just to the primary contact for this one active record (if this is all you wanted to do, there are easier ways) or all the secondary contacts for this record, or to a filter or group that you have already set up.

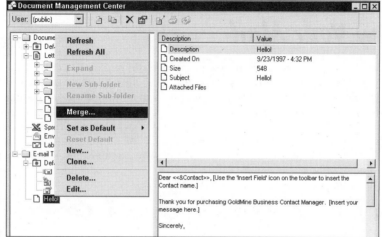

Figure 14-9:
Choosing an
e-mail
template.

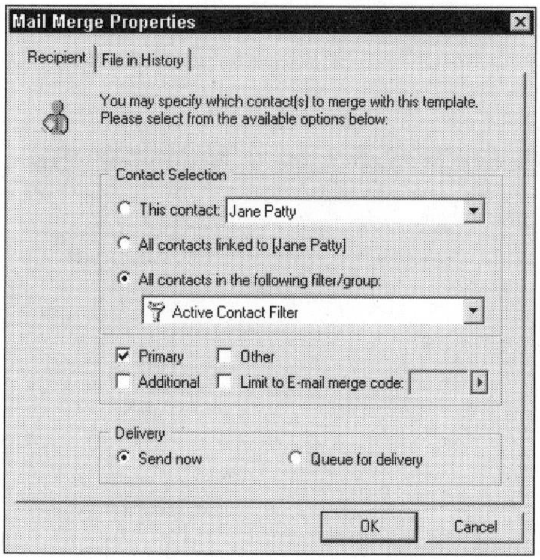

Figure 14-10:
Specify
recipients
for your
e-mails.

3. Choose either the Send Now option or the Queue for Later Delivery option and then click OK.

After you have completed these steps, your e-mail message is on the way to all your recipients (assuming you didn't just put the message into the queue for later transmission), and the message can be registered in the History tab of each account to whom you sent the e-mail.

Getting Your Mail

In the simplest sense, you can use the GoldMine E-mail Center to retrieve your messages, read them, and then either save them or delete them. From the E-mail Center window, you can perform all the usual and simple e-mail functions, but you can also go a step farther and define rule conditions and actions. For example, you can tell GoldMine what to do with your e-mails while you are on vacation, or what to do if the subject line contains the word "complaint." All this can be set up using the E-mail Rules Wizard.

I just wanna get my e-mail already

Life in the e-mail fast lane is really not as complex as all the foregoing implies. After your options are set, retrieving your e-mail is very easy. The E-mail Center icon is on the main screen. Just click the icon to open the E-mail Center window, connect to the Internet (if you're not already connected), and retrieve your e-mail. The E-mail Center window is shown in Figure 14-11.

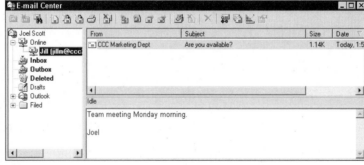

Figure 14-11:
The E-mail
Center
window.

You may have more than one e-mail message waiting for you. GoldMine begins retrieving, and you can see each e-mail message coming in, along with the sender's name, the subject, the size of the message, and the date it was sent to you. As soon as GoldMine is done retrieving these headings for you, you can begin looking at each message.

With your user preferences, you have set a relatively small default amount of text to come in with these headings. This text is displayed in the lower panel of the E-mail Center window so that you can get a little better idea of the topic of the e-mail. To see the full text of the message, double-click the particular From or Subject listing you want. GoldMine then retrieves any remaining text or attached files. At this point, you have a variety of options ranging from reading the message, viewing the attached files, forwarding the message to another person, replying, or saving the e-mail for future reference.

Defining rule conditions

Using the E-mail Rules Wizard, you can define one or more conditions for GoldMine to evaluate when retrieving online messages. If a message meets the conditions, GoldMine then applies the action(s) that you define in the E-mail Rules Wizard.

This means that you can really automate the processing of your incoming e-mails. Examples of the use of such automation includes having GoldMine redirect incoming messages with particular headings to someone else, or sending a return message indicating that you are on vacation and won't be reading your messages until you return to the office.

To define a new condition or to edit an existing condition, follow these steps:

1. **Click the E-mail Center icon on GoldMine's main screen.**

2. **From the E-mail Center, click the Set up E-mail Rules local icon (the fourth icon from the right).**

3. **Right-click in the left panel of the E-mail Rules Center, and choose New Rule Set from the shortcut menu.**

    The E-mail Rules Wizard appears, as shown in Figure 14-12.

The E-mail Rule Wizard gives you the following options to choose from:

- ✔ **Mail Field:** Click to select the e-mail field that you want GoldMine to search for a specified value. For example, if you want GoldMine to look for a specified value that appears as the title of the e-mail, select Subject.

- ✔ **Logical Condition:** Click to select a condition, such as Begins With. By default, GoldMine displays Equal To.

- ✔ **Value:** Type the value for which you want GoldMine to search when evaluating the field that you selected in Mail Field.

Figure 14-12:
Use the
E-mail Rules
Wizard
to define
e-mail rules.

When you're done setting up your new rule, click OK to enter the condition in the Browse part of the Condition dialog box. To add another condition, click the New button. To change a selected condition, click the Edit button. When you're done adding or editing rules, you can specify how GoldMine should apply the rules by selecting either the All Of option or the Any Of option.

When you're done, click the Next button. The E-mail Rule Wizard: Action dialog box appears. The actions you specify are only executed when the conditions you just defined are met.

Defining rule actions

After you have defined the condition(s) that you want GoldMine to check for in incoming messages, you can define the action(s) for GoldMine to apply upon finding a message that meets the condition(s). Click the New button. The E-mail Rule: Action dialog box appears, containing the following options:

- **Action on Mail:** Click to select the operation that you want GoldMine to perform upon detecting a message with the specified condition(s), such as the Move to Inbox option or the Delete Attachments option.

- **Value:** Provides additional information necessary for GoldMine to complete the operation. For example, if you selected the Move to Inbox option in the Action on Mail field, you can click to display a drop-down list from which you can select the subfolder of your Inbox where you want GoldMine to place the messages that meet the condition(s).

The Value field is available only when needed to complete the action. For example, if you select the Delete Attachments option in the Action on Mail field, then GoldMine needs no further information to process this request, so the Value field is not available.

Click OK to enter the rule in the Browse section of the Action dialog box. To add another action, click the New button. To change a selected action, click the Edit button.

When you're finished, click the Finish button. GoldMine adds the rule to the selected rule set. The name of the rule appears in the left pane under the rule set. The selected condition(s) and action(s) of the rule set appear in the right pane.

Chapter 15

Faxing Made Simple

- -

In This Chapter

▶ Selecting fax software

▶ Sending a fax

- -

*F*axing documents to your prospects and clients is an important tool for any contact management system. GoldMine can't fax by itself and depends upon a combination of external word-processing and third-party fax software to accomplish this feat. By far the most popular word-processing software is Microsoft Word, but you have three or four reasonable choices for the fax software itself.

In this chapter, you discover enough of the pros and cons of each type of faxing software (or service) to better help you decide which one to acquire and implement. This chapter focuses on the several software systems you can purchase and emphasizes the most sophisticated of them, OmniRush. You may, in fact, decide to use a combination of in-house faxing software for small jobs and a fax service bureau for big blasts of faxes. You also discover how to use template documents and how to actually send a fax and record the results in the History tab.

Selecting Fax Software

To send a fax using GoldMine, you must use faxing software. The best known and most widely used fax products are WinFax PRO, RightFax, and OmniRush. These systems rely on having one or more fax/modems connected to your computer or to your network. You need to purchase this software, install it, and configure it to work with your copy of GoldMine and with your word processor. The best of these programs interface with GoldMine and automatically create an activity in each record's History tab to indicate the status of every fax you think you have sent.

Another category of faxing systems is made up of service bureau products, such as Xpedite, which allow you to send out a high volume of faxes in a short time. A *service bureau* is typically an outside company that maintains a large array of fax/modems. You use GoldMine to send the service bureau a list of names and fax numbers and one copy of the document you want to be faxed. In less than five minutes, 10,000 or more faxes can be sent out on your behalf. You still need to have one fax/modem or an Internet connection to communicate with the service bureau.

Using third-party software

Whether you buy your own in-house fax software or hook up with a service bureau, you're going to pay for faxing. In the first case, you buy the software and then pay for long-distance telephone charges. In the case of a service bureau, you may not pay up-front charges, but you pay a fee for every fax that goes through the service bureau.

Each third-party, in-house system has its own quirks and credentials:

- **WinFax PRO 10.0:** WinFax is one of the original faxing programs and continues to evolve. This product is one of the least expensive solutions to faxing from your PC, but it is primarily a single-user system. WinFax can also be set up to communicate with network-based faxing systems like RightFax or even with a service bureau. WinFax does not record its results back into GoldMine's history, and therefore, you may not be able to tell later whether a fax was successful. Check out `www.symantec.com/winfax` for more information.

- **RightFax:** This server-based fax solution allows you to send and receive faxes directly from any network workstation through a single fax/modem on the network. Much like WinFax, RightFax doesn't really report back to GoldMine on the status of those faxes that have been sent. You can contact the manufacturer at `www.captaris.com/rightfax` or by calling (520) 327-1557.

- **OmniRush 5.5:** This third-party add-on provides a really integrated fax solution. For details, visit either the GoldMine Web site at `www.frontrange.com`, or the Z-Firm LLC Web site at `www.zfirmllc.com`. My company uses OmniRush because I think it works better with GoldMine than any other fax product. I discuss OmniRush in more detail in Chapter 29. Z-Firm's previous fax product, FaxRush, does not support GoldMine 6.0.

The simplest, and possibly least expensive solution may be WinFax, but it doesn't automatically record its results in the History tab of each of your accounts. OmniRush is the most tightly integrated. It does record its results, but you need to get at least as many OmniRush licenses as you have GoldMine licenses. Consider service bureau software if you anticipate a high volume of faxing. For information about service bureaus, see the following section.

Taking fax speeds into account

If you have ever watched a piece of paper go through a standard fax machine, whether coming or going, you know that a single piece of paper takes almost a minute to go through. This slowness is due to the speed limitations of typical telephone lines and fax machines in general.

If you use any of the in-house faxing programs, you run into the same speed limitation as your good old fax machine has. It takes, at best, almost a minute to send a page. If you want to take advantage of the GoldMine feature to send mass faxes (broadcast faxes), then you could run into a problem. If your intention is to send a large number of announcements to your clients

from GoldMine via fax, you should first do a little calculation to see how long such a method would take. (See the "Using service bureau software" section for more about what software to use to send mass faxes.)

At about one minute per page, 1,200 one-page faxes will take 20 hours to send, assuming that every fax goes through the first time, and the system doesn't have to repeat any due to busy signals or to other problems. This slow pace isn't just a function of which software you select or which hardware you buy — you can't send a fax any faster than the machine at the other end can receive the fax.

Using service bureau software

Service bureau software, such as Xpedite, works a little differently than regular third-party fax software. You use the GoldMine filters or groups (see Chapter 12) to isolate the set of contacts to whom you want to send a fax. Suppose you have 1,200 intended recipients. The link to Xpedite automatically assembles the names and fax numbers for all 1,200 recipients. At the same time, you also send *one copy* of the template document to the service bureau. After this data arrives (and it takes just a minute or so), Xpedite sends your faxes through its network of fax/modems.

Using this method of transmission makes a huge difference. You take only a few minutes to instruct Xpedite and to transmit your data. And within just a few more minutes, all your faxes are delivered to your contacts, and a report is returned to you detailing the results of all the transmissions. You pay a fee for this service, but it may make more sense to pay the fee than to tie up your own fax/modem for hours (or even days, if you're sending a really large number of faxes).

A GoldMine interface with Xpedite Systems, Inc. called XPLINK gives you the ability to fax to some or all of your GoldMine accounts very easily. XPLINK is a utility that, after installation, places a button on the GoldMine toolbar for creating fax lists. After XPLINK and Xpedite's PC-Xpedite for Windows software have been installed on your PC, you may launch a broadcast fax to all or part of your database directly from GoldMine. It's fast, and you get a report back almost immediately detailing which faxes succeeded and which ones failed and why. Call (800) 966-3297 to contact Xpedite, or visit www.expedite.com.

Sending a Fax

GoldMine comes standard with dozens of template documents that can be used for printed material or for faxing. You can initiate a fax by following these steps:

1. **Click the Print Documents icon from the main toolbar.**

   This icon is shown in Figure 15-1.

Figure 15-1:
The main toolbar.

The Document Management Center window opens, as shown in Figure 15-2. The available templates are listed in the left panel.

2. **Highlight the letter, memo, or fax you want to send.**

3. **Click the Fax Template icon on the local toolbar.**

   You can see this icon in Figure 15-2.

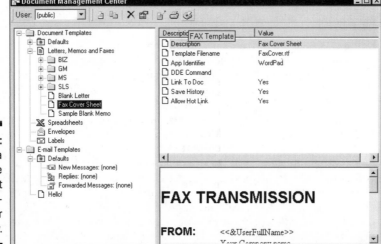

Figure 15-2:
Preparing a fax from the Document Management Center window.

Creating a template

A *template* is a preformatted outline of a document, whether you are talking about faxes, e-mails, or just plain word-processing documents. GoldMine comes with quite a few templates that you can use as is or modify to your taste. Templates may have some boilerplate wording as well as some GoldMine data fields that are automatically filled in for you.

You can use a template to merge contact information into a letter or fax document. You might use a template for something as simple as a fax cover letter, or you could build an entire 30-page template for sales proposals. A template converts into a printable document when you merge contact information, such as the recipient's name and address, into the template. (See this and the next section to find out how to add contact information to a template.)

To view and work with templates, follow these steps:

1. **From the main menu, choose Contact⇨Write⇨Customize Templates.**

   The Document Management Center window appears (refer to Figure 15-2).

2. **Set the User field in the upper-left corner to Public.**

3. **Double-click Letters, Memos, and Faxes.**

   The entire list of available public templates appears.

4. **Highlight the template that you want to use.**

   For example, choose Fax Cover Sheet. Statistics for the template appear in the upper-right pane. The template itself appears in the lower-right pane.

To make changes to the template before printing or faxing, follow these steps:

1. **From the left panel of the Document Management Center, highlight the name of the template you want to edit.**

2. **Click the Merge and Edit Template local icon.**

   GoldMine opens Microsoft Word and loads the template you have specified and also brings in any fields from the current GoldMine record that is open. Now you can modify any text in the document you want.

3. **In Word, choose GoldMine⇨Save as GoldMine Template if you want to save this as a new template; choose GoldMine⇨Update GoldMine Template if you want to overwrite the existing template.**

   After you have saved an edited template, it automatically appears in GoldMine's list of available templates in the Document Management Center.

Sending a fax to one contact

Several simple fax cover sheets are available as ready-made templates. When I want to send a quick fax to a single contact, I usually select either Fax Cover Sheet or Blank Letter from the set of templates that is initially available in the left panel of the Document Management Center. Using a template is almost always easier than starting a new document from scratch.

Sending a fax to multiple contacts

When you have a template that you're satisfied with, you can use it to send a fax to one contact at a time, or you can send a *broadcast fax* when you want to blast out your correspondence to everyone in a filtered set or group of accounts. Using a broadcast fax, for example, you can send an invitation to a seminar to only those people who have an interest in a particular topic. To send a broadcast fax, follow these steps:

1. **Make sure you have a filter that properly identifies the accounts to which you want to send this fax.**

   See Chapter 12 for more information on setting up groups and filters.

2. **From the GoldMine main menu, choose Contact⇨Write⇨Custom Templates.**

3. **Highlight the document you want to fax to these accounts.**

4. **Click the right-most icon from the Document Management Center (Fax Template).**

5. **On the Recipient tab, shown in Figure 15-3, make the following choices:**

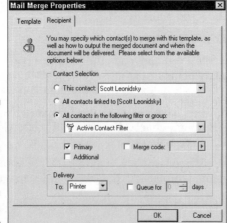

Figure 15-3:
Selecting
recipients
from the
Mail Merge
Properties
dialog box.

- **Contact Selection:** Select either the current record, all contacts linked to this record, or the records belonging to a filter or a group. The latter two choices allow you to send your fax to many accounts at once.

- **Primary and Additional:** Send your fax just to the primary contact of each record, to the additional contacts only, or to both.

- **Merge Code:** Each contact person in your database has an associated Merge Code. If, for example, you filled in an X in someone's Merge Code field, you could enter an X in the Merge Code field on the Mail Merge Properties dialog box. Doing so limits the sending of your fax only to those contacts that also had an X in their Merge Code fields. Use this method to regulate who gets Christmas cards, or newsletters, or seminar invitations.

- **Delivery:** Direct the output either to the fax or to a printer and schedule when to send your documents. To schedule a send time, set the number of days in the Queue field. Entering a 3 in this field causes GoldMine to wait three days before faxing any documents.

6. **Click the File in History tab and choose from the following options:**

   - **Create a History Record:** Choosing this option tells GoldMine to record in each contact record's History tab whether and when the document was sent. Keeping track of such information is a good thing to do so that you can have an audit trail of materials that have gone out to each account.

   - **Save the Template Text in History:** You probably don't want to save a separate copy of the template text for each account, so I recommend that you don't select this option.

   - **Activity:** You may want to develop some special Activity codes here, such as SLS to indicate Sales Activity, or CSS for Customer Support.

   - **Result:** You should enter a code in this field. Usually COM is appropriate because GoldMine uses this code routinely to indicate that an activity is complete. (To find out about completing activities, see Chapter 10.)

   - **Update Reference Field Using a dBASE Expression (optional):** You may also want to enter some phrase (or dBASE expression) in this field. This information also appears in each contact's History tab. By entering a phrase here, you can tell six months from now what you actually sent to this account. So if you're sending a newsletter, a phrase like "11/02 Newsletter" would be helpful.

7. **When you finish making your choices on the Mail Merge Properties dialog box, click OK.**

   GoldMine launches its fax/mail merge system, and you're in business.

Chapter 16

Linking Documents

● ●

In This Chapter

▶ Linking word-processing files and e-mails automatically

▶ Manually linking files and folders

▶ Accessing linked documents

▶ Integrating document management systems

● ●

*D*ocument links are a very powerful feature in GoldMine that allows you to store any type of information with the contact record. Using document links, along with the contact record, you can store forms relating to the contact, incoming facsimiles, voice-mail messages, or contact documents created with a word processor. When you need to view or edit the linked file, GoldMine automatically loads both the application and the file in one operation.

In this chapter, I explain what types of documents and files you can link to contact records, demonstrate how to link documents and files, and show you how to view your linked files. You also discover how to launch the application that runs your linked file, so that you can view the linked file quickly and easily.

With the new GoldMine+View tab, you can customize and store a wide variety of HTML and rich content links and files. You can find more on the GM+View tab in Chapter 27.

Exploring the Links Tab

The Links tab, formerly at the far right of the main GoldMine screen, has been pushed to the second bank of tabs. The Links tab maintains the connections from the clients' records to their linked documents. When you click the Links tab, shown in Figure 16-1, GoldMine displays each of that contact's linked documents. The link to each document shows the name of a file and the name of the application used to edit or display the file.

The needle in the haystack

In my years of being in business B.G. (Before GoldMine), I wrote many letters and proposals. I would often mail a 15-page proposal and then wait for the inevitable signed contract to arrive. I now suspect the arrival of those signed contracts probably could have been expedited and made a more regular occurrence if I had followed up with a phone call. But without GoldMine to remind me to make the calls, it almost never happened — I relied on the innate beauty of the proposal to pull me through.

An equally serious problem typically arose about six months after I mailed a proposal — a phone call from the prospective client. I would pick up the phone and hear something like, "Hi, this is Charlie at Universal. I want to go over that proposal you sent me." My first problem was trying to remember who Charlie was. If I did remember him, I was still left with another issue: What did I do with that proposal? Is it in the pile on my desk, in the pile on the floor, or (hopefully not) in the circular file? "Charlie, I'll call you right back."

GoldMine's ability to keep track of documents and files cured my disorganization. Well, maybe not all of it, but I'm much better off now. Whether it's a 15-page proposal, a spreadsheet, an e-mail, a fax, or a photo of the kids, GoldMine can link the file to the appropriate contact record. Locating any document that relates to the client becomes a snap, so you won't have to call a client back after ransacking your office to find a proposal.

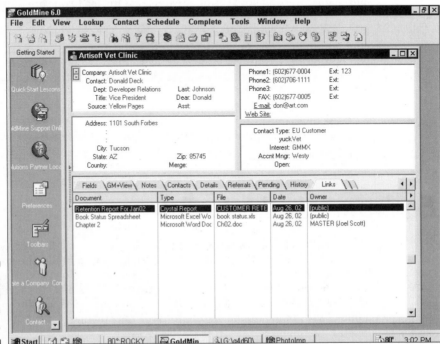

Figure 16-1: A typical view of the Links tab.

The Links tab contains the following information:

- **Document:** Descriptive title of a document or folder that's linked to the contact.

- **Type:** Document type that must match a registered application in the Windows Registration Database.

- **File:** Filename and path of the linked file.

- **Date:** Date the file was linked to GoldMine. This date may be different from the date the file was created or last modified. You can see the document's most recent modification date in Windows Explorer.

- **Owner:** Owner of the document or file, which is typically the user name of the GoldMine user who created the document.

If you right-click a blank area in the Links tab, a shortcut menu enables you to choose from the following options:

- **Launch:** Launches and loads the highlighted file and its application. This option is the same as double-clicking the linked document entry in the Links display.

- **Move:** Moves the highlighted file to a different location.

- **E-Mail document:** Allows you to e-mail the highlighted file to a contact, GoldMine User, User Group, Manual Recipient, or Outlook contact.

- **Find:** Enables you to search the contents of all linked documents for specified text.

- **Output to:** Enables you to send the list of files under the Links tab to a printer, Word, Excel, or the Windows Clipboard. This list includes all the information found under the Links tab (Document, Type, File, Date, and Owner), but not the information found in the actual files.

- **New:** Creates a new link.

- **Delete:** Deletes the highlighted link. The actual file is not deleted.

- **Edit:** Displays the Linked Document dialog box, in which you can edit the highlighted link.

Linking Files Automatically

Some of the more common file types, such as word-processing documents and e-mails, link themselves automatically to records. Certain fax programs also link automatically. Most other files require you to manually connect them to the client record. (See "Manually Linking Files and Folders" later in this chapter for more information.) In this section, you discover how GoldMine automatically links files to a contact record.

Linking word-processing documents

Out of the box, GoldMine comes with links to various versions of Microsoft Word. If you match the proper version of GoldMine with the correct linking file and the correct version of Word, then you can automatically link every document you create to the Links tab. This process is actually easier than it sounds.

When Word is initially installed, you must also install its ODBC (Object Database Connectivity) drivers. If you don't install them, GoldMine can't create mail merge documents for you. If Word already has been installed without the ODBC drivers, you can install them from the original Word or Office CD without reinstalling all the rest of the software.

Assuming that both GoldMine and Word are properly installed, but have never spoken to each other before, you need to connect the two programs. GoldMine comes with several links to Word. Which one you use depends on which version of each program you have. The various possibilities are shown in the following table:

This Document...	Links This Version...	to This Version
GMLINK.DOT	GoldMine 6.0	Word 98, Word 2000, Word 2002
GMLink.DOT	GoldMine 5.0	Word 98, Word 2000
GM4W8.DOC	GoldMine 4.0	Word 97, Word 2000
GM4W6.DOC	GoldMine 4.0	Word 95

You actually make the connection by opening the appropriate GoldMine document (using Word). These documents, listed in the preceding table, are stored in the main GoldMine directory.

If you are using Word 2000 or above, you need to set your macro security to low by choosing Tools➪Macro➪Security; in the dialog box that appears, select the Low radio button, and then click OK. This allows the macros contained in the GMLink file to work properly. Remember to reset the macro security to medium after you've installed the link. Making the connection is automatic after you enable the macros and click Install GoldMine Link, which is displayed with the Word document. See Figure 16-2 for a look at the actual linking system as displayed within Word. Additional information on this linking procedure is provided in the User's Guide that comes with GoldMine, although the system itself guides you gracefully through the process.

After the connection is made, creating Word documents starting from GoldMine is easy, and linking them after they're created is even easier. During the linking procedure, Word creates several blank template documents, one of which is `BLANK.DOT`. You can see it in the list of mail merge documents. You access these documents by clicking the Print Documents icon from GoldMine's main toolbar. Clicking this icon takes you to the Document Management Center window, as shown in Figure 16-3.

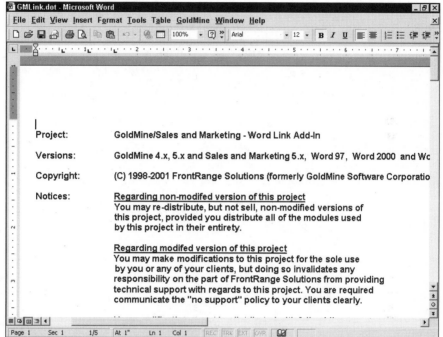

Figure 16-2:
Setting up the GoldMine link from Word.

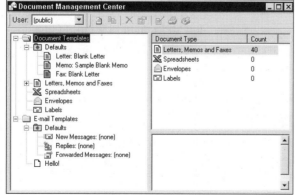

Figure 16-3:
The Document Management Center window.

By selecting Letter: Blank Letter, GoldMine shows you a Word template document that starts creating a letter for you by filling in the salutation portion of a typical letter you might write. You can fill in the actual text of the letter and then save this letter using the Save As option. Make sure you don't simply save the letter, because doing so overwrites the original template. After you save the letter, Word automatically sends the file information back to GoldMine.

GoldMine takes all the file information and lists it within the Links tab of the active contact record for you. You don't need to do anything, assuming you began this process from the Document Management Center window within GoldMine. If you didn't start from the Document Management Center window, Word doesn't send any linking information back to GoldMine, and you have to manually link the document.

Linking e-mails

I discuss the details of sending and receiving e-mails in Chapter 14, but basically, the GoldMine e-mail system is tightly integrated with contact records, but through the History tab, not the Links tab. It's as automated as the Word link, but the results are a little different.

Outgoing e-mails

To automatically attach an outgoing e-mail to a contact record, you must complete the following steps:

1. **Find the record with which you're associating the e-mail and display it on-screen.**

   That record becomes the active record.

2. **Click the E-mail Center icon on the main toolbar.**

3. **Click the Create a New Mail Message icon on the local toolbar.**

4. **Compose the e-mail message and send it by clicking the Send icon on the local toolbar.**

These outgoing e-mails, whether they have attached documents or not, are automatically recorded in the History tab, *not* in the Links tab! If there are attachments to these outgoing e-mails, they can be accessed by double-clicking the e-mail message on the History tab.

Incoming e-mails

Incoming e-mails are automatically registered in the History tab. Any incoming files attached to e-mails are recorded in the Links tab. The e-mail system allows you a good bit of control over exactly which records are associated with particular e-mails. Please refer to Chapter 14 for more details on controlling incoming e-mails.

Linking faxes

You must have a third-party program in order to fax at all. Of the commonly used ones, only one automatically records what it has done in the Links tab. FaxRush (also called OmniRush) is the most tightly integrated fax system. When properly configured, OmniRush automatically links all outgoing and incoming fax activity for you. Please see Chapter 30 for more details on this product.

WinFax, which also integrates with GoldMine and with Word, is not so tightly integrated as to automatically record what it has done in your GoldMine records. It is up to you to manually link or record those files that WinFax has sent or received. (Refer to Chapter 15 for specific detailed information about faxing using GoldMine.) See the following section for details on linking files manually.

Manually Linking Files and Folders

You can manually link virtually any file to GoldMine. You can create document links by using either the local (shortcut) menu on the Links tab of the contact record or by dragging-and-dropping the file with an application that supports file dragging, such as Windows Explorer.

Using the Links shortcut menu

To manually link a file using the local (shortcut) menu, follow these steps:

1. **Click the Links tab on the contact record (the main GoldMine screen).**

2. **Right-click the mouse anywhere in the display area below the tab.**

   The Links shortcut menu appears, as shown in Figure 16-4.

3. **Select New from the menu.**

   The Linked Document dialog box appears, as shown in Figure 16-5.

4. **Enter a name in the Document Name text box that will make sense to you six months from now.**

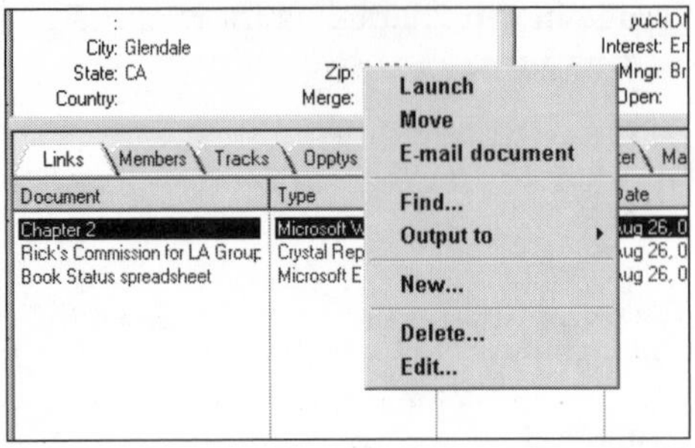

Figure 16-4:
The Links
shortcut
menu.

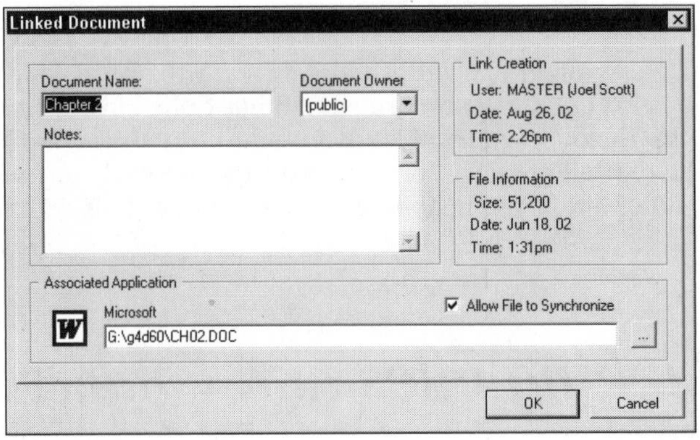

Figure 16-5:
The Linked
Document
dialog box.

5. **Enter a user name in the Document Owner text box if it is someone other than you.**

   Consider using Public as the Document Owner to make this file available to everyone on your team.

6. **Record the exact filename of the file using the Browse button at the bottom of the Linked Document dialog box.**

7. **Select the Allow File to Synchronize check box if you want this file included in a transfer set.**

   See Chapter 24 for details on synchronizing.

8. **Click OK when you are finished, and your file is linked.**

Using drag-and-drop

Using the drag-and-drop method is the quickest way to link a document to GoldMine:

1. **Click the document name in the application that supports drag-and-drop (such as Windows Explorer) to highlight it.**

2. **Hold down the left mouse button, drag the file icon to the currently open record (you don't need to have the Links tab selected), and release the mouse button.**

   GoldMine displays the Linked Document dialog box.

3. **Type the linked document name in the Document Name field.**

In just three moves, you completely link almost any kind of file or document. In no case have you moved the document itself. You merely established a pointer from GoldMine to the document.

Accessing Linked Documents

When a document file is linked with GoldMine, you can launch directly into the application and load the linked file with one operation. This means you can easily start up Word or Excel and immediately display the linked file. To do this, click the Links tab to access the list of linked files, and then double-click a file.

If you select a Word document, for example, GoldMine starts up Word (if it isn't already running in the background) and loads the document you have requested. It does the same for Excel spreadsheets, or for that matter, for any program that allows file access.

By linking all your client-related documents to the appropriate contact record, you're assured that you can always find those documents when you need them.

If you work on a local or wide area network, always store your documents on a server accessible to all who may ever need to reference those documents. Even if others won't need to reference those documents, chances are that only your file servers are being regularly backed up. And you probably want all your documents backed up. The take-home lesson is to save your documents in a standard, agreed-upon location that's accessible to your team and that's backed up regularly.

Integrating Document Management Systems

Several add-on products do an even more sophisticated job of linking and managing documents. One that has been around for several years is Scan2Gold. Scan2Gold is tightly integrated with GoldMine and allows you to scan a document, automatically link the document to the appropriate GoldMine contact record, search for documents with a particular subject, and view the document.

LaserFiche is a somewhat more sophisticated scanning and retrieval system that integrates to GoldMine with the help of an associated product, GoldFiche. One of the fundamental differences between Scan2Gold and LaserFiche is the ease and thoroughness of the search engine that each has. In addition, LaserFiche has a more sophisticated methodology for handling large batches of incoming documents.

For example, in the financial services industry, brokers may receive lengthy reports (as much as 1,500 pages) on the investments for their clients. Pages 3–5 may pertain to one client, and pages 6–9 may be for the next client. With LaserFiche, it is possible to link pages 3–5 to one GoldMine contact record and pages 6–9 to another. In fact, it can be done semi-automatically, which is a big timesaver if you ever run into this situation.

As document security becomes more and more of an issue (particularly in the health care and financial services industries) more companies will need to add document scanning and automated retrieval to their software tool chests.

Part V

Organizing and Distributing Information to Your Team

The 5th Wave   By Rich Tennant

"Sure, at first it sounded great—an intuitive network adapter that helps people write memos by finishing their thoughts for them."

In this part . . .

Information is power. This part of the book is about using the InfoCenter to distribute all sorts of internal information to your staff. It's a poor man's intranet. In addition, you can use the built-in statistical analyses and reports to keep yourself on target and to keep everyone on the team informed.

Chapter 17

The InfoCenter

In This Chapter

▶ Navigating the InfoCenter

▶ Creating new InfoCenter books and topics

▶ Making changes to your InfoCenter

▶ Notifying your staff of important changes

*T*he InfoCenter is like an encyclopedia that you can develop for use by your staff as well as for distributing information to clients and prospects. In many ways, it's like an intranet site. You can use the InfoCenter to catalog your company's rules and regulations, make them available to every employee, and notify staff of any changes to the rules and regulations. You can also stock the InfoCenter with product catalogs and price lists for easy maintenance and distribution.

The InfoCenter window divides its information among three tabs:

- ✔ **KnowledgeBase (KB):** Contains general information relevant to staff and clients alike, such as company rules and product prices.

- ✔ **Personal Base (PB):** Contains information pertinent to an individual user, such as family birthdays and anniversaries.

- ✔ **What's New?:** Presents KnowledgeBase information in chronological order with the most recent information at the top. In addition, this tab enables the creator of a new item to notify each user when that item is added or an existing section or topic is modified.

The KB and the PB are structurally the same and operate in the same way. Whereas only users with Master rights can control access to the KB, determining reading and writing access for individual users, individuals can set up their own sections in their PBs. The PB is designed for use by an individual, and the only way to access a PB is to log on with the same user name as the user who originally created that particular PB.

This chapter explains how to navigate through the InfoCenter to find relevant information, and how to create and post new entries. In addition, this chapter covers alerts, a special type of information distribution system within GoldMine.

Navigating the InfoCenter

You can easily access the InfoCenter from the main menu by choosing View↪InfoCenter. The InfoCenter window, shown in Figure 17-1, appears.

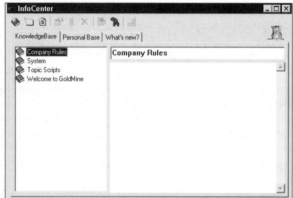

Figure 17-1:
The
InfoCenter
window
with initial
books.

As you can see in Figure 17-1, the InfoCenter window contains three tabs: the KnowledgeBase, Personal Base, and What's New? tabs. The KB and the PB tabs are functionally the same, so this chapter focuses on the KB and What's New? tabs.

How the InfoCenter is organized

The left pane in Figure 17-1, which by default shows the KnowledgeBase tab when you open the InfoCenter, categorizes all the information in the KB into books, sections, and topics. A *book* is the most general grouping. Each book contains one or more sections. *Sections*, in turn, may contain one or more *topics*, or may themselves house information directly. If sections contain topics, then topics are where data is actually stored.

To the right of the KnowledgeBase tab (refer to Figure 17-1) is the Personal Base tab. Again, the PB tab is structurally identical to the KB tab; the only difference being the access rights.

To the right of the PB tab is the What's New? tab. This tab lists all the topics entered into the KB in reverse chronological order. You see every topic for which you have read access rights. By clicking the What's New? tab, you immediately see what topics have been most recently changed in the KB.

When you first install GoldMine, two books exist — Topic Scripts and Welcome to GoldMine. Each of these books is further divided into sections. You can see this structure simply by double-clicking one of the book icons, as shown in Figure 17-2. As soon as you open a book, the icon changes from a closed book symbol to an open book symbol.

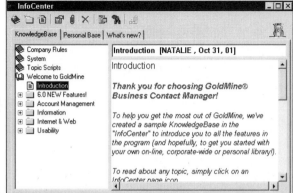

Figure 17-2:
Section and topic detail in the InfoCenter.

Searching the InfoCenter

As you begin expanding your InfoCenter, finding any particular item within the InfoCenter can become challenging. Fortunately, a search tool exists that can help. The Search icon on the local InfoCenter toolbar allows you to search for keywords or phrases that may be in some folder or topic in the InfoCenter. Clicking this icon brings you to the Search dialog box, as shown in Figure 17-3.

Figure 17-3:
Enter a term you want to search for in the InfoCenter Search dialog box.

In the Search For field, you can either type the keyword or phrase you want to search for, or you can select a previously searched-for item from the drop-down list.

In the Search Scope section, you can specify the range of entries that you want GoldMine to search. You have the following choices:

- ✔ **Entire contents:** Searches through every book, section, and topic in the InfoCenter for the term you entered in the Search For field. This is often a good choice unless you have so much material in your InfoCenter that a full search takes a long time.

- ✔ **Selected node:** Searches just the book, folder, or topic you currently have highlighted in the left pane of the InfoCenter window. In the example shown in Figure 17-3, Welcome to GoldMine is highlighted, so the option shows up as Welcome to GoldMine.

- ✔ **Last pages found:** Searches only the pages that were identified by the last search you performed. This function allows you to drill down to find further detail.

The following options allow you to determine how closely a phrase must be matched during the search:

- ✔ **Match whole words only:** Considers the term in the Search For field as a unit, so an exact match must be made to the entire value. In other words, if you enter "Joe" as the term you want to look for, and "Joel" exists in one of the topics, then "Joel" won't show up as a match.

- ✔ **Match case:** The exact upper- and lowercase letters must match between your phrase and those phrases found in the InfoCenter. If you turn on this option, "Sun" will not match with "sun."

In the Search Area section, you can identify which areas of the InfoCenter to search for potential matches. Your choices are

- ✔ **Keywords**
- ✔ **Topic name**
- ✔ **Folder name**
- ✔ **File names** (of attached files)
- ✔ **Topic text**

After you specify your search criteria, you can begin the search by clicking the Search button at the bottom of the Search dialog box. Figure 17-4 shows the results of a search for any book, folder, or topic containing the word *e-mail.* To continue searching for a second, third, or further match, click the Search Next icon, which continuously moves through the text looking for additional matches.

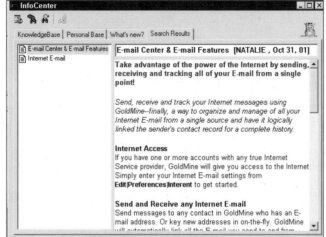

Figure 17-4:
The results
of a search
for e-mail
references
with the
InfoCenter.

Creating New InfoCenter Books, Folders, and Topics

You can set up a virtually unlimited range of material in your InfoCenter. I have found it particularly useful for housing my company's employee handbook. Other useful topics include such things as product catalogs, price lists, and competitive information.

Creating an InfoCenter book

The following procedure illustrates how to create a new book in the InfoCenter. The procedure for creating books, folders, and topics is the same in both the KB and the PB, except that you don't need to be concerned with access rights in the PB.

1. **From the InfoCenter local menu, click the New Book icon (the left-most icon).**

   A temporary name, New Book, appears within brackets.

2. **Type over <New Book> with the actual title of the new book you are creating and press Enter to save your new title.**

   If you're creating a handbook of company rules, you might call it something clever like *Company Rules*.

After you have a new book, you can add folders and topic pages. You can create a folder or a topic page by following these steps:

1. **Highlight the book in the left pane of the InfoCenter and then right-click it.**

2. **Choose New from the shortcut menu.**

   Choose book, folder, or page.

3. **Enter your new text in the right pane.**

4. **When you're done typing, click the left-most local icon (Save) to save this new text in the InfoCenter.**

Figure 17-5 shows a more fully developed book of Company Rules.

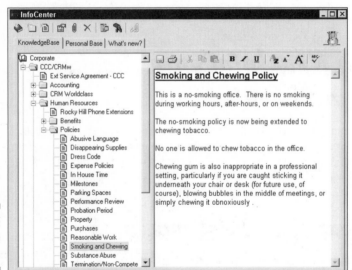

Figure 17-5:
A Corporate
Rules book.

After you create a topic page, you have three methods of getting information into it. You can

✔ Type the information directly into the right pane of the InfoCenter.

✔ Paste a document from another source, such as your word processor.

✔ Attach an existing file of any type, such as a text file, data file, picture, and so on.

Editing entries in your InfoCenter

Editing a topic in the InfoCenter is easy. Highlight the folder or topic page in the left pane of the InfoCenter. In the right pane, you see the actual text, to which you can make necessary edits.

Notifying Your Staff of Important Changes

One of the most important features of the InfoCenter is its ability to automatically let your staff know that something new is in the InfoCenter. That's the whole point of the What's New? tab. Another way to do this — when a new situation affects just one account — involves the Alert System.

Using the What's New? tab

The What's New? tab of the InfoCenter allows you to automatically notify all the other users that a revision has been made in the InfoCenter. That revision could be the addition of a new topic or a change to an existing topic. Each user will receive an automatic notification when signing on to his or her copy of GoldMine.

One of the User Preferences settings is critical to the operation of the What's New? feature in the InfoCenter. Each user must be sure to select the Show What's New in the InfoCenter When Logging In option on the Misc tab of the User Preferences dialog box. (See Chapter 3 for more information on changing the User Preferences settings.) As long as this option is set, the user will be notified when any information is changed in or added to the KnowledgeBase.

Within the InfoCenter itself, you can click the What's New? tab and see all the various topics listed chronologically (most recent on top) based on the date and time the last change was made.

The InfoCenter can act like a mini-intranet, and the What's New? feature ensures that everyone is notified of changes in a timely fashion.

Assigning an alert to a contact record

Alerts are not actually part of the InfoCenter, but they have a role that is similar to the What's New? tab of the InfoCenter. You can attach an alert to a particular record in GoldMine and make sure that everyone on your team is notified about some important condition relating to that record.

Just recently, I received a notice from a bankruptcy court that one of my clients had just declared bankruptcy. I checked the account and discovered that my company was scheduled to provide them with training in two days. I used the Alert System to make sure that we didn't run off to their office without securing payment first.

You can warn other GoldMine users of a special status or situation regarding the contact. Three-character codes, such as CRH for Credit Hold, can be defined to cover a variety of issues. Figure 17-6 shows an already configured Alert System.

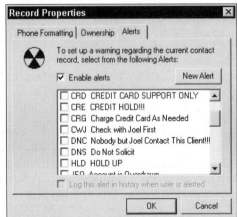

Figure 17-6:
The Alert
System.

You can issue an alert for a record by following these steps:

1. **Activate the record.**

2. **Choose Edit⇨Record Properties.**

    The Record Properties dialog box appears (refer to Figure 17-6).

3. **Click the Alerts tab.**

4. **Select the Enable Alerts option.**

5. Select one or more alerts for this record.

6. Click OK when you're done.

By default, GoldMine displays the alert seven seconds after anyone calls up the record. It's important to understand that the only time someone will actually see your alert is immediately after that person activates that particular account. No general message goes out when you program an alert. Alerts continue to show for a record until someone goes back into the Alert System and either disables alerts or removes the selection for every previously selected alert.

Unfortunately, I have not found a way to assign the same alert to a defined group of accounts, nor have I discovered how to use Automated Processes to set alerts. Setting alerts is very much a manual process, record by record. If you need a more automated method of creating and removing alerts, check out KnowledgeSync, which is discussed in Chapter 29.

Chapter 18

Graphical and Statistical Analysis

. . . .

In This Chapter

▶ Displaying account statistics

▶ Using quota and sales analysis

▶ Going over the statistical analysis

▶ Foreseeing with the forecast analysis

▶ Drawing up the graphical analysis

▶ Looking up the leads analysis

. . . .

GoldMine has a substantial amount of graphical and statistical analysis capability built into it. Using this analysis capability, you can focus on one individual account, on a GoldMine user, or on a group of users.

If you're a sole practitioner using GoldMine by yourself, you can use these analysis tools to monitor your performance and to keep yourself on target. Resist the urge to check your stats only when you think you're doing well. Use the tool the same way a manager might. Check consistently, and make mid-course corrections whenever needed.

If you're a manager, resist the urge to use the analysis tools in a Big Brother type of way. Use them to help your staff achieve goals. Your team probably wants to achieve its goals as badly as you do. Don't ask, "When are you going to close that deal?" Instead, you should ask, "What can I do to help you with this opportunity?"

In this chapter, you find out how to get those statistics to help you chart your course.

Displaying Account Statistics

Using GoldMine, you can track a variety of up-to-date statistics for any contact in your database. To access this statistical data, follow these steps:

1. **Open a contact record and then click the History tab.**

2. **Right-click in the display area and choose Options from the shortcut menu.**

3. **Choose Analyze from the next menu that appears.**

   The Contact Record Statistics dialog box appears, shown in Figure 18-1, giving you information such as the amount of time you're dedicating to the contact and the amount of sales generated by the account.

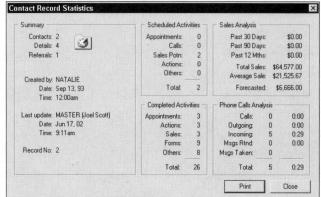

Figure 18-1:
GoldMine
displays
tons of
statistics in
this dialog
box.

The Contact Record Statistics dialog box displays important information about the contact, grouped into the following categories:

- ✔ **Summary:** Displays the number of additional contact records, detail records, and referral records; information about the creation and updates to the record; and the record number of the contact record.

- ✔ **Scheduled Activities:** Shows the number of appointments, calls, forecasted sales, next actions, and other actions currently scheduled for the account.

- ✔ **Completed Activities:** Lists the number of appointments, sales, forms, and other actions that have been completed for the account.

- ✔ **Sales Analysis:** Displays the total dollar amount spent by this account over the past 30 days, 90 days, and 12 months; the total amount the account has purchased; the average sale amount; and how much is currently forecasted for the account.

- ✔ **Phone Calls Analysis:** Shows a breakdown, by number and total duration, for each type of phone call to and from this account.

Setting Quotas and Measuring Performance against Them

The sales analysis section of GoldMine can be independent of setting quotas but is much more meaningful if quotas or guidelines are set up ahead of time.

Whether you are a one-person operation or a multinational conglomerate, you should always be setting performance goals, standards, and quotas. In my company, toward the end of each year, I sit down and develop a game plan for the coming year. That includes some strategic analysis and planning, detailing the expected expenses for my company, and then setting sales goals with the idea of bringing in sufficient revenue to handle all those expenses.

GoldMine's quota analysis is a big part of that effort. By setting each sales-person's goals (quotas) for each product line, you can decide whether your goals are reasonable and obtainable. Then, by comparing your forecasted and completed sales against that quota, you can make midstream adjustments as needed.

Assigning a quota

To assign a quota to a user, follow these steps:

1. **From the main menu, choose View➪Analysis➪Quota Analysis.**

   The Quota Listing dialog box appears, as shown in Figure 18-2.

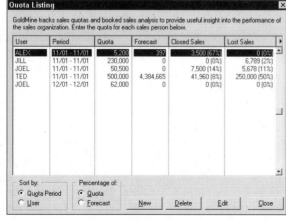

Figure 18-2: View your quota in the Quota Listing dialog box.

Quota Listing

GoldMine tracks sales quotas and booked sales analysis to provide useful insight into the performance of the sales organization. Enter the quota for each sales person below.

User	Period	Quota	Forecast	Closed Sales	Lost Sales
ALEX	11/01 - 11/01	5,200	397	3,500 (67%)	0 (0%)
JILL	11/01 - 11/01	230,000	0	0 (0%)	6,789 (2%)
JOEL	11/01 - 11/01	50,500	0	7,500 (14%)	5,678 (11%)
TED	11/01 - 11/01	500,000	4,384,665	41,960 (8%)	250,000 (50%)
JOEL	12/01 - 12/01	62,000	0	0 (0%)	0 (0%)

Sort by:
○ Quota Period
○ User

Percentage of:
○ Quota
○ Forecast

New   Delete   Edit   Close

2. **To develop a new quota, click the New button.**

The Assign New Quota dialog box appears, as shown in Figure 18-3.

Figure 18-3:
Assign
quotas to a
user in the
Assign New
Quota dialog
box.

The Quota Profile tab contains the following information and options:

- **User:** By default, GoldMine displays the name of the currently logged-on user. To choose a different user, click the down arrow to the right of the User field. The name of the selected salesperson appears in the User column of the Quota Listing dialog box.

- **From Date:** Starting date of the quota period. By default, GoldMine displays the first day of the current month.

- **To Date:** Ending date of the quota period. By default, GoldMine displays the last day of the current month.

- **Quota:** Dollar amount of sales that the salesperson is expected to make during the quota period.

- **Forecast:** Displays the total dollar amount of sales scheduled on the calendar for the period. This entry changes as the salesperson schedules sales he or she expects to close during the quota period.

- **Closed Sales:** Displays the total dollar amount of sales completed successfully during the quota period. This entry changes as the salesperson completes sales during the quota period.

- **Lost Sales:** Displays the total dollar amount of sales that are completed as lost or unsuccessful during the quota period. An uncompleted sale is neither closed nor lost and remains in the Forecast field.

- **Goals & Objectives:** You can store up to 32,000 characters of information related to the quota.

3. **When you finish entering information, click OK to leave the Quota Profile dialog box.**

Doing so adds the new or updated quota entry to the Quota Listing. To edit a previously defined quota, right-click the appropriate user and choose Edit from the shortcut menu.

The Quota Profile dialog box has a Recurring tab, as shown in Figure 18-4. The recurring feature makes it easy to create quotas for daily, weekly, or monthly sales. You enter one period's quota and then immediately click the Recurring tab. From this tab, you specify the rate at which the quota should increase (or even decrease), as well as the period over which this should occur. Before version 6.0, you had to manually enter each month's quota. Now you can do many in one fell swoop.

Figure 18-4:
The Recurring tab of the Assign New Quota dialog box.

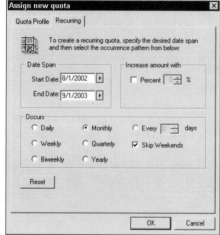

Analyzing sales versus quota

As soon as your quotas are established and entered, you can check your progress against these quotas. For this process to work at all, you must be forecasting and completing all your sales (discussed in Chapter 11). Assuming you are religiously doing this, go to the main menu and follow these steps:

1. **Choose View➪Analysis➪Sales Analysis to view the Sales Analysis dialog box, as shown in Figure 18-5.**

The Sales Analysis and the Select Users dialog boxes appear. Select at least one user's name in the Select Users dialog box.

2. **Select individual users, multiple users, or groups by highlighting an entry in either the User List or the Group List and double-clicking.**

3. **When you have chosen all the users you want, click OK.**

   The Select Users dialog box disappears, leaving you with a blank Sales Analysis dialog box. It is blank because you have not yet asked it to do any analysis. Before asking for your analysis, make sure that the range of dates in the lower-left corner is correct. You may also want to enter a particular activity code or result code if you want to analyze just those types of sales. If you leave the Activity Code and Result Code fields empty, GoldMine uses all sales activity within the date range you picked.

4. **When you are satisfied with the dates and other codes, click the Analyze button.**

   You then see the resulting analysis.

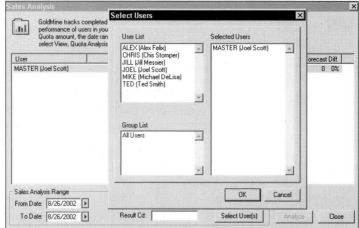

Figure 18-5:
Select which users you want to analyze sales for.

Stats, Stats, and More Stats

The Statistical Analysis of Completed Activities dialog box displays completed activity information for an individual user, a group of users, or on a system-wide basis. Analyzing completed activities can provide useful insight into your performance or into the performance of others in your organization.

You can access the Statistical Analysis of Completed Activities dialog box, as shown in Figure 18-6, from the main menu by choosing View⇨Analysis⇨ Statistical Analysis.

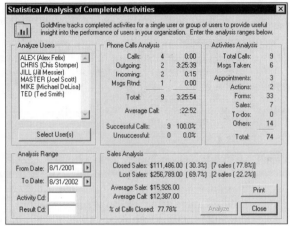

Figure 18-6:
Viewing
completed
activities.

The Statistical Analysis of Completed Activities dialog box contains the following options:

✔ **Select User(s):** Click the Select User(s) button to display the Select Users dialog box, from which you can pick GoldMine users for activity analysis. The list box above the button displays the users who will be included in the analysis; your user name is displayed by default.

✔ **From Date:** Sets the first date of the period to be included in the analysis.

✔ **To Date:** Sets the last date of the period to be included in the analysis.

✔ **Activity Cd:** Enter an activity code into this field, and GoldMine includes in the analysis only those completed activities that have the activity code you specify. When the field is left blank, GoldMine includes all completed activities.

If you code your activities as billable versus non-billable, you could enter the activity code for billable activities here and get an analysis of these activities only.

✔ **Result Cd:** Enter a result code into this field, and GoldMine includes in the analysis only those completed activities you specify by the result code. When the field is left blank, GoldMine includes all completed activities.

✔ **Phone Calls Analysis:** Shows the total number of completed telephone calls of the specified type in the history file. Call-backs, outgoing calls, incoming calls, and returned messages are listed, as well as the total duration of calls in each category. GoldMine displays the average duration of calls below the total line for this section. Successful Calls shows the number and percentage of calls with a satisfactory outcome, while Unsuccessful calls are those calls that were not answered at all.

Unsuccessful outcomes (such as *lost the sale* or *they told me to buzz off*) should be recorded through the result code. When you mark a call as Unsuccessful, GoldMine labels that call Attempted in the Summary tab, as opposed to Last Contact.

✔ **Activities Analysis:** Lists the total number of completed activities in the history file, including to-do actions, sales, received messages, appointments, and other actions.

✔ **Sales Analysis:** Displays the completed sales statistics. Closed Sales shows the total number of closed sales activities in the history file. The totals are displayed on the right. Look at % of Calls Closed to compare the number of completed sales as a percentage of completed call activities. The average sales value per completed call activity is also displayed.

✔ **Analyze:** Recalculates the totals in the display. Until you click this button, your analysis window remains blank. After clicking the Analyze button once, the Print button appears, which enables you to print this window.

After you select Analyze, GoldMine presents you with a Print button that allows you to print out the results of this statistical analysis. This print option also applies to the forecast analysis, discussed in the next section.

Using the Forecast Analysis

The forecast analysis is different than the sales analysis. Although sales analysis contains information on quotas, forecasted sales, and completed sales, the forecast analysis focuses on just those opportunities that have not yet closed.

To access the Forecasted Sales Analysis dialog box, as shown in Figure 18-7, choose View➪Analysis➪Forecast Analysis. This dialog box provides the following information about projected sales or cash flows for individuals, groups of individuals, or the entire organization:

✔ **Analyze Users:** Lists the users who will be included in the analysis; your user name is selected by default. To add or change the analyzed users, click the Select User(s) button.

✔ **Period:** Shows forecasted sales statistics divided into several periods. The top portion of the analysis window shows forecasted sales statistics by week for the next four weeks. Total amounts for the four-week period are displayed below the weekly section.

Below the weekly section, forecasted sales for the next four months are broken down by month. The Beyond line includes all forecasted sales scheduled to close after the next four months. Grand totals for the lower section are displayed at the bottom of the screen.

✔ **# of Sales:** Displays the total number of forecasted sales activities scheduled on the calendar for the period.

✔ **Forecasted:** Presents the total dollar amount of sales scheduled on the calendar for the period.

✔ **% Prob.:** Unveils the average probability that a sale will close in this period. This value is calculated by averaging the values entered in the Probability field for all the Forecasted Sales activities scheduled in the period.

✔ **Potential:** Lists the expected value (or weighted value) of sales that will be closed in this period. This value is determined by multiplying the total forecasted sales amount (Forecasted) by the average close probability (% Prob.).

✔ **Select User(s):** Click this button to display the Select Users dialog box, from which you can select GoldMine users for activity analysis.

✔ **Code:** Displays forecasted sales that have the entered activity code. You can use wild cards to select multiple activity codes. By default, this field is blank, and the resulting analysis includes all activity codes.

✔ **Analyze:** Click this button to calculate the totals in the display.

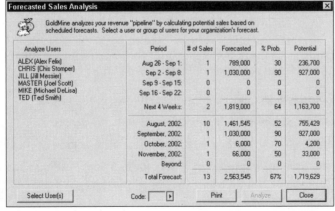

Figure 18-7:
Analyzing
your sales
forecast.

Analyze Users	Period	# of Sales	Forecasted	% Prob.	Potential
ALEX (Alex Felix)	Aug 26 - Sep 1:	1	789,000	30	236,700
CHRIS (Chis Stomper)	Sep 2 - Sep 8:	1	1,030,000	90	927,000
JILL (Jill Messier)	Sep 9 - Sep 15:	0	0	0	0
MASTER (Joel Scott)	Sep 16 - Sep 22:	0	0	0	0
MIKE (Michael DeLisa)					
TED (Ted Smith)	Next 4 Weeks:	2	1,819,000	64	1,163,700
	August, 2002:	10	1,461,545	52	755,429
	September, 2002:	1	1,030,000	90	927,000
	October, 2002:	1	6,000	70	4,200
	November, 2002:	1	66,000	50	33,000
	Beyond:	0	0	0	0
	Total Forecast:	13	2,563,545	67%	1,719,629

Forecasted Sales Analysis

GoldMine analyzes your revenue "pipeline" by calculating potential sales based on scheduled forecasts. Select a user or group of users for your organization's forecast.

Select User(s)   Code: Print   Analyze   Close

Using Graphical Analysis

If you prefer graphs to columns of numbers, then graphical analysis is for you. The GoldMine graphical analysis tool generates summary graphs of user activity data based on a variety of criteria. You can display your data as a bar graph or a line graph. GoldMine can represent all activity for a defined period of time, or one of several defined types of activity. Graphs can also represent total activities, a comparison of all users, or selected users.

To generate a graph, from the main menu choose View⇨Analysis⇨Graphical Analysis. The Graphical Analysis Options dialog box appears, as shown in Figure 18-8.

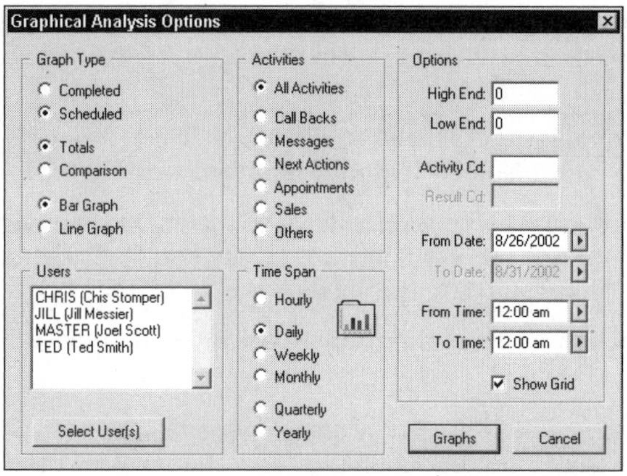

Figure 18-8:
Choose how
your graph
will look
in the
Graphical
Analysis
Options
dialog box.

The Graphical Analysis Options dialog box contains options that determine the time range and activities to be included in the graph:

- ✔ **Completed:** Displays completed activities in the graph.

- ✔ **Scheduled:** Shows scheduled activities in the graph.

- ✔ **Totals:** Charts together activity data for all specified users on the graph.

- ✔ **Comparison:** Graphs activity data for individual users as specified.

- ✔ **Bar Graph:** Generates a bar graph. Bar graphs are generally used to compare different periods or users.

- ✔ **Line Graph:** Creates a line graph. Line graphs are generally used to show trends over time.

✔ **Select User(s):** Click the Select User(s) button to access a list of users. If the Comparison option is selected under Graph Type and more than one user is selected, data for these users will be displayed on one graph with color-coded entries to differentiate between users.

✔ **All Activities:** Displays scheduled or completed data for all activity types in the graph.

✔ **Call Backs:** Generates a graph for either completed or scheduled call backs, depending on whether Completed or Scheduled is selected under Graph Type.

✔ **Messages:** Churns out a graph for either completed or scheduled messages, depending on whether Completed or Scheduled is selected under Graph Type.

✔ **Next Actions:** Creates a graph for either completed or scheduled next actions, depending on whether Completed or Scheduled is selected under Graph Type.

✔ **Appointments:** Generates a graph for either completed or scheduled appointments, depending on whether Completed or Scheduled is selected under Graph Type.

✔ **Sales:** Shows a graph for either completed or scheduled sales, depending on whether Completed or Scheduled is selected under Graph Type.

✔ **Others:** Displays a graph for either completed or scheduled other actions, depending on whether Completed or Scheduled is selected under Graph Type.

✔ **Time Span:** Allows you to specify a time range for your graph. Selecting the Hourly option provides a full day's worth of hourly data, starting at the beginning of the time period specified. The Daily option gives you about 10 days of data. The Weekly option provides about three months of data graphically.

✔ **High End:** Type a numeric value that corresponds to the uppermost number you want displayed on the vertical axis of the graph. For example, if experience shows that users rarely schedule more than 30 appointments per week, entering 30 in the High End field generates a graph with a vertical axis that ends at 30. The default, zero (0), allows GoldMine to generate the high-end value based on included data.

✔ **Low End:** Type a numeric value that corresponds to the smallest number you want displayed on the vertical axis of the graph. For example, if experience shows that users have never scheduled fewer than five call backs per week, entering 5 in the Low End field generates a graph with a vertical axis that starts at 5. The default is zero (0).

✔ **Activity Cd:** Generates the graph from activity records with the specified activity code. You can use wild cards to select multiple activity codes. By default, this field is blank, and the generated graph includes all activity codes.

✔ **Result Cd:** Type a result code to be used as the basis for graph data. Only activity records with this result code will be included in the graph. You can use wild cards to select multiple result codes. The default value for this field is blank, and all result codes will show up in the generated graph. This field is available only if you select Completed for Graph Type.

✔ **From Date:** Enter the beginning date from which data will be graphed. The default is the current date. This field is available only for a graph of completed activities; the ending date for scheduled activity graphs is always the current date.

✔ **To Date:** Enter the ending date to which data will be graphed. The default is the current date. This field is available only for a graph of scheduled activities; the beginning date for completed activity graphs is always the current date.

✔ **From Time:** Place the beginning time of a range you want to include in the graph. The default is 12:00 a.m. When combined with the default To Time entry of 12:00 a.m., the graph will display data for a 24-hour period. This field is not available when generating hourly graphs for completed activities.

✔ **To Time:** Place the ending time of a range you want to include in the graph. The default is 12:00 a.m. When combined with the default From Time entry of 12:00 a.m., the graph will display data for a 24-hour period. This field is not available when generating hourly graphs for scheduled activities.

✔ **Show Grid:** Displays lines that represent the horizontal axis of the graph (default). To generate a graph without this grid, remove the check from the check box.

✔ **Graphs:** Click the Graphs button, and GoldMine generates a bar graph or line graph based on your selections in the Graphical Analysis Options dialog box.

Using Leads Analysis

If you ever wondered what that Source field on the main screen is really for, read on; you find out in this section.

GoldMine enables you to track valuable information on the current status of sales efforts and on the effectiveness of various advertising and promotional efforts in generating inquiries and sales. Employed in this way, GoldMine becomes a strategic asset. GoldMine can provide timely and accurate information to help managers make better decisions on deploying their resources.

You can use the Source field to determine the profitability of individual marketing campaigns or groups of campaigns. GoldMine can report the total number of leads generated from each seminar, advertisement, or trade show from each Source value, the total sales volume generated from each Source value, and the potential sales pending from each Source value. You can then easily identify the most effective lead sources in terms of total leads or total sales volume generated.

Further, if you also know the cost of each lead, you can calculate the profit for each lead, easily locating the most profitable lead source. For example, if this lead source is an advertisement, you have an excellent tool that helps you determine whether to run that ad again.

When the analysis is complete, the Leads Analysis dialog box contains one record entry for each unique value found in the selected field in the contact database. These records appear in the Source column.

To generate a leads analysis, from the main menu choose View⇨Analysis⇨ Leads Analysis. The Leads Analysis dialog box appears, as shown in Figure 18-9.

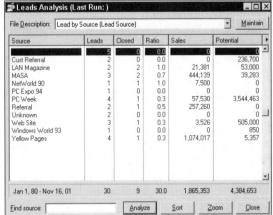

Figure 18-9: The Leads Analysis dialog box.

The Leads Analysis dialog box contains the following fields, each of which controls a portion of the analysis you can get:

✔ **File Description:** Profile name of the currently open leads analysis file, followed by the filename (in parentheses). You can select a different leads analysis from the drop-down list.

✔ **Maintain:** Click the Maintain button to display the Open Leads Analysis File dialog box, from which you can add, modify, or delete a leads analysis.

✔ **Source:** Name of the lead source, such as LAN Magazine. This entry appears in the Source field of the contact record.

✔ **Leads:** Total number of accounts in the database with this value in the selected field.

✔ **Closed:** Total number of accounts with this source that have at least one purchase, as recognized by the presence of a sales activity record in the history file.

✔ **Ratio:** Percentage of closed sales based on number of leads.

✔ **Sales:** Total dollar amount of sales generated by this lead source. This value is calculated by summing up all sales activity history records linked to the accounts with this source.

✔ **Potential:** Total dollar amount of future sales activities scheduled on the Calendar. This value is calculated by summing up all the Forecasted Sales records linked to the accounts with this source.

The Leads Analysis dialog box also contains the following additional options:

✔ **Find Source:** Moves through the Source entries to position the list at the first record that starts with the specified letter. For example, type C to select the first Source that starts with the letter C, such as Comdex.

✔ **Analyze:** Click the Analyze button to regenerate the leads analysis information for the current leads analysis database. You must select the field on which to base the analysis and the range of dates to be scanned for calculation of statistics. If you don't click this button, no analysis is performed.

✔ **Sort:** Click the Sort button to display the Leads Analysis Sort Menu dialog box, from which you can select the ordering of the records in the Leads Analysis dialog box.

✔ **Zoom:** Click the Zoom button to see more detailed information about the highlighted leads analysis record in the Leads Analysis Zoom dialog box.

Chapter 19

The Reporting System

In This Chapter

▶ Choosing a report category

▶ Sorting and selecting records for reports

▶ Printing and displaying reports

▶ Modifying reports

▶ Creating brand-new reports

▶ Discovering alternatives to the built-in reporting system

*G*oldMine comes with 60 or 70 reports already developed for your immediate use. These reports are divided into six report categories so you can more easily find the one you are looking for. In this chapter, I show you how to generate, view, and print a GoldMine report.

While GoldMine provides a report for almost every purpose, you may still find a need to modify an existing one or even create one from scratch. Thus, GoldMine has the ability to revise any existing report or to develop new reports from scratch. In this chapter, you also discover how to build a customized report.

If the built-in report generator proves too limiting, a number of very good third-party, report-generating utilities exist that work directly with GoldMine files. I also discuss a few of these third-party utilities in this chapter.

Choosing a Report Category

GoldMine generates six different categories of reports. Each category enables you to construct a report containing specific information. The following list details the six report categories and the information each one contains:

✔ **Contact Reports:** Print contact and activity data to meet a variety of needs, such as phone lists and completed activity logs.

✔ **Calendar Printouts:** Print scheduled activity data in graphical formats, such as monthly calendars.

✔ **Analysis Reports:** Print statistical information similar to the analyses available from the View menu, such as phone-call statistics and quota analyses.

✔ **Labels and Envelopes:** Print selected data in formats that conform to various Avery label types and envelope dimensions.

✔ **Other Reports:** Present a variety of useful information, such as organizing information from your personal Rolodex entries and a listing of available merge forms.

✔ **System Reports:** Contain a smorgasbord of reports, including activity logs, printouts of each of the tab folders, and reports on the Opportunity Manager and Literature Fulfillment Center.

Generating a GoldMine Report

In this section, I show you how to generate a GoldMine report. To create your report, you must do the following:

✔ Select the type of report you want to create.

✔ Specify the order in which you want your data organized.

✔ Choose the actual data you want to include in your report.

Choosing the report type

From the main GoldMine menu, choose File⇨Print Reports. The Reports Menu dialog box appears, as shown in Figure 19-1. You can see the six report categories in the upper-right corner. (See the "Choosing a Report Category" section, earlier in this chapter, for detailed information about the six types of reports.) Select the report you want by clicking it.

The next step in creating a report is to select and sort the information each report requires. See the next section for more details.

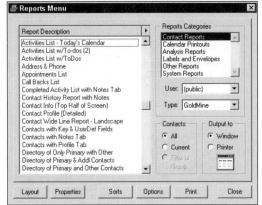

Figure 19-1:
Choose the
type of
report you
want in the
Reports
Menu dialog
box.

Sorting and selecting data for your reports

Contrary to popular belief, sorting and selecting are not the same thing. *Sorting* a report means that the items on the report are alphabetized or, perhaps, listed numerically. *Selecting* involves specifying a subset of all your data — for example, only the accounts in California, or only those accounts that are on credit hold. You may very well need to select a portion of your database for your report and specify sorting criteria as well.

Sorting report data

When you prepare a report, typically you want to control the order in which data is shown; that is, you want to list data in a sequence that makes the information clear and meaningful. Sorting allows you to arrange data in a specified order by one or more fields. GoldMine provides up to three levels (primary, secondary, and tertiary) by which each report can be sorted. For example, if you select the Company field as the first sort field, then all the records listed in the report will be ordered alphabetically by company name.

The Sorts option is available for only Contact Reports, Analysis Reports, Labels and Envelopes, and Other Reports. This option is not available for Calendar Printouts or System Reports.

With many canned reports, if you change the sort field, the report does not work without many other changes. If you're a GoldMine rookie, I suggest that you *not* change the sort option on a canned report without training or a real knowledge of database report writing.

Because GoldMine allows three levels of sorting, you can also select a secondary sort order if the Company field is the same for two or more records. For example, if you select the Company field as the primary sort, and the secondary sort is the Last Name field, then the records will be ordered by company name in the report. However, when two records have the same company name, they will be further ordered alphabetically by last name.

When a field is selected for tertiary sort, the records are ordered by the third sort field only when the first- and second-level sort fields are identical. For example, if the first- and second-level sorts are the State and City fields, and the third-level sort is the Zip field, then records will be ordered by zip code only when two or more records share the same state and city.

Without a second- or third-level sort, records in the report are ordered by date and time of entry in the database when the first-level sort is the same over several records. Listing records by the order in which they were entered is known as the *natural order of records.*

When selecting the sort order for your report, keep in mind that GoldMine queries the database in the most efficient way. If you select a multilevel sort, or a single-level sort with a field that's not already indexed, GoldMine builds a report sort table. This additional step allows other users to access GoldMine data while the report prints, and it also speeds the printing process.

To sort records in a GoldMine report, click the Sorts button on the Reports Menu dialog box. The Report Sorting dialog box appears, as shown in Figure 19-2.

Figure 19-2:
Choose
sorting
options in
the Report
Sorting
dialog box.

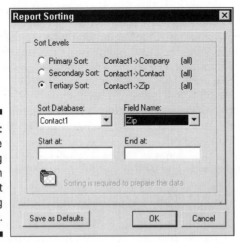

Use the following options to specify your sort:

- ✔ **Primary Sort:** Specifies the first set of parameters for ordering records. To complete the sort definition, select the Sort Database and Field Name by which you want GoldMine to order records in the report. To specify a range of records, specify a value in the Start At and/or End At fields.

  Every GoldMine report must have at least a primary sort defined to operate properly, even if no sorting is required. To preclude any sorting, set the Sort Database option to (none).

  If the Primary Sort option is defined as (none), the data preparation entry dims, indicating that GoldMine will sort records by the natural order of record entry.

- ✔ **Secondary Sort:** Specifies the second set of parameters for ordering records. To complete the sort definition, select the database and the field by which you want GoldMine to sort records. To specify a range of records, specify a value in the Start At and/or End At fields.

  You must define a first-level sort before you can define a second-level sort. If you want a report with only one sort level, define the first-level sort only.

- ✔ **Tertiary Sort:** Specifies the third set of parameters for ordering records. To complete the sort definition, select the database and the field by which you want GoldMine to sort records. To specify a range of records, specify a value in the Start At and/or End At fields.

  You must define a second-level sort before you can define a third-level sort. If you want a report with only two sort levels, define the first-level sort and the second-level sort only.

- ✔ **Sort Database:** Selects the contact database that contains the field on which records will be sorted for the selected sort level — that is, primary sort, secondary sort, or tertiary sort. The selected database appears to the right of the sort level.

  To display a list of contact databases, click the arrow to the right of the field.

- ✔ **Field Name:** Selects the field on which records will be sorted for the selected sort level. The selected field appears to the right of the sort level and the contact database name. To display a list of contact databases, click the arrow to the right of the field.

- ✔ **Start At:** Specifies the beginning value of a range that defines how the selected sort level will order records. If the Start At and the End At fields are blank, (all) appears to the right of the sort level database and field, and all records will be sorted in ascending order. For example, `Primary`

`Sort: Contact1->Lastname (all)` indicates that the first-level sort will order all records by the Lastname field of the database in alphabetical order.

You can enter a value in the Start At field alone to define a range; that is, without entering a value in the End At field, to specify a beginning point from which you want GoldMine to select and order records. The resulting report will include and order records from the specified starting point to the implied end of the range. For example, if the Start At field contains 06/11/03, the report will order records by the selected field from June 11, 2003, to the current date.

✔ **End At:** Specifies the ending value of a range that defines how the selected sort level will order records. If the Start At and the End At fields are blank, (all) appears to the right of the sort level database and field, and all records will be sorted in ascending order.

You can use the End At field alone to define a range; that is, without entering a value in the Start At field, to specify an ending point to which you want GoldMine to select and order records. The resulting report will include and order records from the earliest or smallest value through the value entered in the End At field. For example, if the End At field contains M, the report will order records by the selected field from the beginning of the alphabet through records with field entries that start with M.

✔ **Save as Defaults:** Saves the sort settings for future printings. If you want to apply the sort settings to the currently generated report only, do not click this button.

Playing with report specifications can be hazardous to the health of the original report. You should not generally try any major modification unless you are sure you have a backup of your files.

When you finish choosing your sort options, click OK.

Selecting data for a Contact, an Analysis, or a Labels and Envelopes report

Four of the six report categories allow you to select further options before printing. After you choose how you want your data sorted, select the data you want to include in a Contact, an Analysis, Other Reports, or a Labels and Envelopes report. In the Reports Menu dialog box, highlight the report you want to set data options for and click the Options button. The Contact Record Options dialog box appears.

The Contact Report Options dialog box, shown in Figure 19-3, is divided into three sections. Each section contains options that you use to control which data appears in the report.

✔ **History Data:** This section enables you to include activity data from history records (completed activities), as well as the date, time, and user who created the history record, and any reference information associated with the record. Select one or more types of data by checking the appropriate boxes in the dialog box (see Figure 19-3). In other words, if you want appointments included in your report, check that option. You can check multiple activity types.

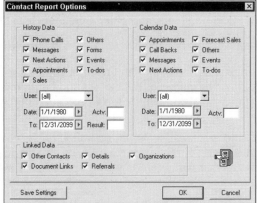

Figure 19-3:
The Contact
Report
Options
dialog box.

You can also select the individual user who created history records, or you can select all users. You can also specify a range of dates as well as an Activity (Actv) code and a Result code.

If an Actv code and a Result code have been entered, the two codes work as an AND condition to include events that have been assigned both to the specified Actv code and to the Result code. If no code is specified, GoldMine includes data with all activity codes.

✔ **Calendar Data:** The Calendar Data section, on the right side of the dialog box shown in Figure 19-3, allows you to select which kinds of scheduled activities to include in your report. You can check off as many activity types as you like, in the same way as you can in the History Data section.

The User and Date fields function in the same way here as in the History Data section. So does the Activity (Actv) field, but there is no Result field. That's because scheduled activities have not yet been completed, so they don't have a Result code associated with them.

If no items are checked under Calendar Data or no data exists for any of the checked data types, GoldMine suppresses the scheduled activities from the report and continues with the next section for which data is available.

✔ **Linked Data:** The Linked Data section, at the bottom of the Contact Report Options dialog box, allows you to choose what types of additional data to include on the report. Each of these warrants a little further definition.

- **Other Contacts:** Includes data about individuals entered as additional contacts for the contact records, including additional contact name, title, telephone number, and any reference data associated with the additional contact.

- **Document Links:** Includes documents linked to the contact records and provides information about the document, such as the creating application, the user who created the document, and the path and filename of the document.

- **Details:** Includes detail information linked to the contact records, such as birthday, and provides data about the Detail record, any reference data associated with the Detail record, and the date it was created.

- **Referrals:** Includes referral information linked to the contact records, such as the source of the referral (of:), to whom the referral was made (to:), and any reference data associated with the referral.

- **Organizations:** Includes Org Chart information linked to the contact records.

Displaying and Printing Reports

In the lower-right corner of the Reports Menu dialog box (refer to Figure 19-1), you can specify where to send your report output by using the radio buttons. Your choices are Window or Printer. In this case, selecting the Window option means that the report will be displayed on-screen.

If you're not sure about how much data will be printed, or if you're unsure of your own report specifications, you should generally send your output to the window first. After the report is displayed on-screen and you're satisfied with it, you can easily send it directly to your printer from the window display.

Setting up your printer

Before you can print your report, however, you have to configure your printer — not each time, just once. From the main GoldMine menu, choose File➪Setup Printer. The Print Setup dialog box appears, as shown in Figure 19-4.

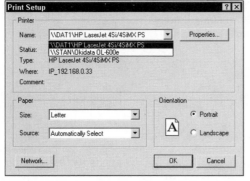

By supplying the information that GoldMine asks for in this dialog box, you can control which printer to use (if you're on a network with more than one printer), the orientation of the printout, and the size and feed source of the paper. The Print Setup dialog box contains the following options:

✔ **Name:** Indicates the printing device that will produce the report. To display a list of installed printers, click the arrow to the right of the field. For each installed printer, GoldMine displays the following information:

  • **Status:** Indicates whether the selected printer is the default printer, and whether the printer is available for printing.

  • **Type:** Lists the driver used by the printer; typically, this value is the same as the printer's name. The optional Comment line displays any additional information helpful to using the printing device.

  • **Properties:** Displays the Properties dialog box, in which you can set additional parameters specific to the selected printer. For example, the Properties display for a PCL-type printer, such as a LaserJet, is different than the display for a PostScript-type printer, such as a LaserWriter.

    When you finish selecting additional printer options, click OK to enter the parameters for the selected printer.

✔ **Size:** Specifies the dimensions of the paper on which GoldMine is to print the report. To display different paper sizes, click the arrow to the right of the field. After a paper size is selected, it remains in effect until a different paper size is selected.

✔ **Source:** Specifies the origin of the paper feed, such as Upper Tray. To display different sources, click the arrow to the right of the field.

✔ **Portrait:** Arranges the report in an orientation that's taller than it is wide. For example, on a letter-sized page, a portrait orientation would print 8½ inches wide by 11 inches tall.

✔ **Landscape:** Arranges the report to be wider than it is than tall. For example, on a letter-sized page, a landscape orientation would print 11 inches wide by 8½ inches tall.

When you finish, click OK to enter the printer configuration.

Chances are, particularly if you're on a computer network, that you have more than one printer. Within GoldMine, you can point your report to the desired printer by choosing File⇨Printer Setup from the main menu. The dialog box shown in Figure 19-4 appears.

In the first field on the dialog box shown in Figure 19-4, notice the list of all the printers available to you. These printer specifications got there when Microsoft Windows was initially installed or perhaps later when additional printers were installed. In any event, this list comes from all those printers that Windows believes are available to you. It's not a GoldMine function.

Sending a report to a printer

To print an entire report without previewing it on-screen, click the Printer radio button in the lower-right corner of the Reports Menu dialog box, and then click the Print button. The Printing in Progress status window appears, displaying information about the selected printer, the number of pages printed, and the number of records printed.

To stop printing at any time, click the Cancel button. Otherwise, the Printing in Progress status window closes when GoldMine finishes sending the report to the printer.

Sending a report to display on-screen

GoldMine can generate a report on-screen just as the report would look if printed on paper. To make a report appear on-screen, simply select the Output to Window radio button on the Reports Menu dialog box, and then click the Print button. GoldMine may chug for a little while as it sorts and selects, but your report shortly appears on-screen. From that window, you are given the option to look at the data and cancel out of the report, or print the report.

The selected printer affects the window display a little because each printer driver has unique spacing definitions.

To print one or more selected pages from a report displayed on-screen, follow these steps:

1. **Click the Print icon on the local Print toolbar.**

   The Print Pages dialog box appears.

2. **Type the page number values in the First Page field and in the Last Page field corresponding to the range of pages you want printed.**

3. **Click OK to start printing.**

Modifying Existing Reports

The idea of a report is to have all the information you need, exactly the way you want to see it, not the way the programmers think you want to see it. GoldMine allows you to modify its already existing reports to meet your specific needs. However, this is another thing you may not want to try at home.

The best advice if you want to modify a report is to make sure you don't destroy the original, existing report. Make a clone, or copy, of the report you want to modify and rename it to ensure that you don't lose the original report as follows:

1. **Choose File⇨Print Reports.**

   The Reports Menu dialog box appears.

2. **Highlight the report you want to modify, right-click, and select Clone from the shortcut menu.**

   The Report Profile dialog box appears.

3. **Enter the report description, any notes you feel appropriate, and the report filename.**

   Make sure you give the cloned report a unique filename. If anyone else uses this same report filename, it will overwrite your report. Also review the User option. If this report is one that everyone should have access to, you can leave User as Public; if this report is for your eyes only, change it to your user name. If you do change a public report to one with another user name, be sure to select the correct user (on the Reports Menu dialog box) the next time you try to access that report.

4. **Click OK.**

   You now have a cloned copy that you can feel free to modify.

Structuring your report

Modifying reports is not usually a fun task for poets, but if you need to, then choose Reports⇨Layout to display the selected report in its design layout. A typical report layout is shown in Figure 19-5. The field labels and the fields themselves are designated by a series of Xs.

The first section is the Page Header. Any field in the Page Header prints on the top of each page. The next section on a report is the Report Header, which contains the title of the report. The data contained in the report header prints only on the first page. The next section down is the sort headers, in which the break field is defined. *Break fields* group the data within the report and specify the database that is linked to a particular section of the report. You can only define break fields in a sort header. GoldMine limits the number of sort headers to nine. Information such as company, contact, address, and phone is contained in the sort header as well as the column labels for the Detail sections. The sort header prints only once per company. The Detail section is where the meat of the report displays. Working in conjunction with the sort header, this section displays all the information in the sort header based on the break field. The Page Footer is on the bottom of each page of the report. Included in this section are the date the report was printed and the page number. The date and page number are system fields that GoldMine automatically updates.

To modify the design of a report, from the Reports Menu dialog box, follow these steps:

1. **Select Contact Reports from the categories listing and highlight the Contact Wide Line Report — Landscape.**

2. **Click the Layout button at the bottom of the dialog box.**

   The programming involved in specifying this report appears in the window.

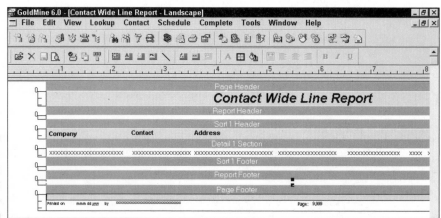

Figure 19-5:
A report
layout
window.

The Page Header contains the title of the report (refer to Figure 19-5). The Sort 1 header contains the company contact, address, phone, and text labels for the information that will be displayed in the Detail 1 section. If you want to see the actual field names instead of just Xs, right-click in any blank area of the report and choose Edit⇨Show Field Names.

To view the filter and break field for the Sort 1 header, shown in Figure 19-6, double-click the dark bar labeled Sort 1 Header. The Sort 1 Header dialog box appears, and you can choose break field or the filter from the buttons at the bottom of the window. Click the Break Field button. In this report, it's set to "Contact1->Owner." No filter exists on the sort header or detail header in this report.

Adding new fields

One of the most common modifications you may make to existing reports is to add a field that isn't already on the report. For example, you might want to include the Account Manager's name along with the account itself; for example, I want to add Key 4, Acct Mngr, under the company and address. Follow these steps to add a field to your report:

1. **Increase the size of the Detail 1 Section to accommodate the additional field by clicking the Detail 1 Section label and dragging down to make the section larger.**

   Two small black squares appear at the top and bottom of the section when you first click it. After you have dragged the section label to make it larger, you have room for some extra fields.

2. **In an empty area of the report, right-click and choose Insert⇨Data Field from the shortcut menu.**

   The Select a Field dialog box appears. The top drop-down list allows you to choose what database you want to add a field from. Choose the field from the database in the second drop-down list. To add Accnt Mngr, choose Contact1 from the top drop-down list, and then Accnt Mngr from the second drop-down list.

3. **Click OK.**

   Your mouse pointer changes into an outlined field that you can move.

4. **Move the cursor to where you want to place the field; in this case, under Company, and then click to place it there.**

   After you place the field, you can use the black squares that appear to resize the display of the field. You can move or change the size of the field at any time. You may want to indent the Accnt Mngr field under company for easier visual reference.

Figure 19-6:
Filters and
break fields
in a report.

5. **To change the font of the field, right-click in the field and choose Edit⇨Fonts.**

   The Font dialog box appears. Pick out a font you like and make any other tweaks to the font's appearance; click OK when you're done.

In order to preview the changes, GoldMine asks whether you want to save the modifications you have made. If you choose Yes, a sample of the report with your changes appears. *If you choose No, you lose all changes you have.* To change back to the Layout view, simply click the Layout icon on the Reports toolbar.

Adding a label

Of course, what good is adding a field if you don't label it? To add the label for Accnt Mngr, you need to make the Sort 1 header larger. Click the Sort 1 header label and pull down the bottom black square. Notice that the shading doesn't increase with the size of the header.

1. **Right-click, choose Insert⇨Label, and click OK.**

   A rectangle appears in the window with dashed lines surrounding it. The word "Label" appears in this box.

   In order to distinguish between Company and Accnt Mngr, indent the field slightly under Company and click to place it.

2. **To define the label, double-click it to see the Text Field Parameters dialog box; in the text box, type** Accnt Mngr **and click OK.**

   The shading for the Sort 1 header is defined in the Company label. To increase the shading, you need to resize the Company label.

3. **Click the Company label and drag the bottom black square down until the label meets the top of the Detail 1 header.**

   The shading now encompasses the entire Sort 1 header. Notice, however, that Company has moved down and is centered in the header.

4. **To correct this problem, double-click the Company label, and in the Text Position section of the Text Field Parameters dialog box (shown in Figure 19-7), select the Top option; click OK.**

   Company now aligns at the top of the header.

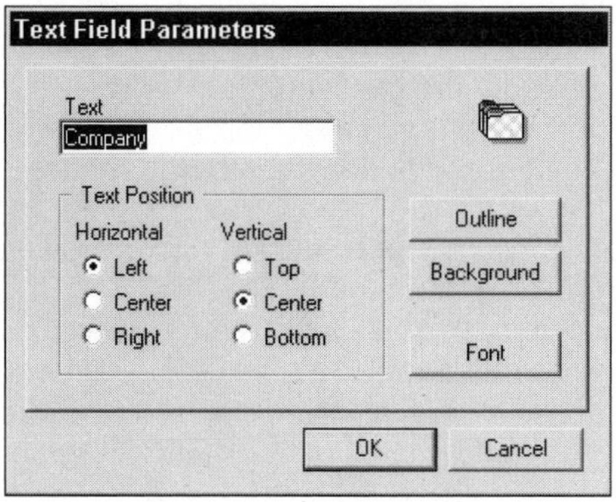

Figure 19-7:
Adjust the text in your report with the Text Field Parameters dialog box.

Text Field Parameters

Text
Company

Text Position
Horizontal
○ Left
○ Center
○ Right

Vertical
○ Top
○ Center
○ Bottom

Outline
Background
Font

OK   Cancel

5. **To view the changes, click the Preview icon in the Reports toolbar.**

6. **Make sure to save your modifications by clicking OK.**

To get a better understanding of report design and modifications, choose different reports and go into each layout and see how they are set up. Look at the break fields, filters, and general layout of the report. Doing so can give you a good idea of how to make the modifications you desire.

Creating Custom Reports

Most of your reporting needs can be met by the reports that come with GoldMine or by making some minor modifications to them. However, you may find it necessary to create your own reports based on your company's specific needs.

To create a new report:

1. **Choose File⇨Print Reports.**

   The Reports Menu dialog box appears.

2. **In the Report Description section, right-click and select New from the shortcut menu.**

   The Report Profile dialog box appears.

3. **Fill in the Report description, make any notes you may want to add, and give the report a unique name; click OK.**

   You are returned to the Reports Menu dialog box.

4. **Highlight the new report in the Reports Menu dialog box and click the Layout button.**

   GoldMine automatically gives you a Page Header, Sort 1 Header, Detail 1 Section, and Page Footer. Using the instructions from the example in the "Modifying Existing Reports" section, earlier in this chapter, you can add the labels in the Sort 1 header and fields in the Detail section.

If you want to add a filter to the entire report, click the Report Filter icon from the Reports local toolbar (in layout mode). This brings up the Record Selection Criteria dialog box, where you can build a filter for your report. See Chapter 12 for more information on filters.

Using Alternatives to the Built-in Reporting System

Because the GoldMine file structure is built on well-known and well-established dBASE files, you can use many third-party utilities to create reports. I discuss some of the more common ones I have used in the following sections. Others are available. Basically, any report system that can handle dBASE files can produce reports from your GoldMine data.

Excel

Almost everyone has a spreadsheet program, and most of us have Excel. Almost all the GoldMine data files are standard DBF files, which Excel can read directly. If Excel can read the file(s), then Excel can also manipulate the data for you.

By opening a GoldMine file with Excel, you can then reformat the data, perform all sorts of calculations, and generate graphs and charts. You can also use Excel to save these same files in some other format if you need access to the data from another program.

Do not open your GoldMine files with Excel or any other utility while GoldMine is being accessed by another user. And, most importantly, do not save the Excel files using the original name of the file. After you have made any changes to the data or the file structure with Excel, GoldMine will not be happy trying to use that file later. Even if it looks like it is working, you will probably have destroyed GoldMine's ability to synchronize its data.

In order to successfully use Excel to manipulate your GoldMine data, you need some understanding of the GoldMine file structure, or you at least need to know what data is contained in which files. The GoldMine Reference Guide details all this information.

Access

Consider Microsoft Access to be Excel's big brother. You can use Access to do almost anything Excel can do. In addition, Access has much more reporting capability than does Excel. The downside is that you need to have some serious experience with Access before trying to do too much with GoldMine files.

Other report generators

Seagate's Crystal Reports is one of the best-known standard report generators. There's a bit of a learning curve, but after you've mastered Crystal Reports, you can create a wide variety of custom reports and build them into GoldMine almost as if they came from GoldMine's own system.

Stonefield Query is a query builder and report writer with a simple wizard interface. Its wizard is easy to use and allows you some flexibility that Crystal Reports just doesn't have. MasterMine is another well-respected tool that generates Excel-based pivot tables from GoldMine data. For more about Crystal Reports and Stonefield Query, see Chapter 29.

Part VI

Customizing GoldMine

The 5th Wave — By Rich Tennant

"I find it so obnoxious when people use their cellular phone in public that I'm making notes about it on my HPC for a future opinion piece."

In this part . . .

One of the secrets to success with GoldMine is the art of fine-tuning it to your needs. You can add any custom fields you need, create lists of legitimate choices for most data fields, and electronically import and export data to avoid doing all that dirty work by hand.

Chapter 20

Creating New Labels and Fields

In This Chapter

▶ Adding new fields to your database

▶ Organizing and creating field views

▶ Changing field labels and data on the fly

▶ Modifying an existing field

*O*ne of the most powerful aspects of GoldMine is its capability of conforming to your business. You can customize the labels for individual fields so they more closely fit your needs. You can create an almost unlimited number of additional fields, and you can rearrange where many existing fields appear in the window.

Modifying fields and labels has been the domain of GoldMine dealers. The relatively straightforward modifications have gotten even easier in version 6.0, but very significant and powerful new features have been added to this version, still giving you a reason to maintain a relationship with a knowledgeable dealer.

This chapter helps you break into some of the secret tools of those dealers so that you can do some of your own customization, rather than pay someone else to do it.

Adding New Fields to Your Database

You can add up to 999 additional custom fields, or about 4,000 total characters, whichever is less. Several steps are involved. The first step is to add the new field to the database structure. The second step is to rebuild the database, and the third step is to position the field somewhere in the window so that you can see and use it.

If you are ever going to upgrade from the dBASE version of GoldMine to the SQL version, you're going to have trouble converting more than about 255 custom fields. Beware of this gotcha.

A somewhat new Screen Design utility presents an alternate method of adding new fields to your database. The older method, which I describe in this chapter, allows you to see your existing fields while adding new ones. I think this is a significant enough advantage that I recommend the older method and ignore the new one.

To begin adding fields to the database, from the main menu, choose File⇨ Configure⇨Custom Fields. The User Defined Fields dialog box appears, as shown in Figure 20-1.

Figure 20-1:
Use this
dialog box
to define
custom
fields.

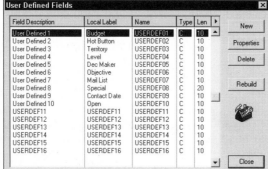

The User Defined Fields dialog box contains the following information:

- ✔ **Field Description:** Description of the field that typically describes the contents or purpose of the field; for example, Business Type.

- ✔ **Local Label:** Displays the default label that will ultimately appear on-screen.

- ✔ **Name:** Name that GoldMine uses to identify the field in the contact database.

- ✔ **Type:** Identification code for the data type of the field from one of the following values:

    - C — Character
    - N — Numeric
    - D — Date

- ✔ **Len:** Length of the field in number of characters. The length of the field determines how much data the field can hold, or the total number of characters that can be stored. For numeric fields, you must count the decimal point and the plus or minus sign, if you anticipate using one.

When adding a field type, you should know the types of fields and when you should use them. You can add three different field types:

- **Character fields (C)** can contain any keyboard character and are generally used to hold text. While the maximum length you can define is 254 characters, a practical limit is imposed by the size of your screen. The largest field that can be displayed across the screen and without room for a field label on the same line is 76 characters. You can, of course, have a field larger than 76 characters, and you can scroll from right to left within the field.

- **Numeric fields (N)** have a maximum length of 16, including any plus or minus signs. You can have from 0–9 decimal places. This limitation should never be a problem if you design your numeric fields properly.

  One of my clients in the financial services industry insisted she needed 20-digit numeric fields. Some of her clients, she said, had very large accounts. The entire United States national debt is currently about $6 trillion, which would take up 13 digits in a numeric field. She and I finally settled on 16 digits because that was all GoldMine can handle anyway.

  Very few human beings can look at a number like 5,132,563,436,666 and have any appreciation for what it represents. If you need to keep a number in the billions or trillions or more, you should label it as such and keep the number itself to a reasonable length. Examples include the following:

Field Label	Data Field
Bank balance (billions)	498.5
Avogadro's number (10^{23})	6.023

- **Date fields** must contain a valid date only and always have a length of eight characters. Dates are represented in a MM/DD/YY format.

Creating a new field

To create a field and add it to your existing database, follow these steps:

1. **If you don't already have the User Defined Fields dialog box open, choose File➪Configure➪Custom Fields, and then click the New button.**

   (Refer to Figure 20-1 to see the User Defined Fields dialog box.) After you click the New button, the User Defined Field Profile dialog box appears, as shown in Figure 20-2.

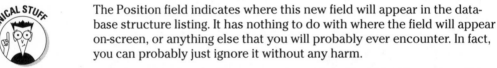

Figure 20-2:
The User
Defined
Field Profile
dialog box.

2. **Enter the name of your new field.**

   The Field Name field itself already has a *U* as the first character. *U* stands for *user-defined* and must be the first character in all fields you build. All user-defined fields

   • Must begin with the letter *U*.

   • Can contain up to, but not more than, ten alphanumeric characters.

   • Must have unique field names.

   The Position field indicates where this new field will appear in the database structure listing. It has nothing to do with where the field will appear on-screen, or anything else that you will probably ever encounter. In fact, you can probably just ignore it without any harm.

3. **In the Description field, enter a short, plain-English phrase describing the contents or purpose of this field. Spaces are allowed.**

4. **Select what type of data the field will contain and the length of the field.**

   As I mentioned previously, you have three choices of field type: character (C), numeric (N), and date (D), and you must select one of these options in this dialog box.

   If you're adding a field for a phone number, the field name should start with UPHONE. You can use either upper- or lowercase. Designating a user-defined field name with these first six characters forces GoldMine to format the data into typical phone-number format, with parentheses and dashes.

5. **When you're finished entering the information for a new data field, click OK.**

   You return to the User Defined Fields dialog box. (Refer to Figure 20-1.)

You can continue with this procedure, adding as many new fields as you need. After you finish adding all the new fields, you have one more step to complete before you can actually use these fields: You must *rebuild* your database. In fact, GoldMine has a reminder message that awaits should you forget the rebuild process. See the next section to find out how to rebuild your database.

Note that only users with Master rights are allowed to rebuild your database.

Rebuilding your database

Rebuilding your database creates a new dBASE data file structure according to the specifications you entered on the User Defined Fields dialog box. GoldMine then copies all the existing data from the old files into the newly created files.

To rebuild your database, simply click the Rebuild button in the User Defined Fields dialog box. GoldMine asks whether you're ready to rebuild the database; click OK. The rebuild function appends all your new fields to the CONTACT2.DBF file. This process takes only a moment or two if you do it while very few accounts are in your database. As the number of accounts grows, so does the time it takes for a rebuild.

A little planning at the beginning of your project may save you a considerable amount of time later if you have to do a few rebuilds with 25,000 existing accounts in the database. Try your best to plan for new or additional fields *before* you add a ton of data to the database. Then, rebuilding is quick; later, it may be painfully slow. In fact, if you're not completely sure how many fields you may need, it might be clever to add a couple of spare character, numeric, and date fields before you stock your database with 25,000 records.

Keep the following in mind when rebuilding:

- ✔ Always back up your entire database before rebuilding. GoldMine 6.0 has a new built-in Backup/Restore function. Use it.

- ✔ No one else should be running GoldMine while a rebuild is happening.

- ✔ Make sure you have enough free disk space available before rebuilding. GoldMine will be adding each of your new fields to every record in your database. You can find a formula for figuring free disk space in the GoldMine Reference Manual, but a common guideline is to never allow your hard drive to get more than about 70 percent full. Beyond that level, your disk efficiency begins to deteriorate anyway, and you run the risk of running out of space whenever GoldMine or any other program creates temp files or backup files.

Rebuilding usually only takes a short time, and then you will be ready to display or use the fields.

Organizing and Creating Field Views

Field views are groups of fields organized into logical groupings and shown together in one window display. GoldMine comes with basically one field view: the one directly under the Fields tab. To further organize the data, GoldMine enables anyone with Master rights to design custom views. Before you can display a newly created field in a field view, you need to create that view.

One of the benefits of custom field views is that you can organize your data logically. If you have a dozen fields related to accounting, you can put them all together in one accounting view. Marketing fields can be placed together, as can the fields for customer service and those for sales.

In addition, you can control the access rights to individual field views. If you don't want people in the Marketing department to view or to manipulate data in the Accounting view, you can preclude them from doing so. This is often a valuable tool.

To create and maintain custom user-defined field views, follow these steps:

1. **Click the Fields tab to highlight it.**

2. **Right-click anywhere in the Fields area and select Screens Setup from the shortcut menu that appears.**

   The Custom Screens Setup dialog box appears, as shown in Figure 20-3.

3. **Click the New button to create a new field view.**

   The Custom Screen Profile dialog box appears, as shown in Figure 20-4.

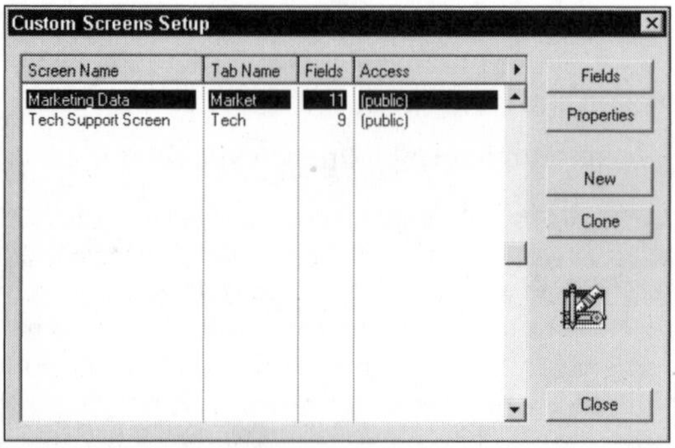

Figure 20-3: Create a custom view with the Custom Screens Setup dialog box.

Figure 20-4:
Name the
custom
view and
tab in the
Custom
Screen
Profile
dialog box.

4. **Fill in the following three fields on the Custom Screen Profile dialog box:**

- **Screen Name:** This is the name for the new dialog box and will be shown in the Custom Screens Setup dialog box.

- **Tab Name:** Designing a tab name creates a custom tab in one of the banks of tabs behind the standard tabs. Although you can enter up to 20 characters for a tab name, only 7 or 8 characters actually appear within the tab itself. Make sure the first 7 or 8 characters you use are sufficient to clearly describe what this view is all about.

GoldMine orders its custom tabs alphabetically from left to right. If you're concerned about ordering them differently, place a number at the beginning of the tab name. The number doesn't appear on the tab but determines the position of the title in the bank of custom tabs. For example, if you want the Marketing tab to appear to the left of the Accounting tab, enter **1Marketing** and **2Accounting** for their respective tab names.

- **Access:** This field allows you to direct who has access to this particular custom dialog box. To restrict access to this dialog box, select a user or a group of users who may access the dialog box. To allow everyone to have access, leave the access rights set to (public).

The last check box on the dialog box controls whether this custom dialog box is accessible from this particular contact database. Generally, you want to leave the default setting as is.

5. **When you're finished, click OK.**

Sometimes you will have several custom views that are very similar and actually contain many of the same fields. Rather than painstakingly recreating the second or third such view, you can copy all the individual view and field specifications from one view to another. You can do this by clicking the Clone button on the Custom Screens Setup dialog box, as shown in Figure 20-5.

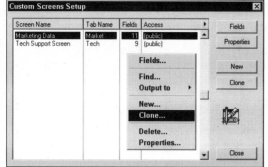

Figure 20-5:
Cloning a
view from
the Custom
Screens
Setup dialog
box.

Clicking the Clone button brings you to the Custom Screen Profile dialog box, allowing you to give the old view a new name and then automatically copy all the fields that are included into a brand-new field view.

Displaying New Fields

After you create all the field views (custom dialog boxes) that you need, you can begin placing individual fields on those dialog boxes.

Quite a few methods exist for displaying individual fields. In this section, I discuss a method that was introduced in GoldMine 5.0. This method is the most streamlined and logical method of them all.

To display a new field that already exists in your database, you must first locate the proper field view. You can maneuver through the various tabbed file folders by clicking the scroll arrows to the right of the row of tabs. After you locate the custom screen tab on which you want to display your field(s), follow these steps:

Creating hot keys

If you want to gain access to a particular field view by using *hot keys* (a special key sequence that accesses a command), you can create a custom hot key. For example, you may want to go to the Accounting tab by simply pressing Ctrl+A. To designate this hot key for the Accounting tab, type **&A** in the tab name. Actually, the ampersand (&) can appear anywhere within the tab name, but the following letter will become the hot key for that tab.

1. **Highlight the custom tab.**

2. **Right-click in the blank area below the tab and select Screen Design from the shortcut menu.**

   A series of local icons appears, as shown in Figure 20-6.

3. **Click the New icon.**

   The Place Field dialog box appears, which allows you to select the specific field to place on this tab. Assuming you have already created the field and rebuilt the database since then, you can find this field by clicking the arrow to the right of Field, as shown in Figure 20-7.

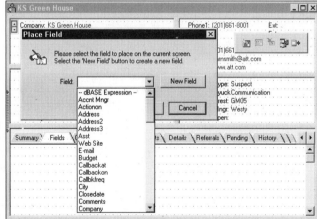

4. **After you identify the field you want, click OK.**

   You are brought back to the selected field view, with your new field highlighted in a red or white box. A red box indicates that the field is currently positioned on top of an existing field. You don't want two fields overlapping each other, so you have to move at least one of them. A box with a white background indicates that it doesn't conflict with any other field, but you may want to reposition it anyway.

You can reposition the field, whether it is highlighted in white or in red, by clicking and dragging it to an empty place in the window. When you have it in approximately the right place, double-click the box with the field you're displaying to show the Field Properties dialog box. Doing so allows you to do some further fine-tuning of the field, as shown in Figure 20-8.

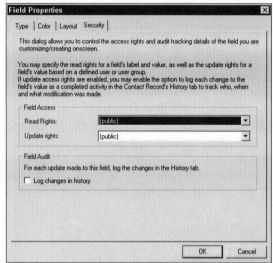

Figure 20-8:
Fine-tune
your field
definitions
in the Field
Properties
dialog box.

Click the Security tab on the Field Properties dialog box. Among other options in this tab, you can also specify who has rights to read and/or to change the data on a field-by-field basis by choosing from the following options:

✔ **Read Rights:** By default, this field is listed as (public), which allows all users to see the data in this field. You can enter either an individual or a group name into this field, and thus control who can see the data in this field.

✔ **Update Rights:** This option is similar to the Read Access field. By default, everyone can edit the data in each field. If you turn off Read Access rights, you also turn off Update Access, but situations may exist where you want someone to be able to see the data but not change it. An example might be a Credit Limit field. You may want anyone in the Accounting group to be able to read it and update it, but you may want the folks in the Sales group to be able see the data but not update it.

✔ **Field Audit:** If you turn on this option, GoldMine automatically keeps a historical log of all changes to the data in this field. This log includes the time, the date, and the user who changed the data. I have this set in the Account Manager field just in case a salesperson decides to reassign all the best accounts to him- or herself.

On the Layout tab, you specify the size and window positioning of each field you are displaying, as shown in Figure 20-9:

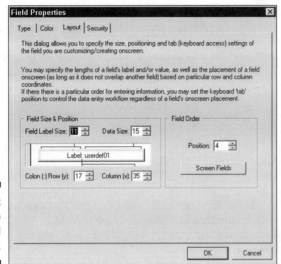

Figure 20-9:
Setting up
the field
layout.

✔ **Field Label Size:** You may need to adjust the length of the label you are using for this field. You can increase or decrease the size of the label by simply changing the number in this field. This may allow you to adjust the window location of the data by making more room if you need it.

✔ **Data Size:** You can also adjust the actual size of the data display for the field. This doesn't affect the data itself but may affect how much of the data you can see at one time without scrolling right and left.

✔ **Colon:** You can specify the position of the colon, which separates the field label from the data itself. This essentially positions the entire object, which is the label plus the data.

✔ **Field Order:** The integer in the Field Order field determines the order in which you normally tab from one field to the next. GoldMine takes you sequentially from one field to the next based on the number in the Field Order field.

You can change a field that has already been placed for display by double-clicking the label while you hold down the Ctrl key. The field and label become highlighted, and you can then double-click the highlighted area. The Field Properties dialog box reappears, and you can then make whatever changes are needed.

Changing Field Labels and Data On the Fly

Any user with Master rights can change the labels of the fields on the main screen, including those fields above the file folders as well as all the user-defined fields in the Fields tab. For example, for a contact database that contains only educational institutions, you can change the label of the Company field to School.

In addition to changing a field label for every record, GoldMine 6.0 can now change field labels on the fly based on the data entered in that or in other fields. For example, if you enter Canada as the country for a particular record, you can have GoldMine automatically display Postal Code as opposed to Zip Code in the prior field.

You can also change the data in particular fields on the fly based on what is entered in other fields. While this can also be done using the LOOKUP.INI file (see Chapter 21), there is at least one key advantage to doing this with the new facility, as shown in Figure 20-10.

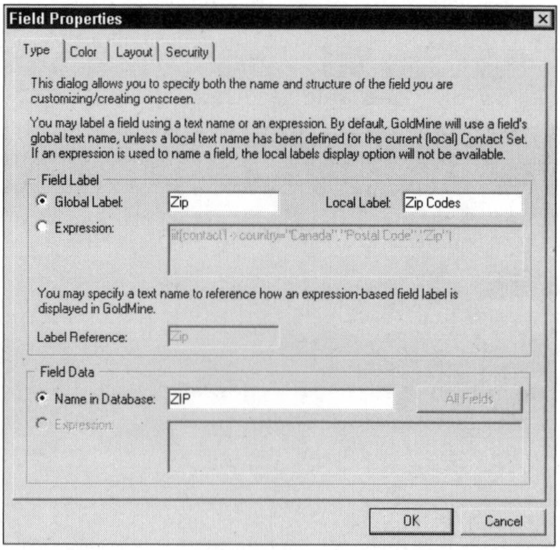

Field Properties

Type | Color | Layout | Security

This dialog allows you to specify both the name and structure of the field you are customizing/creating onscreen.

You may label a field using a text name or an expression. By default, GoldMine will use a field's global text name, unless a local text name has been defined for the current (local) Contact Set. If an expression is used to name a field, the local labels display option will not be available.

Field Label
- Global Label: Zip   Local Label: Zip Codes
- Expression: iif(contact1->country="Canada","Postal Code","Zip")

You may specify a text name to reference how an expression-based field label is displayed in GoldMine.

Label Reference: Zip

Field Data
- Name in Database: ZIP   All Fields
- Expression:

[OK] [Cancel]

Figure 20-10:
Changing
data on
the fly.

Using LOOKUP.INI, you can automatically have GoldMine assign an Account Manager based on, say, the state the account is in. This only happens, however, when you actually move the cursor into and out of the Account Manager field. You may still need to resort to this original methodology if you have more conditions than allowed in a typical dBASE expression.

You can only use expressions to change data in non-indexed fields in GoldMine 6.0. For example, none of the fields in Quadrant 4 are eligible for this treatment. See Tables 2-1 through 2-4 in Chapter 2 for a complete list of indexed fields. If you can use a field to locate records, it's an indexed field.

Another common section where field labels are often changed is within Quadrant 4 of the main screen (see Chapter 2), which contains the key fields. You probably want to have the five most important fields for your company's use right here on the main screen. First, you must decide what the five most important fields are; then you can modify the field labels accordingly.

To change the label of a field, follow these steps:

1. **Select the field label by holding Ctrl and double-clicking the field.**

   All the other fields in the window become highlighted in yellow, while the selected field remains in a white box. Refer to Figure 20-1.

2. **Double-click again in the white area where the original field is.**

   The Field Properties dialog box appears (refer to Figure 20-8). The Field Properties dialog box allows you to change not only the labels that appear in the window, but also a number of other properties as well, including the size and position of the label. See the "Adding New Fields to Your Database" section, earlier in this chapter, for details.

   The Field Label section focuses only on the labels themselves:

   • **Global Label:** Specifies field label text. GoldMine uses the text in the Global Label field unless you have specified a value in the Local Label field (see the next bullet). Global labels appear consistently throughout all contact databases. If you want to use a different label for this field in each contact database, use the Local Label field to store the label text.

   • **Local Label:** Specifies the text of a field label for only the currently open contact database. This option allows you to use a different field label for the primary field in different databases. An entry in the Local Label field overrides whatever is in the Global Label field for the one database that is open.

   The following limitations apply to local labels:

   • Local labels can be used only with fields, not expressions.

   • Local labels can be used only with character fields.

   • Local labels can be no more than 15 characters in length.

3. **When you're finished choosing labels and properties, click OK.**

   GoldMine updates the contact record display to show the new field label. Changing the field label has no effect on the data in the field.

Modifying an Existing Field

Suddenly in GoldMine 6.0, you have much more control over labels and data fields. This is one of the most powerful innovations introduced in version 6.0.

Assigning an account manager

Every account, whether big or small, whether prospect or active client, should have a real live person in charge of it. This should be a basic principle of your client retention strategy. You can assign account managers in many different ways, based on product lines or geography, for example. If you pick geography, you can base the assignment on a state, counties, a range of zip codes, telephone area codes, or a few other pieces of data.

If you decide states are most appropriate way to assign an account manager, you can enter a field expression in the Account Manager field that automatically assigns the salesperson as soon as you enter the state. With the old LOOKUP.INI technology, you could do the same thing, but the user needed to move his or her cursor into the Account Manager field for an assignment to happen. This is much better. Figure 20-11 shows how to make this happen.

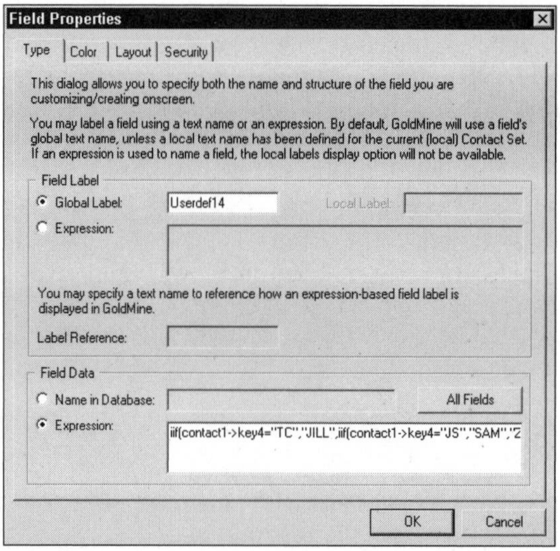

Figure 20-11: Assigning account managers on the fly.

Changing the face of GoldMine

You can use this new facility to make really profound changes to the way in which you use GoldMine. Perhaps you want to have several different kinds of records in the same database. For example, perhaps you want records for clients, vendors, and employees as well.

If you had a single field for Record Type, you could specify whether a particular record was a vendor, a client, or an employee. Based on the data you enter, GoldMine can completely reconfigure the entire screen. Virtually every field you see on the Vendor window can be different from what you see on the Employee window.

To be more specific, you might want the first Key field in the Employee window to house a social security number. For the Vendor window, you might want a federal ID number. For the Client window, you might want an account number.

Based on that Record Type field, the label for Key 1 would automatically change to accommodate to whatever type of information is appropriate. Taking this a step further, you can change virtually every label to coincide with the type of information this account has.

The new GM+View tab (see Chapter 27) can also be controlled this same way. The limits are your imagination, or the experience of the GoldMine dealer with whom you are working.

If you select the Expression toggle switch, you can then enter a valid dBASE expression to have GoldMine calculate a value for the field. For example, if you have a field for Lease Signing Date and a field for Length of Lease, you could have a third calculated field for the Lease Termination Date.

Chapter 21

Creating and Modifying Lookup Lists

In This Chapter

▶ Using existing lookup lists

▶ Customizing lookup lists

▶ Deleting standard entries

▶ Creating new entries

▶ Setting search options

▶ Using correct punctuation

Many of the GoldMine standard fields come equipped with lookup lists. These lists contain prerecorded logical choices for entry into each such field. A number of advantages exist to having and using these lists.

These lists are a particular boon to those who never took or didn't like typing class. So if you belong to the hunt-and-peck school of typing, you'll find each lookup list to be a real timesaver. If you got an A in typing class but flunked spelling class, the lookup lists are there for you, too.

More important, the lookup lists can help ensure that entries into a field are consistent with those of everyone else on your team or with what you did last month. This consistency pays off when you want to generate reports that are sorted on one of these fields because Schenectady will be spelled the exact same way in every record. So the accounts from Schenectady will appear together in reports sorted by city. Otherwise, who knows?

Frequently throughout the various GoldMine manuals and in the help files, you see these lists referred to as F2 lookup lists. The term F2 is a holdover from the days of DOS when users pressed particular function keys (in this case, F2) to access lookup lists. F2 and lookup lists are the same thing, and so you sometimes see them together in the same phrase.

Prior to GoldMine 5.0, one of the main menu choices was Query. In GoldMine 5.0, the Query menu was changed to the Lookup menu. The Lookup main menu choice has nothing to do with lookup lists in particular fields. This situation has the potential to be a little confusing, and I want to make sure you understand the distinction.

Using Existing Lookup Lists

If you used a version of GoldMine prior to version 5.0, you had no obvious way to know whether a field has a lookup list. (See Chapter 2 for a series of tables showing which fields have lookup lists.)

An addition in version 5.0 was an arrow to the immediate right of each field that has a lookup list. You can see this arrow as soon as you click in any field that has access to a lookup list. If you see this arrow, you know a list exists that you can use. Figure 21-1 shows the default lookup list associated with the Title field on the main screen.

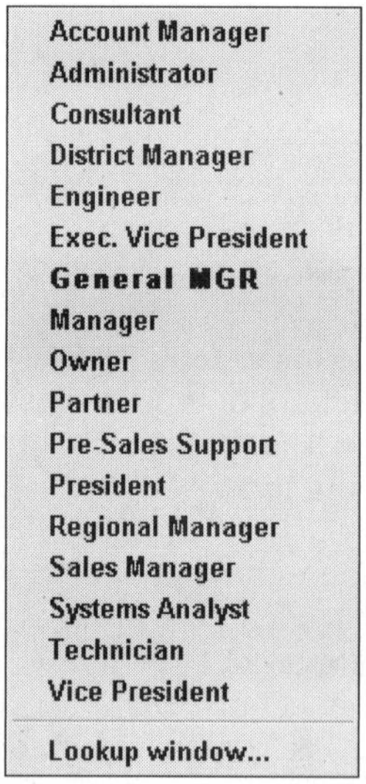

> Account Manager
> Administrator
> Consultant
> District Manager
> Engineer
> Exec. Vice President
> **General MGR**
> Manager
> Owner
> Partner
> Pre-Sales Support
> President
> Regional Manager
> Sales Manager
> Systems Analyst
> Technician
> Vice President
>
> Lookup window...

Figure 21-1: The lookup list for the Title field.

As soon as you click the right arrow next to the field, a list similar to that shown in Figure 21-1 appears. If data was already in the field you just came from, that selection is highlighted in bold within the lookup list. Throughout the list, all the choices are arranged alphabetically. If more choices exist than can fit in one display window, you can scroll up and down using the scroll buttons on the right side of the lookup list.

If the choice you want is visible in the window, you can simply click it to send it into the data field. Unless some special punctuation exists (see the "Using the punctuation tools" section later in this chapter), this choice replaces whatever is already in the data field.

Customizing Your Own Lookup Lists

As long as you have appropriate access rights, you can easily modify lookup lists. From the Lookup Window dialog box, you can delete, add, edit, or select special properties for each lookup list. To start customizing your own lists, open the Lookup Window dialog box:

1. **Click the right arrow next to a field with a lookup list to get a display of all the existing choices.**

2. **Select the last choice just below the horizontal line — Lookup Window.**

   The Lookup Window dialog box (in this case, for the Title field lookup list), shown in Figure 21-2, appears.

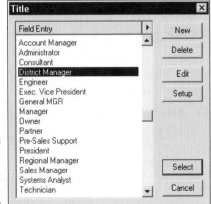

Figure 21-2:
Modifying a
lookup list.

One of the first things you need to do after installing GoldMine is to manually delete most of the lookup lists. Next, you need to assemble all the lookup entries you want to use. Solicit from the key people using the system what choices they need in each field.

To avoid the drudgery of manually deleting all the irrelevant lookup lists that come with GoldMine, during the installation process, you can instruct GoldMine to forget about including them in the first place. While you may lose a few good ones that way, you're probably better off starting from scratch. If you're reading this Tip after you installed GoldMine, check out the next section.

Deleting the standard lookup entries

For some reason, in version after version, the developers of GoldMine continue to supply a standard set of lookup lists whether you want them or not. Likely, you don't want most of the standard GoldMine lookups. To delete an existing entry, follow these steps after you have displayed the particular field's lookup list:

1. **Choose Lookup Window from the options in the lookup list.**

   The Lookup Window dialog box appears (refer to Figure 21-2).

2. **Highlight the choice you want to remove.**

3. **Click the Delete button.**

4. **Confirm that you really want to delete this choice.**

5. **Repeat Steps 2 through 4 until you have removed all the entries you want to get rid of.**

Creating new entries

The Lookup Window dialog box contains the New button (refer to Figure 21-2) that allows you to enter new items into a lookup list. To create a new lookup list choice, follow these steps:

1. **Click the New button on the Lookup Window dialog box to gain access to all the existing lookup choices for a particular field.**

2. **Enter your choice in the F2 Entry dialog box.**

3. **Confirm your entry by clicking OK.**

Your new entries are automatically placed alphabetically into the lookup list for that field.

Setting lookup list options

In addition to deleting and creating lookup list entries, you can also customize your lookup lists to make them easier for others (as well as yourself) to use. Click the Setup button in the Lookup Window dialog box (refer to Figure 21-2). The dialog box shown in Figure 21-3 appears, which contains the following options:

✔ **Allow blank input:** Allows you to enter and leave the field without entering any data.

✔ **Force valid input:** Forces you to enter data that corresponds exactly to some entry in the lookup list.

✔ **Insert closest match:** Allows GoldMine to select the closest match from the lookup list and enter it into the field. This option can help shorten data entry time for experienced data entry operators.

✔ **Capitalize first letter:** No matter how you capitalize your data, GoldMine automatically overrides it and capitalizes the first letter.

✔ **Pop-up when selected:** Forces the lookup list to appear immediately as soon as you enter a field.

✔ **Allow adding:** Allows users to add entries to the lookup list.

Adding to, editing, and deleting from lookup lists should be an administrative task that I recommend you assign only to one or two key people for coordination. Otherwise, you'll end up with a complete hodgepodge of conflicting and confusing codes and choices. Major mess.

✔ **Allow editing:** Allows users to edit entries in the lookup list.

✔ **Allow deleting:** Allows users to delete entries from the lookup list.

✔ **Auto Fill:** As you type, GoldMine automatically places the closest matching entry from the lookup in the field.

✔ **Import lookup entries from another field:** Often, one field in GoldMine uses the exact same set of lookups as another. This new option allows you to essentially copy one field's lookups to another field. If you already have items in your lookup list and you import entries from another field, these new entries are merged alphabetically with those that already exist in the lookup list.

Figure 21-3:
Customize
your lookup
list in the F2
Field Setup
dialog box.

Using the punctuation tools

You can include four special punctuation tools in your lookup lists. These tools allow you to program some advanced functionality into your lookups. I explain these tools in the following sections.

Making remarks (//)

The double forward slash (//) separates your actual data from comments you want in the lookup list. Nothing that appears to the right of the slashes is actually put into the data field.

A typical example of the use of these slashes is in the Acct Mngr field. Especially when you need multiple entries, you want to use short codes for each account manager. If you were to spell out each manager's entire name and wanted three or four of them in one field, all the names just wouldn't fit. So you probably need to use their initials.

The downside of using initials is that other people on the team may not recognize the initials. The double slashes allow you to have the full name of the account manager following their initials, so you can use the short codes and still ensure that everyone else understands the meaning of each code. Figure 21-4 shows a typical example of the use of the double forward slash.

Only your data in the lookup list actually goes into the data field. Nothing to the right of the slashes is transferred.

Appending data (;)

Normally, when you select a choice from a lookup list, your choice overwrites whatever was already in the data field. The semicolon, as well as the percent sign, allows you to add your selection to the already existing data without removing the original data. Figure 21-5 illustrates the use of these semicolons.

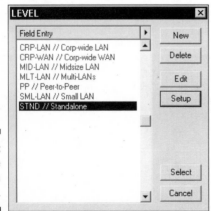

Figure 21-4:
Sample remarks in a lookup list.

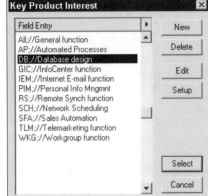

Figure 21-5:
Using
semicolons
in a lookup
list.

If a choice in your lookup list has a semicolon immediately after the data itself, selecting that choice places it in the data field following the existing data, separated by a comma and a space. Using this technique, you can have multiple selections in your data fields.

When using multiple selections, you can quickly run out of space in your data field. Be aware that you need to count not only the actual characters in each selection, but also the comma and the space that separate each choice in the data field.

Putting data up front (%)

The percent sign is similar to the semicolon, but the percent sign mandates that the new data go in front of the existing data. The other major difference between the semicolon and the percent sign is that the percent sign includes no punctuation or separation between data. For example, if you already have DEF in the data field and you select G% from the lookup list, you end up with GDEF in the data field. Figure 21-6 illustrates this.

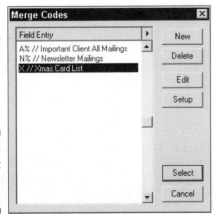

Figure 21-6:
Percent
signs in a
lookup list.

This tool is useful if you want to use very short (usually one character) codes and there is a premium on space in your data field.

If you use the percent sign to add data to a field and you need to find fields with a particular code in them, you must use a filter that tests for fields that *contain* a particular code. Also, using semicolons does not work unless the Force Valid Input option is *not* checked in the F2 Field Setup dialog box (refer to Figure 21-3).

One field begets another (~)

The tilde (~) is the most sophisticated of the punctuation options in the lookup lists. You can use the tilde to specify that whatever follows is a dBASE expression that will compute the entry into the field. For example, you can set a field equal to another field, or you can set a field equal to today's date, as shown in Figure 21-7.

The following are some examples of adding dBASE expressions to compute an entry:

- ✔ **~Company** places whatever data is currently in the Company field into this field.

- ✔ **~dtoc(date())** places the current date in the field in character format; for example, 09/08/03.

- ✔ **~Contact2->UserDef03** takes the information from the third user-defined field in the `Contact2.dbf` file and puts it into this field.

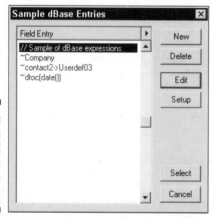

Figure 21-7:
Coding
dBASE
expressions
in a lookup
list.

You can also use this programming technique to improve upon the standard lookup list associated with the Dear field. Out of the box, GoldMine has Dear field choices of Dr., Mr., Mrs., and Ms. You can keep these choices, but you may want to add several expressions that append last names to these salutations.

Chapter 22

Importing and Exporting Data

In This Chapter

▶ Using the Import Wizard

▶ Importing and exporting XML data

▶ Converting data from ACT

▶ Using GoldBox

▶ Exporting your data from GoldMine

*Y*ou can import data into GoldMine in three basic ways: Type it in manually, scan papers to convert hard copy to electronic copy, or import the data that's already in electronic form to GoldMine.

Manually entering your data into GoldMine means you, or your designated droid, will be doing a lot of typing. Typing your data may be your fate if your records are currently stored in the heads of your account managers, or are so randomly structured that an automated method of getting the data into GoldMine is impossible.

One step above typing is scanning. If your data only exists on paper, scanning the data may be possible using your scanner with Optical Character Recognition (OCR) software and GoldMine's import system. Document scanning systems, such as LaserFiche, are useful for scanning documents and attaching these documents to accounts in GoldMine. (For more about LaserFiche, take a look at Chapter 29.) These kinds of systems are not really that useful for placing data into specific fields, however.

Electronic data can come from your accounting system, a competitive system, or a spreadsheet. Enough tools are available to you that the computer should do most of the grunt work involved in initially stocking your new system with your current data. *Warning:* Importing data is far more involved and far more time-consuming than you may think. You can never have a machine too fast, and you can never allocate too much time to the job.

In this chapter, you discover many of the basic ingredients of both importing and exporting data with GoldMine, and you're introduced to some important third-party utilities, such as GoldBox and ACT-Out.

Using the Import Wizard to Import Data

GoldMine comes to you with its own built-in wizard to aid in importing the most common kinds of data. The data that you can import comes in the form of electronic files, and GoldMine accepts several file types:

- ✔ **DBF:** This standard dBASE format is one of the most popular file types. If you have a choice, use DBF format because it's faster than any other type, and setup is generally easier.

- ✔ **ASCII:** These are text files with delimiters (usually commas and spaces) between each field, which is another very common format.

- ✔ **SDF:** This type is a holdover from the old mainframe days. Each field is a fixed length and is identified by its beginning position and its length. It is not very common anymore.

- ✔ **SQL:** You may encounter this format if you import from an SQL database table.

GoldMine offers you two ways to import files. You can import new data in some never-before-seen format, or you can import previously defined files by using import profiles. (See the "Importing new files" section, later in this chapter, for more information.) Import profiles are simply maps showing which fields in the original data format correspond to which fields in GoldMine.

GoldMine comes with a small collection of predefined import profiles. These profiles supply a method of getting data from four other competitive products, including ACT, into GoldMine. It's in GoldMine's interest to supply these methods so that you'll have an easier time converting from some other system to GoldMine. Table 22-1 lists each of the systems from which you can convert your data.

Table 22-1	Predefined Import Profiles in GoldMine
Data Structure	*Competitive Product*
ASCII	Maximizer
DBF	ACT! For Windows 1.1
DBF	ACT! For Windows 2.0 and higher
DBF	TeleMagic

The bottom line is that if your data is in one of the programs listed in the table, GoldMine provides you with a relatively easy, but not foolproof, way to convert your data.

While GoldMine supplies a built-in ACT import utility, it doesn't handle Details, Pending, and History activities too well. If you are concerned about these things (and you should be), consider using Innovative Marketing's ACT-Out product. Also, if you have a lot of records to import (10,000 or more), please be advised that GoldMine's utility is just a little slower than molasses in January.

Importing new files

To import a file from another program using the Import Wizard, follow these steps:

1. **From the main GoldMine menu, choose Tools➪Import/Export Wizard➪Import Contact Records.**

   The Import Wizard begins, as shown in Figure 22-1.

2. **Select the Import a New File Using an Existing Profile radio button.**

   Selecting this option allows you to select a predefined import profile or one that you have previously created. (See the next section, "Creating your own import profiles," for detailed information on creating import profiles.)

3. **Click Next, and GoldMine moves on to the next appropriate part in the Import Wizard.**

   The wizard walks you through a sequence of steps, all of which are simple and self-explanatory. Make your selections based on your knowledge of your data.

Creating your own import profiles

If your incoming data is already in DBF, ASCII, SDF, XML, or SQL format, you can create your own custom import profile in addition to using the four pre-built profiles. You would want to create a custom import file if you have a data source that you repeatedly use (you buy mailing lists, for example). If you create a profile specific to that format and save it for future use, you'll save time later when you need to import more data from that source.

To create your own custom import profile from a typical DBF file, follow these steps (these steps are basically the same for ASCII, SDF, XML, and SQL files, too):

1. **From the main menu, choose Tools⇨Import/Export Wizard⇨Import Contact Records.**

   The GoldMine Import Wizard appears, as shown in Figure 22-1.

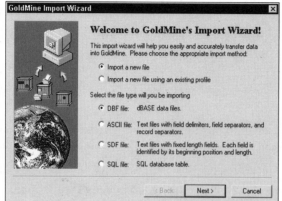

Figure 22-1:
Define the type of file from which you want to import data.

2. **Click the Import a New File radio button.**

3. **Click the DBF File radio button, and then click the Next button.**

   The wizard asks where to find the file you want to import, as shown in Figure 22-2.

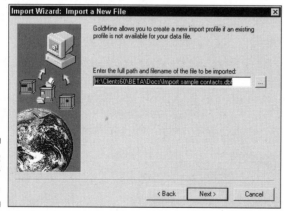

Figure 22-2:
Locate your import file.

4. Tell the wizard where your import file is located and click Next.

You can use the square browse button to forage around until you find the file. After you locate and specify the data input file and click the Next button, the wizard shows you a preview of the data in your import file, as shown in Figure 22-3.

Figure 22-3:
Preview the data in your import file.

5. To change a field label name, click the label to highlight it, and then right-click.

Within the wizard's Import File Profile dialog box, you see the following options and buttons:

- **Label Name:** Shows you an identifying designation assigned to each field in the import file. For DBF files, the designation is an actual label. For SDF files, it's a numeric position.

- **Field Name:** Shows the name, position, or range of the field in the receiving file within GoldMine.

- **Preview Record:** Displays actual data from the input file so that you can make sure the data is what you think it is. You can scroll from one input record to the following one by clicking the top Next button.

- **Convert OEM to ANSI:** This check box allows you to convert European standard international characters to the U.S. standard.

When you finish making your choices, click the Next button to continue. The wizard next enables you to map fields from your import file to the corresponding GoldMine field, as shown in Figure 22-4.

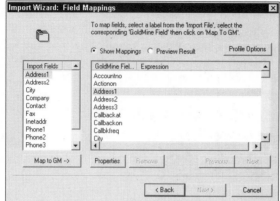

Figure 22-4:
Map fields
into
GoldMine.

6. **Highlight a field name in the Import Fields list, highlight the corresponding field name in the GoldMine Field list, and then click the Map to GM button.**

   The wizard lists the Import File's fields, GoldMine's fields, and any expressions that you may want to use to relate these fields. For example, you could use the Expression area to concatenate two separate fields. The following options provide you with some additional tools in designing your import profile and for testing to make sure GoldMine's going to do what you want it to do:

   - **Show Mappings:** If you select this radio button, the Expression column displays either the label of the field being imported or the expression being applied to the data being imported.

   - **Preview Result:** If you select this radio button, the Expression column displays actual data.

   - **Profile Options:** This button allows you to specify a GoldMine indexed field to use for duplicate record checking — very important when you import into an existing database. Duplicate records often exist, and you want to avoid creating duplicates, if possible. If you use this option, during the import, GoldMine searches the receiving database for a record with the same value as contained in the import database. If a match is found, GoldMine updates the existing GoldMine record with information from the import record instead of adding a new record. GoldMine will replace a blank field with a value, but it will not replace a value with a blank.

   - **Map to GM:** This button allows you to match one or more import file fields with a GoldMine field. Just highlight the import field and the GoldMine field you are mapping it to and click the Map to GM button.

- **Properties:** Click this button to build a dBASE expression that combines fields or formats the data in specific ways. The Import Expression Builder dialog box appears, as shown in Figure 22-5. One of the most common uses of the Import Expression Builder dialog box is the Convert to Proper Case option. This option takes an incoming text field, capitalizes the first letter, and makes the following characters lowercase.

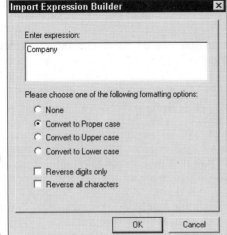

Figure 22-5:
Converting text to proper case.

Proper case is excellent for names and parts of addresses. For example, this option converts JOHN DOE to John Doe. That's just fine, but it also converts IBM to Ibm and NY to Ny, which may not be quite what you intended.

7. **After you finish your mappings and build your expressions, click Next.**

   The wizard next asks you to match fields between your original data and your GoldMine fields. You must select at least one field to match, and logically you probably want to make sure to have a company name or at least a contact name included in your imported data, although GoldMine allows you to proceed (after asking you if you really know what you're doing) even without these fields.

   If you select a match field from the Import Match field, the Record Matching Options dialog box appears, asking you what to do if a matching record is found during the import process. Otherwise, you can click Next, elect to save your new Import Profile, and then your import is ready for primetime.

Estimating import time

Importing files takes longer than you would think. This job has two phases: The first phase is general preparation of the data, and the second is the actual importing itself. Both phases can be tedious and time-consuming, but they're not too difficult.

The best time to clean up your existing data is before you bring it into GoldMine. You just don't need to transfer useless or outdated records. Get rid of them first, if you can.

Providing a guideline regarding how much time the preparation phase will take is difficult. It's a function of how clean the current data is and how well your current field definitions correspond to GoldMine's. I have never seen any database that didn't need some attention before importing. If you're good with Excel, this tool is excellent and quick for examining, cleaning, and rearranging data.

The actual import process is a function of the speed of the computer you're using, the number of records you're importing and, very significantly, the amount of historical information you're importing.

You don't need to use your GoldMine machine for importing. Commandeer the fastest machine you can get your hands on for the import. Make sure it has plenty of available hard drive space — at least twice the size of the incoming files. Nothing is worse than coming in the next morning to discover the import you expected to run all night bombed out at 2:30 a.m. when the computer ran out of disk space.

SQL-based files import much faster than DBF files. If nothing else, rehosting (or converting from dBASE to SQL) is great for this process.

Reduce, as much as possible, the amount of history you bring into GoldMine. If you don't really need notes and activities from three years ago, don't import them.

Importing and Exporting XML Data

XML is fast becoming the industry de facto standard for exchanging data from one system to another. The ability to import and export XML data is new in GoldMine 6.0. The purpose of this is to open the database structure to allow developers to more easily interface other applications. For example, if someone wanted to pass data back and forth from GoldMine to an accounting package, using XML might be a way to do so.

Even more interestingly, if someone wanted to post GoldMine data on a Web page, XML is just the trick for that. I believe that someone will create a customer self-help system where a customer could request some information about his or her account and could see that information automatically displayed on a password-secured Web page. Well, anyway, that's food for thought.

The XML Import and Export functions are accessed by choosing Tools⇨ Import/Export Wizard⇨Import GoldMine Data from an XML File (or Export GoldMine Data to an XML File), as shown in Figure 22-6.

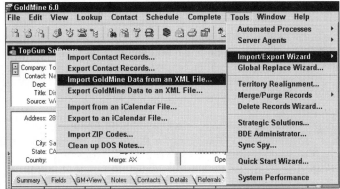

Figure 22-6: Import or export XML data to GoldMine.

After you choose this command, the XML Wizard appears, allowing you great flexibility regarding the precise data that is coming in or going out. Unlike GoldMine's original Export utility (see the "Exporting Data from GoldMine" section, later in this chapter), virtually all fields can be exported, including the fields from the top half of the main screen, scheduled and completed activities, and messages. In addition, you can specify activities of particular users or groups of users.

This is a potentially very powerful tool and, I suspect, many ingenious uses will be found for it.

Converting Data from ACT

Converting from some version of ACT to GoldMine is the most common upgrade, so I focus on that to the exclusion of the other worthy competitors' products. ACT is one of the import profiles GoldMine supplies, and it is worthwhile to review some of the key issues involved.

Whatever version of ACT you're converting from, you must have the actual software available and running during the import. Also, you should pack the ACT database (or any database) before importing!

Importing ACT's user-defined fields

ACT has 15 user-defined fields. When ACT was initially configured, these fields could have been designed to be almost any size. When you perform a data import, the data in ACT's user-defined fields will be placed into GoldMine's user-defined fields. Some differences exist, however.

GoldMine comes to you with only ten user-defined fields, and each field is exactly ten characters long. Because you can't get 15 fields into 10 fields, you may need to increase the number of user-defined fields within GoldMine. See Chapter 20 for this method. You need as many user-defined fields in GoldMine as there are in the ACT database.

You can't put 14 pounds of concrete in a 10-pound bag, and you can't put a 14-character field into a 10-character field. You need to review the length of each of ACT's user-defined fields, and then make sure that each corresponding GoldMine field is at least as long.

Importing additional ACT fields

Table 22-2 shows a mapping of additional fields in ACT and where they will land when they go into GoldMine.

Table 22-2	Additional Fields from ACT
ACT Source	*GoldMine Target*
Referral	Source
Record Mgr	Key 1
Id/Status	Key 2
Alt Phone	Phone 2
Alt Phone Ext	Ext 2
Mobile Phone	Phone 3
Pending activities	Pending tab and Calendar
History activities	History tab

ACT Source	GoldMine Target
Assistant info	Contacts tab
3rd Contact info	Contacts tab
Home info	Contacts tab

More ACT conversion words of wisdom

After many years of doing ACT imports, my team that specializes in ACT imports assembled the following list of issues, tips, and gotchas:

- ✔ Calendar items marked as private don't transfer into GoldMine. The obvious solution is to go through all the scheduled ACT activities and remove the private designations before importing into GoldMine.

- ✔ Calendar activities will transfer to GoldMine if you use the wizard, but remember: If the GoldMine user name is different than the ACT user name, you must edit each activity's property and switch to the GoldMine user.

- ✔ Group membership in ACT doesn't transfer into GoldMine. You have to manually create it in GoldMine. The same concept applies to record ownership; it doesn't transfer automatically from ACT.

- ✔ Web page information from ACT doesn't transfer to GoldMine. It should to go into the Detail section of GoldMine, but it doesn't, which means more manual work for someone.

- ✔ Notes in ACT's Notes/History section goes into the Notes tab section of GoldMine. All others go into the History tab of GoldMine.

- ✔ ACT's history type becomes an entry in the reference section in GoldMine's history.

- ✔ If no time is specified for a pending activity in ACT, GoldMine will show the priority level in the Time field.

Advanced Importing Using GoldBox

GoldBox is a utility that many GoldMine dealers use to handle the more sophisticated imports. As good as the GoldMine built-in utilities are, a number of things still exist that the Import Wizard wasn't designed to handle, such as complex comparisons to avoid duplicate records, or the creation of fields calculated from other fields.

Importing with GoldBox is faster and more flexible than doing it with the GoldMine Import Wizard. Besides importing into the Main Contact File, you can also import into Details, Additional Contacts, Calendar, History, Referrals, and Document Links. Importing into one or more of these tab sections, however, is a multistep process.

GoldBox handles imports from incoming files in dBASE3/Clipper, dBASE4, ASCII Delimited, or SDF formats. You can set many options that will save you hours of work in reformatting the incoming data.

If you're concerned with remote users being able to properly access and synchronize this new data, GoldBox properly handles all synchronization issues. This critical issue is one that many novice data importers overlook.

If your data import is a one-time event, then consider having an experienced dealer do it for you. If you anticipate importing as an on-going event, investing in GoldBox software and investing in the time you need to learn to use it properly may be worth your while.

GoldBox is one of several import tools available. It was a DOS-based utility, but a Windows version came out in summer 1999 and has been further enhanced in 2002. Redstone SoftBase Company (310-839-6530) developed GoldBox, and you can purchase it through most authorized GoldMine dealers. See Chapter 29 for more details on GoldBox.

Exporting Data from GoldMine

You may want to export data from GoldMine for several reasons. You may need this data to feed into some other application, like an accounting system. You may want to use GoldMine data as the basis for sophisticated reporting, graphing, and/or statistical analysis. Or, for some completely inexplicable reason, you may want to export it into some other contact manager.

The Export Wizard encompasses the same basic steps as the Import Wizard. You access it the same way, and many of the questions are the same also. Please refer to the "Using the Import Wizard to Import Data" section, earlier in this chapter, for details.

To get to the Export Wizard from the main menu, choose Tools⇨Import/ Export Wizard⇨Export Contact Records. The Export Wizard appears, as shown in Figure 22-7.

You can use a preexisting export profile if you have one, or you can start a new one. In addition, you can select from three different export file formats:

✔ **DBF:** dBASE format.

✔ **ASCII:** Essentially characters and numbers. Each field is enclosed in quotation marks and separated from the other fields by a comma. This format and DBF are the two most common.

✔ **SDF:** Standard Delimited Format, where each field is a preset size. You don't see this format very much since the early days of big iron (mainframes).

Figure 22-7:
The Export
Wizard
welcomes
you.

After you select the best options, click Next. The wizard next asks you to select a filer or group, as shown in Figure 22-8. Make your selections, and then click Next.

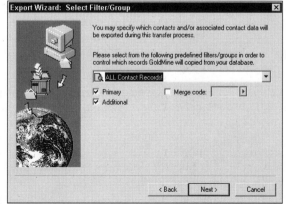

Figure 22-8:
Choose a
filter or
group to
export from
GoldMine.

The wizard next enables you to map the GoldMine fields you are exporting, as shown in Figure 22-9. On the left side of the wizard, GoldMine lists all the fields available for exporting. It doesn't matter what order you select them in because GoldMine automatically puts them in alphabetic order, whether you want that or not. You can continue selecting fields by simply double-clicking any field you want. If you change your mind, you can remove any field by selecting it from the main browse box and then clicking the Remove button.

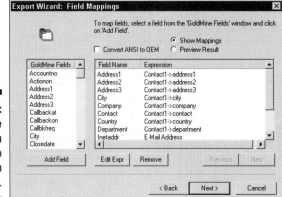

Figure 22-9:
Map the
fields you
want to
export from
GoldMine.

You can click the Preview button to see the current record's data displayed. By previewing, you can ensure the right data is going to the right place. You can also scroll through as many records as you want by using the Previous and the Next buttons.

When you're satisfied with your map, click the bottom Next button; proceed though to the last step of the Export Wizard. GoldMine asks for a filename to store your output; enter a name and click the Finish button. Then you have it — a perfectly created export file. You can then read it with a spreadsheet or a database program, or use some programming language to manipulate it.

Part VII
Advanced Stuff

The 5th Wave   By Rich Tennant

"So, what kind of roaming capabilities does this thing have?"

In this part . . .

This part of the book is for power users, the people I affectionately call GoldMine geeks. When you master the basics, you can set up GoldMine to help you with complicated sales and projects, accessing your data from afar, or with automating some of your best business practices.

Although tradition says GoldMine is for *hunters* (those who run around looking for new accounts), it also works beautifully for *farmers* (those in charge of the proper care and feeding of existing accounts). In this part, I present some of my best thinking on client retention powered by GoldMine.

GoldMine just doesn't do it all. But recently the developers have begun adding interfaces to some of the most important products like Outlook and various handhelds (like Palm Pilots and Windows CE devices). This has added tremendous power and begins to turn GoldMine into a real business management system. In this part, I also describe the pros and cons and the ins and outs of linking GoldMine to these products.

Chapter 23

Opportunity and Project Manager

· ·

In This Chapter

▶ Using the Opportunity and Project Manager

▶ How the Project Manager differs from the Opportunity Manager

· ·

*O*pportunity tracking is the next step up from just forecasting sales. You use the Opportunity Manager to track complex sales. A complex sale involves either an individual or a team trying to close a sale that may have more than one decision-maker on the other side. These sales might also include multiple products or services. Often these complex sales have a long sales cycle compared to simpler sales.

While the use of the Opportunity Manager is not directly related to the dollar value of a potential deal, very often the more complex sales are the ones with greater-than-average value. It is probably not a coincidence that these larger deals also seem to attract the most competitors. The Opportunity Manager allows you to track those competitors.

After you close a complex sale, it usually becomes a complex project. And GoldMine lets you easily turn that opportunity into a project. A project is the natural next step for an opportunity that you managed well. When you have a project to track, you can manage your team of workers, the timeline, and the money involved using Project Manager.

Initially setting up the Opportunity and/or Project Manager is a lot of work. You need to build lookup lists for many fields. Monitoring an opportunity or a project in detail is also a lot of work. You should probably consider using these tools only for those opportunities and projects that really are complex or are very important. This caution notwithstanding, these tools are potentially valuable when used under the right circumstances.

In this chapter, you discover when and how to make use of the Opportunity/Project Manager (O/PM).

The Opportunity/Project Manager

The Opportunity Manager and the Project Manager contain similar types of information, and thus their windows look similar. The first icon on either window allows you to toggle back and forth from an Opportunity to a Project. Each of these tools contains two major sections. The upper section displays general information about a selected opportunity or project. The lower section consists of a series of tabs. To access either of these windows, from the main menu, choose View⇨Projects. The Opportunity/Project Manager appears.

GoldMine displays either the Opportunity Manager or the Project Manager view, depending upon which view you selected last. Chances are if this is your first time anywhere near the Opportunity Manager, nothing has been entered.

GoldMine's use of wizards has finally extended to the Opportunity and Project Manager. This addition is welcome, as manually going through all the steps to create a new opportunity was sometimes a daunting task that is much easier now.

The Opportunity Wizard

Clicking the second icon at the top of the Opportunity Manager window brings you to the new Opportunity Wizard, as shown in Figure 23-1. Using the wizard is a terrific way to start a new opportunity — you never forget your first time.

On the first wizard dialog box, as shown in Figure 23-1, you relate the new opportunity to a contact record and to a particular person at that company. You should use the browse button to the right of the Company field to assist in locating the correct company. When you've filled out the Company and Contact fields, click the Next button.

Figure 23-1: Building a new opportunity.

Naming your opportunity

The wizard next asks you to enter a unique and descriptive name for this opportunity, as shown in Figure 23-2. Please remember that you may have multiple opportunities with the same customer, and you may have similar opportunities with completely different customers. So you should select names that are descriptive enough to allow you and others on your team to recognize which opportunity this really is. Examples of reasonable names might be "Designing Our Retention Workshop," or "Competitive Bid on Space Shuttle."

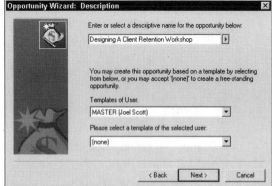

Figure 23-2:
Give your
opportunity
a name.

You can create a template (similar to synchronization profiles), but in this chapter, I discuss creating opportunities from scratch. After you have named your opportunity, click the Next button.

Specifying opportunity details

The wizard next wants to know details about your opportunity, as shown in Figure 23-3. Here you begin really specifying the details of this opportunity with the following fields:

- ✔ **Manager:** Designate a manager for the opportunity in this field, or you can accept the default manager, which is you (your user name).

- ✔ **Code:** Classify your opportunities with a three-letter code from the lookup list associated with this field. You may want to consider using some departmental codes or product category codes.

- ✔ **Probability:** Enter the likelihood of successfully capturing this opportunity as a percentage in this field. The Probability field comes with a preset lookup list that you will likely want to modify to your own situation.

✔ **Stage:** Enter more detailed information related to the level, or stage, of the process in this field. The entry is given as a number and a descriptive reference, such as "10 - Initial Contact."

✔ **Source:** This field is taken by default from the Source field on the main window of the contact record linked to this opportunity. You have the same lookup list available to you, but you can enter a new selection if you want.

✔ **Start Date:** This date relates to projects more than to opportunities, so you can pass this one by for opportunities.

✔ **Close Date:** The date by which you expect to close this deal. By default, GoldMine sets it to be the current date, so take care to put in a more realistic date. If this date comes and goes without someone actually closing this deal, GoldMine sends you an alarm about it.

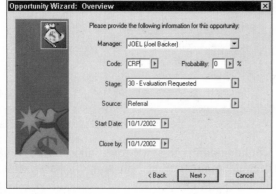

Figure 23-3:
Enter details
about
the new
opportunity.

After you have entered information into these fields, click Next.

Pointing the finger at influencers and contacts

The wizard asks you about the contact's role and about influencers for your new opportunity, as shown in Figure 23-4.

Influencers are the people on the other side of the table who are involved in the ultimate decision-making process. After an opportunity becomes a project, these same people are referred to as *contacts,* which is the usual terminology throughout GoldMine.

To add an influencer or a contact, select either New Linked Contact or New Unlinked Contact from the Contact section of the wizard. A *linked contact* is anyone who is already in your database, not necessarily a contact at the particular account that this opportunity is with. A *new unlinked contact* is someone who is completely unknown in your database.

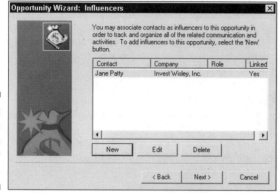

Figure 23-4:
Entering the
influencers
for your
opportunity.

The Role field is for the specific contribution that this influencer or contact is likely to make to the decision-making process.

The Response Mode field (in the Opportunity Manager only) specifies the perceived attitude of this person toward your product or service. By default, a few sample entries are already in the lookup list, such as Even Keel or Trouble. Feel free to make up your own — see Chapter 21 to find out how.

Forecasting your opportunity

The Opportunity Wizard next asks you to divide the total opportunity into its component sales, assuming that you have more than one product or one stage of the sale. An example is selling a GoldMine consulting project that involves the software itself, a pilot or test phase, and then a full rollout to an entire sales force.

An opportunity must already exist before you can link a forecasted sale to it. In the normal course of business, you may create a simple sales forecast without any initial intention of using the Opportunity Manager. Then, as the complexity of the potential sale begins to grow, you might decide to create an opportunity record. If this happens, you can edit the original sales forecast record and link it to the just recently created opportunity.

The Forecast dialog box that you use within the Opportunity Manager is identical to that of the general Sales Forecast dialog box. Please see Chapter 11 for more details. You can, however, have multiple forecasts linked to one opportunity. In fact, this situation is fairly common with complex sales.

Teaming up

You next need to tell the Opportunity Wizard which people are on your team and with whom you are working to close this deal. You can even put someone from your prospect's team or someone else from outside your own firm on the team. Doing so is sometimes appropriate when you have someone from the other side acting as a coach. The wizard's Type field, shown in Figure 23-5, allows you to either specify a *User,* which is someone from your own team, or an *Other Contact,* which is anyone else in your database.

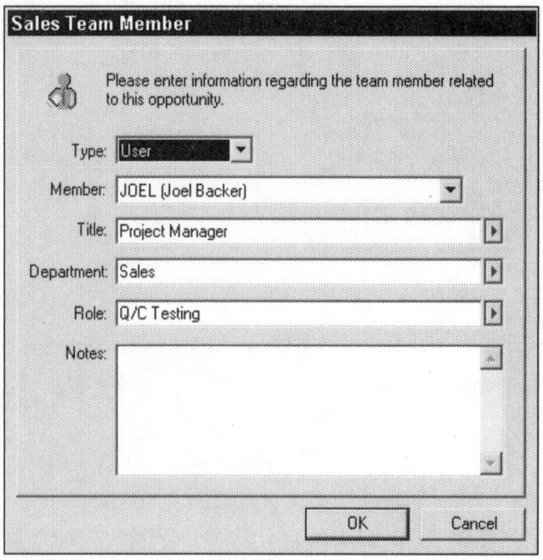

Figure 23-5:
Tell the
Opportunity
Wizard
who's on
your team.

In the Role field, you can enter each person's anticipated role in the opportunity or project. Examples might be Write RFP Response or Q/C Testing.

Dealing with the opportunity's issues

The wizard now asks about the issues concerning the opportunity, as shown in Figure 23-6, to help you keep track of the issues that come up and need to be addressed. As you pursue an opportunity, you may, for example, become aware of a pending price increase that will go into effect next month. Because this increase would conflict with the budget your prospect has already set up, it could potentially be a serious problem and could have an impact on your schedule for closing the deal. Enter information into the fields as follows:

- ✔ **Issue:** Enter a brief description of the issue your team must handle in this field, or you can select a previously defined issue from the lookup list.

- ✔ **Status:** Type a brief description of the issue's status in this field, or you can use its lookup list.

- ✔ **Priority:** Specify a rank-order of this issue in the Priority field. You generally should assign numbers in ascending order, so the more important issues have smaller or lower numbers.

✔ **Date:** Set a date for this issue. You can either enter the date the issue became known, or you can use the Date field to indicate when the issue needs to be resolved. You must be consistent, however. I like to use the resolution date in this field.

✔ **User:** Assign a member of your team to this issue in this field.

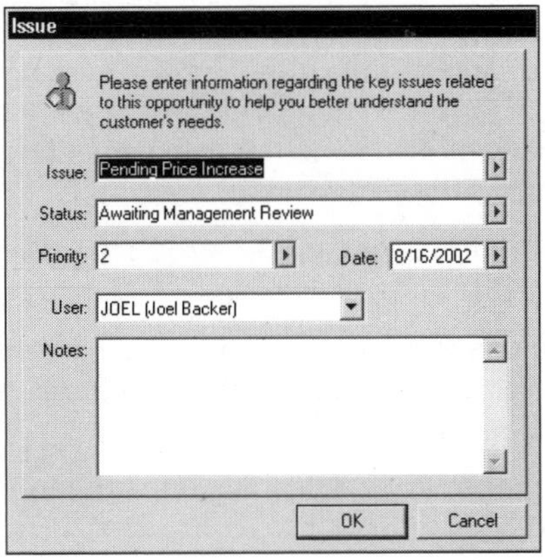

Figure 23-6:
Keeping track of the issues for the new opportunity.

Keeping an eye on the competitors

The Opportunity Wizard next wants to know about the competition, as shown in Figure 23-7. Entering information here allows you to track companies and products with which you are competing for this opportunity. (Competitors do not apply to Project Management because after you close the deal, you don't need to worry too much about competitors. Hopefully.)

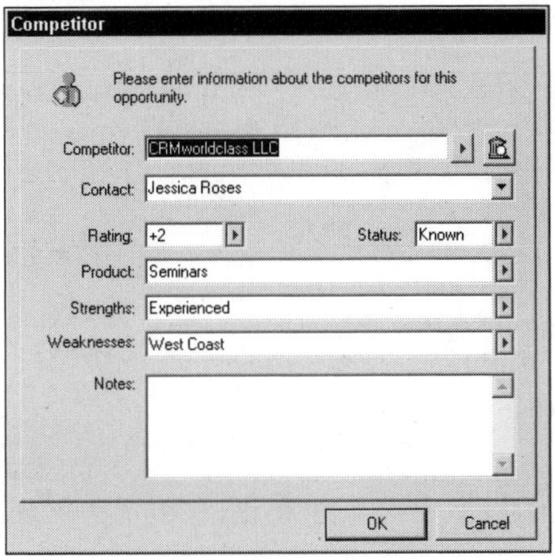

Figure 23-7:
Monitoring the competition.

Enter the information about your competitors, paying special attention to the following fields:

- ✓ **Rating:** Use this field to indicate just how strong a competitor you're dealing with. The standard ratings range from –5 to +5; they're a little out of order due to the vagaries of alphabetic order in lookup lists.

- ✓ **Status:** Enter in this field a description of your prospect's attitude, as best you understand it, toward this competitor. You can use or modify the lookup list for this field. An example might be if you're trying to upgrade a prospect from ACT to GoldMine, but they already have 30 users who know ACT. You might describe that prospect's attitude toward your competition as Entrenched.

- ✓ **Product:** Enter the name, if there is one, of the product against which you are competing in this field.

- ✓ **Strengths:** Use this field to describe the most attractive features of this competitor. Please note that this field refers more to your competitor than to their product, although you can use it either way.

- ✓ **Weaknesses:** Enter your competition's least attractive features in this field. The Weaknesses field is, of course, the exact opposite of the Strengths field.

Tracking details

Using the Details dialog box, you can track custom information associated with the opportunity (or project). This section is similar to the Detail tab associated with the main records. You can define an unlimited number of items. Each item has an associated Reference field that actually houses the data. In addition, you can link an external file (a Word document or an Excel spreadsheet, as examples) to each item.

Crossing the finish line

On the last screen of the Opportunity Wizard, you finish your data entry with essentially the remaining parts of your sales forecast. That is, you enter the probability, total revenue, and potential close date for this deal. Click the Finish button, and you're done!

The Opportunity Manager and its functions

An opportunity (or a project) complex enough to merit tracking by the Opportunity Manager usually involves multiple tasks that start and end over differing time periods. Some tasks might overlap in time, or occur at different times, or be dependent upon the completion of prior tasks. In a complex sale, tracking these individual tasks is essential to successfully completing that sale. A completed set of task specifications is illustrated in Figure 23-8.

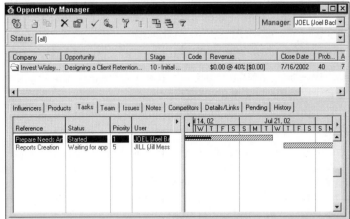

Figure 23-8:
Task
descriptions.

To view or add tasks to an opportunity or to a project:

1. **Make sure you have the proper opportunity or project displayed and highlighted in the upper section of the Opportunity/Project Manager window.**

2. **Click the Tasks tab.**

3. **To add a new task, right-click below the Tasks tab and select New from the shortcut menu.**

4. **In the Reference field, type a descriptive name for the task, such as** Survey for number of users.

5. **Fill in the Status field from its lookup list.**

6. **In the Begin Date field, set the beginning date by either typing it in or by right-clicking to access the calendar.**

7. **Enter the user who is responsible for this task or for the entire opportunity.**

8. **Use the Color field to designate the type of task.**

   These colors will be displayed on the Gantt chart associated with the opportunity or project. I like to use the same color scheme as I describe in Chapter 8.

9. **In the Begin Date field, enter the date by which the task must be completed.**

10. **In the Priority field, enter a ranking order for the task.**

    You can use numerals (1, 2, 3, and so on) or an alphabetical scheme (A, B, C, and so on). Just be consistent.

11. **In the %Done field, enter the percentage of the task that has been completed.**

    You need to enter this information on an ongoing basis.

12. **Use the Notes field for any additional free-form information.**

13. **When you're done, click OK.**

Pending

This tab may contain the scheduled activities relating to an opportunity or to a project. A complex opportunity or project usually involves many activities to be performed by various members of your team. Although you can add these activities from the Schedule main menu, you can view and manage each one from the Pending tab of the Opportunity/Project Manager (O/PM).

History

This tab contains all the activities that have been closed in pursuit of the opportunity. The History tab in the O/PM relates to the O/PM just as the Pending tab does. You can edit activities either from the main screen or from the History tab within the O/PM.

Closing and Converting Opportunities

When an opportunity closes, it becomes a project. You close an opportunity by right-clicking the opportunity and selecting Convert to Opportunity/Project from the shortcut menu that appears. You can also convert a project into an opportunity. Converting projects back into opportunities is a function of your Sales Prevention Team. Hopefully, you don't have such a team and won't need to do this.

Chapter 24

Remote Synchronization

*O*nce upon a time, being out of the office and still being in touch with everything that was happening was virtually impossible. Using GoldMine, you can be on the road but still stay in touch and exchange information with other GoldMine users. This process is called *remote synchronization*. GoldMine's old standby remote synchronization utility, GoldSync, can help you with remote synchronization. In addition to communicating remotely with other GoldMine users, GoldMine now allows you to talk to a variety of very portable devices like the Palm Pilot, Windows CE devices, or SmartPhones. So today, you have a number of options to keep connected when you're out of the office.

Although GoldMine 6.0 has somewhat simplified configuring GoldSync, it still deserves a certified GoldSync technician to actually implement it so that it works correctly. Implementing GoldSync is another one of those tasks that you just don't want to do by yourself.

In prior versions of GoldSync, a variety of modems were supported. No longer. Plan on synchronizing via the Internet. Dial-up is no more. DSL or a cable connection is your best bet from home.

In this chapter, you discover what remote synchronization is and how to take advantage of it. I show you how to transfer data to others both manually and automatically. GoldMine provides different types of synchronization, and I explain the basic ideas behind each type of synchronization. Then you'll be armed with the knowledge necessary to start planning your implementation and can tell the technician what you need.

In addition, you find out about a couple of alternatives to GoldSync using Internet-based technologies in this chapter.

Synchronizing Your Data

Remote synchronization of data means transferring the data to another user or system. One GoldMine user creates a transfer set of all the data that has changed at one location, and then another user retrieves that transfer set and incorporates it into his or her database. A *transfer set* is an encrypted and condensed file containing information one user wants to share with another. Usually, the transfer set contains just those pieces of data that have changed since the last time a transfer set was created. See the "Creating a transfer set for sneakernet" section, later in this chapter, for specific information on how to create this file.

The actual transfer of information can be done manually, without GoldSync, by using floppy disks, or automatically by using GoldSync. See the "Using sneakernet to share data" and "Sharing Data Automatically by Using GoldSync" sections, later in this chapter, for specific information on these two methods.

Using sneakernet to share data

If you have a very small user community, the old sneakernet methodology may still work for you. *Sneakernet* involves putting your changes on a floppy disk and then running (hence the *sneaker* in sneakernet) to another computer and loading the changes into it. The sneakernet method then usually requires you to run the changes from the second computer back to the first computer.

The sneakernet method may work if you have a system in the office and you also have a machine at home that you occasionally use, or if you have a notebook computer that you occasionally take on the road and you don't need updates while you're on the road with it.

I can't think of another scenario where it is reasonable to consider the sneakernet method. But, if this is your situation, the following instructions show you how to create a transfer set for use on a sneakernet system.

Creating a transfer set for sneakernet

GoldMine provides a wizard that leads you through the creation and retrieval of transfer sets. To access the wizard and create a transfer set, follow these steps:

1. **From the main menu, choose File⟶Synchronize⟶Synchronization Wizard.**

   The Welcome dialog box of the Synchronization Wizard appears, as shown in Figure 24-1. If this is your first synchronization session, you need to create a transfer set from scratch. If you anticipate doing this regularly, you can save your *sync profile* (a set of synchronization specifications) for repeated use.

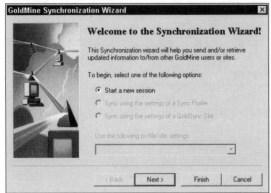

Figure 24-1: The Sync Wizard welcomes you.

2. **Assuming this session is your first time, select the Start a New Session option, and then click Next.**

   The next wizard dialog box appears, as shown in Figure 24-2.

   You can ignore the Connection Method section. You don't need to specify any particular connection method because you're just creating a file to be manually transferred to another computer.

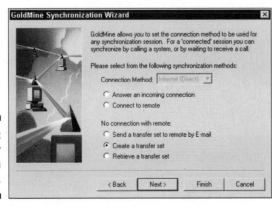

Figure 24-2: Specify your connection method.

3. **Select the Create a Transfer Set radio button, and then click Next.**

   On the next wizard dialog box that appears, shown in Figure 24-3, you can specify where GoldMine should put the transfer set it's going to build. In this example, you're putting it on a floppy disk to take home later.

Figure 24-3:
Creating
and storing
your
transfer set.

4. **Enter** a:\xfer **as the directory on the floppy disk where you will place the transfer set.**

   You can select an update cutoff time if you want to.

   GoldSync builds your transfer set to include only data that has changed since the update cutoff time. If you created a transfer set previously, GoldMine kept track of the time and date it was created. By default, your next transfer set only includes changes to the database since that last transfer set was created. If that previous transfer set has been deleted, or it didn't work correctly, you can adjust the cutoff time on this dialog box. Click Next to move to the next step.

5. **On the Send Options dialog box, shown in Figure 24-4, specify what types of data to include in your transfer set.**

   By default, all types of data are included. Click Next to continue.

   On the Send Contact-related Options dialog box, shown in Figure 24-5 and Figure 24-6, you can further select the specific data that is to be included in the transfer set you're building.

6. **Click Next to continue.**

   The Cutoff Date/Time dialog box appears.

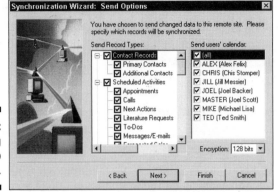

Figure 24-4:
Specifying
the data to
send.

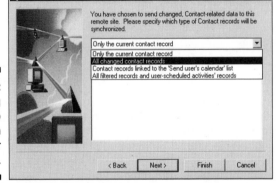

Figure 24-5:
Specifying
accounts to
include in
your
transfer set.

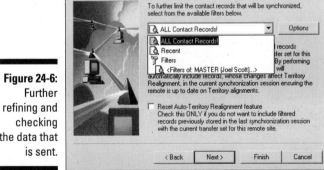

Figure 24-6:
Further
refining and
checking
the data that
is sent.

7. **On the Cutoff Date/Time dialog box, shown in Figure 24-7, specify a date and time other than the default.**

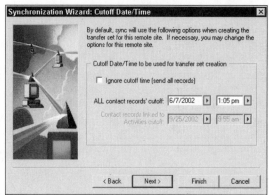

Figure 24-7:
Enter the
cutoff date.

The default is established each time you successfully complete a synchronization session. The next session reads the previous date and time and selects all changes that have been made after that date and time. Click Next.

8. **On the Ready to Synchronize dialog box (see Figure 24-8), make the final preparations before actually creating the transfer set.**

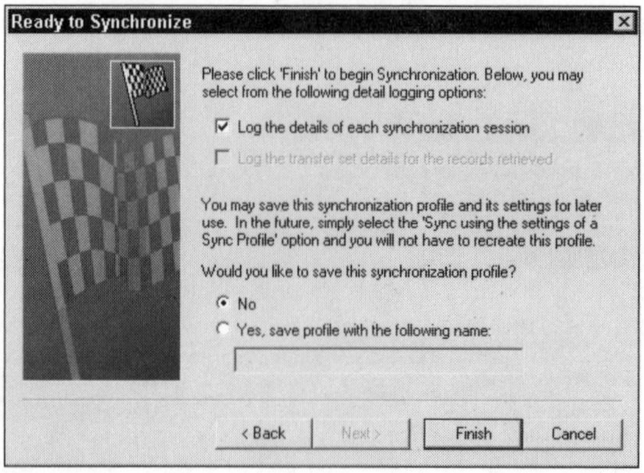

Figure 24-8:
The final
GoldSync
dialog box.

Selecting either of the first two radio buttons allows you (or anyone with master rights) to view the sync logs within the Reporting section of GoldMine. The sync logs are a complete audit trail of all activity during a sync session. You can view these logs if you need to troubleshoot your synchronization.

You can also save the specifications for this transfer set if you expect to ever use a similar transfer set in the future.

9. **Click the Finish button to build your transfer set.**

Manually retrieving a transfer set

Retrieving a transfer is the logical opposite of creating one. You access the retrieval system from the same Synchronization Wizard that creation uses. On the Synchronization Wizard dialog box (refer to Figure 24-2), just below the radio button for creating a transfer set is a radio button to Retrieve a Transfer Set. Selecting this option brings you to the window shown in Figure 24-9. From this point, you can easily fill in requested information about file locations and retrieval options. When you are done, GoldMine automatically incorporates this new data into your current database.

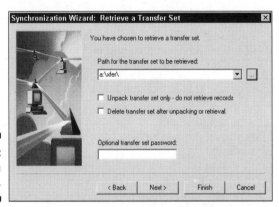

Figure 24-9:
Retrieving a
transfer set.

Palm Pilot, Windows CE, and Outlook

The Palm Pilot is a popular handheld device that holds names, addresses, and appointments. Windows CE devices are also handheld computers with a little more sophisticated operating system (like Windows-lite). Windows CE machines are a little larger and a little more expensive than the Palm Pilots. Outlook is Microsoft's version of a contact management system. Many people use handheld devices when they are on the road and want really quick and simple access to at some of their data. Outlook has become such an industry standard for keeping contact and calendar information that many people use both Outlook and GoldMine now. All of these can now communicate with GoldMine.

This communication is done, in most cases, by physically connecting the Palm Pilot or your Windows CE machine to your computer and running the interface software.

Sharing Data Automatically by Using GoldSync

GoldSync is an advanced feature within GoldMine. For the most part, GoldSync just automates the manual sneakernet system. If you are going to do more than a once-in-a-while data exchange, you really need GoldSync. If you have the standard version of GoldMine, then you must purchase a separate license for GoldSync so you can use it at all. The SQL version of GoldMine includes GoldSync.

This process of creating, transferring, and retrieving sets of data sounds simple, but it isn't. An almost unlimited number of ways exist for the process to get messed up, and more ways are being discovered all the time. Nevertheless, after it's set up properly, it tends to run smoothly and is certainly a handy thing to have. If you've heard horror stories about synchronization, for the most part, these are a thing of the past. In the past two years, GoldSync has been steadily improved and is now a solid performer.

Whereas GoldMine allows you to have as many different databases as you want, GoldSync expects you to have only one. If you have more than one active database and you intend to use synchronization, consolidate these databases into one master database first. If you plan to use synchronization, your life will be less complicated if all the data to be synchronized is located in just one database.

Reviewing GoldSync terminology

GoldSync is filled with strange words and phrases. In this section, I list the most common terms, and those terms that you need to understand in order to intelligently converse with a certified technician:

- **Client privileges:** Privileges determine the type of activities that each remote user is allowed to perform, as well as the types of information that the remote user may request from the central system. For example, the remote user may not be allowed to delete records from the main system.

- **Cutoff date/time:** Every field in GoldMine has an associated date and time stamp. This record is not visible to you as the user, but it is in the background. GoldMine keeps track of the last time the data in every individual field was changed. When a transfer set is created, only data that has changed since the last successful synchronization is put into the transfer set. This is the default cutoff date/time, although each user can manually change the default setting.

✔ **Queue connection methods:** Three distinct methods, called transport methods, exist for getting the data from the main server to the remote sites:

- The server and remote systems can place the data in common directories that all the PCs share.

- The server and remote systems send and retrieve transfer sets via the Internet either directly in real time, or as attachments to e-mail. The direct Internet connection is the most reliable and trouble-free method and is the one that I usually recommend.

- The server and remote systems can exchange transfer sets on a WAN (wide area network) or via RAS (Remote Access Server).

✔ **Queue options:** Queue options regulate the direction in which data is transferred. Data can be transferred as follows:

- The server retrieves data from the remote systems but doesn't send any data.

- The server sends data to the remote systems but doesn't retrieve any data.

- The server sends and retrieves data from the remote systems.

- The server continually processes local data and data from remote systems, and at each end, the computers regularly pick up this data.

✔ **Remote site:** A remote site is made up of one or more computers that usually contain just a portion of your entire database and are not physically connected to the main system. Examples of remote sites include:

- You travel with your notebook, which has just your own accounts in it.

- You have a workstation at home with just your accounts.

- You have one or more field offices that are not connected via a LAN or WAN.

✔ **Synchronization methods:** Two methods exist for preparation of transfer sets. These are selections within the GoldSync Wizard that allow GoldSync to automatically create your transfer sets.

- **Contact record synchronization:** This method creates transfer sets from either the entire database or just those records specified by a filter.

- **User's schedule synchronization method:** This method creates transfer sets based on changes to those records that are attached to a user's schedule. If nothing is scheduled for an account, no information is included in the transfer set.

Looking at sync logs

You can display the date and time of each attempt to synchronize, as well as the details of records sent and retrieved by synchronizing. You access these logs by choosing View⇨GoldMine Logs or View⇨Sync Retrieval Logs.

The sync logs display a date/time entry for each attempt by your system to synchronize. If a transfer set was sent or retrieved during synchronization, GoldMine displays folders under the date/time entry. These folders contain the files for which the transfer set included updates.

The first set of file folders contains updates for the selected contact set file(s). When you click a folder, such as CONTACT1, the details of record updates appear in the right panel. The right-pane display is the same as that for the contact files logs.

The second set of folders contains updates for GoldMine files. When you click a folder, such as InfoMine, the details of record updates appear in the right panel.

When you finish viewing the log entries, you can either select another folder or system log, or close the System Logs window.

Troubleshooting GoldSync

Three distinct phases of synchronization exist — creation of transfer sets, retrieval of transfer sets, and merging of data into an existing database. Problems can develop in any one of these areas and are typically listed in the GoldSync logs.

The best starting point for problem resolution is the GoldMine help file. You can access specific information about GoldSync troubleshooting by choosing Help⇨How Do I⇨Index and typing **Troubleshooting synchronization** in the Search field.

You have several additional resources for setting up and for assistance with synchronization. You can avail yourself of help directly from FrontRange Solutions, or you can contract with a GoldMine dealer. Make sure the dealer is GoldSync certified before getting involved, however.

Chapter 25

Automated Processes

● ●

In This Chapter

▶ Designing Automated Processes

▶ Developing tracks

▶ Programming events

▶ Running the processes

● ●

*A*utomated Processes are routines that sit quietly in the background, looking for events or conditions within each record that trigger some action, or even a whole series of actions. You can use the Automated Processes feature to perform a set of actions to accomplish a specific task. The Automated Processes feature is one of the key features that differentiates GoldMine from the vast majority of its competitors. I am convinced that properly implemented Automated Processes are the most powerful tools for growing your business that you will ever encounter.

You can design an unlimited number of Automated Processes to emulate a wide variety of already-existing processes within your business. You can also design some of the processes that have never been manually implemented due to lack of resources. The clear advantage of the GoldMine Automated Processes is that they never forget to do their assigned tasks, never call in sick or go on vacation, and never ask for a raise. Automated Processes just keep doing their job for you without complaint and without fail.

In most industries, selling something to a prospect for the first time takes a considerable effort, and staying in touch enough after the sale to have a reasonable expectation of a repeat sale takes further effort. Many sales consultants estimate that it takes about six touches before you can close a new sale. A *touch* is some sort of communication, whether in person, on the phone, via mail, fax, or e-mail.

The average professional salesperson gives up after fewer than three touches due to the pressures of other commitments and other opportunities. The whole concept behind the GoldMine Automated Processes is to provide the ability to perform most of these touches without any human intervention. (Of course, the best scenario is when the prospect or customer doesn't realize that the computer, and not the salesperson, is doing the touching.) This chapter presents some simple examples of how to get the computer to do the work that salespeople or administrators are either doing now or that they are supposed to be doing, but never seem to get to.

In addition, I show some examples of more complex Automated Processes that may be effective after the initial sale. Anyone with a background in marketing knows that selling something to an existing customer is easier and more cost-effective than finding a brand-new customer for one of your products or services. I have seen many statistics claiming that finding a new customer is six times more expensive than selling to an existing one. I don't have a clue where that statistic came from, and my work in client retention tells me otherwise, but any salesperson would be wise to put the GoldMine Automated Processes to work to keep his or her clients.

Designing Automated Processes

Every successful business has processes. A process may be as simple as an edict that when the sales manager gives a salesperson a lead, he or she must follow up within one day. Another example is that whenever a salesperson returns from an initial sales call, he or she should immediately send a follow-up thank-you letter.

A more sophisticated process may be one that performs a series of follow-up steps after talking with a prospect at a trade show — an initial thank-you letter via e-mail, a second mailing with brochures, and then a scheduled follow-up phone call by the salesperson. (Check out the sidebar, "My favorite Automated Process," elsewhere in this chapter, for a good example of such a process.)

A good starting point when you're designing an Automated Process (AP for short) for GoldMine is to examine all those processes you already have in place. You want to have the computer, as opposed to people, performing as many of the grunt-work steps as you can. This step is often the place where a good, experienced consultant can help you take a fresh look at procedures and policies.

Next, you should examine all the potential areas of your business where no processes exist, but where they could be implemented and could be beneficial.

Keep in mind that just because you have a process in place doesn't mean you should just blindly stick it into GoldMine. While implementing just one good AP can have a huge positive effect on your bottom line, implementing a not-so-well-thought-out process may not have the positive effect you hoped for. In fact, automating a poor procedure, or implementing a good procedure poorly, will only cause your new system to screw you up faster and more efficiently than you could ever imagine. This is a great time to reexamine all your business processes and do some reengineering.

My favorite Automated Process

FrontRange suggests implementing several key types of Automated Processes: performing administrative tasks, managing leads, following up on contacts, sending warranty renewal reminders, automating direct-mail campaigns, and validating data. You can design and implement an Automated Process to help you accomplish any task that you want done automatically.

When I first began my computer consulting business, I occasionally exhibited at trade shows, which were expensive and a lot of work. I wanted to take advantage of any leads I got at these shows. After several days of standing in our booth, I went back to my office with a stack of business cards. These cards were like manna from heaven — hot leads that I just couldn't let go to waste.

After being out of the office for a few days, I returned to a handful of crises that demanded my immediate attention. Before I knew it, my stack of hot leads were in my desk drawer, forgotten. I did this for three straight trade shows, and I just couldn't understand why trade-show results were so poor!

So my company turned over a new leaf and implemented an Automated Process for trade shows that never fails us. At the end of the first day of a trade show, as the other vendors head for the bar, we grab our computer and head for my hotel room. All day long we collected leads and put them directly into GoldMine. We plug the notebook into the phone line and then head

for the bar ourselves: Step One of the Trade Show Automated Process has begun. The computer e-mails and faxes each new lead, sending a letter that basically says, "Thanks for stopping by our trade-show booth today. We were just overwhelmed by all the interest and activity today, but nonetheless, your account would be very important to us. When we get back to our office on Monday, we will send out the literature you requested. If you can't wait until then, call Jane at our office. . . ."

We repeat this process after each day of the trade show. When we get back to the office, Step Two begins. A notice is sent, directing the appropriate person to mail the requested literature. GoldMine assigns an account manager to the account based on geography and also generates a cover letter. After all these processes are done, GoldMine schedules the account manager to make a follow-up call in one week. The process checks to see whether the prospect has called us already, which prevents us from appearing out of control.

The response to this Automated Process is amazing. Literally 35 percent of the people we contact each night call us the next day, stunned that we responded so quickly. The early bird catches the worm: While our competitors celebrate down in the bar, we do our follow-up marketing to make sure they have as little to celebrate later as possible. And it works!

I classify processes into three categories that represent all the major life stages of an account:

✔ **Hunting:** This stage is the entire sales cycle from suspect to prospect to a closed deal. Many steps exist that most companies routinely follow, or should, to move an account from suspect status to becoming a client.

✔ **Farming:** After prospects become clients, they should get just as much, if not more, attention as they got before. A well-known fact is that it's more cost-effective to get additional business from an existing account than it is to find a new account to replace one you've lost or failed to penetrate.

✔ **Resurrecting:** Sometimes accounts are lost; it happens to everyone. Sometimes it happens for reasons beyond your control, or sometimes due to neglect. Just because a client has left the fold doesn't mean you should give up. Implementing some Automated Processes to stay in touch with former clients often reaps some surprising and positive results.

Developing Tracks

One of the confusing aspects of Automated Processes is the terminology, which is probably all new to you. One of the key terms to understand is *track*. GoldMine uses this term interchangeably with *process*. Tracks consist of one or more *events*, which are step-by-step instructions that GoldMine evaluates to perform a series of activities. Each event is composed of a trigger and an action. A *trigger*, such as a warranty period about to expire, causes a specific *action*, such as sending a letter about your extended warranty plan.

Setting process options

To set up a new Automated Process or to view existing Automated Processes, choose Tools⇨Automated Processes⇨Automated Process Center from the main menu. The Automated Processes Center window, shown in Figure 25-1, displays a summary of what has already been developed. The window lists all your processes, each one's options as well as the associated events. You can develop a new Automated Process by using the AP Wizard, which guides you through setting up your Automated Process as follows:

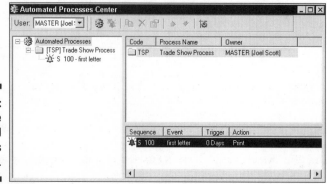

Figure 25-1:
The Automated Processes Center.

1. **To start the Automated Process Wizard, choose Tools⇨Automated Processes⇨Automated Processes Center, and then click the New Automated Processes icon.**

   The Automated Process Wizard appears, as shown in Figure 25-2. The first two fields in the AP Wizard enable you to name the process and to give it a code number. The name of each process should indicate the function or purpose of that track. Tracks are arranged alphabetically by the process code you enter and are displayed this way in various AP dialog boxes. If a process has no code (another possibility), it will be listed first.

Figure 25-2:
The
Automated
Process
Wizard.

2. **Give your process a name and a code (and possibly assign ownership of this process to someone else) and click Next.**

   On the second page of the AP Wizard, shown in Figure 25-3, the following options appear:

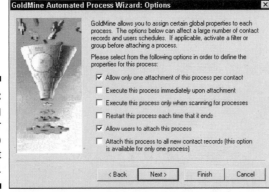

Figure 25-3:
Attaching
your
process to
contact
records.

- **Allow only one attachment of this process per contact:** Prevents the track from being attached more than once to a particular record. For example, you would use this option for a process that sends a thank-you letter to a first-time customer.

- **Execute this process immediately upon attachment:** Starts processing the track as soon as a user attaches it to one or more records.

- **Execute this process only when scanning for processes:** Prevents a track from being executed even if you select the preceding choice.

- **Restart this process each time that it ends:** Reattaches the track as soon as processing for the track is done.

- **Allow users to attach this process:** Allows manual attachment of the track by the system users. You would use manual attachment for a process that is not run for every account.

- **Attach this process to all new contact records:** Causes GoldMine to automatically attach the track to each new contact record, which could be useful in conjunction with use of a monitor track (see the sidebar, "The monitor track: An elegant approach," later in this chapter).

3. **Select the options you want and then click Next.**

   The next step in the AP Wizard, the Events page, appears. If you are creating a new Automated Process, this page is empty, as shown in Figure 25-4. Events are the actual activities the AP is causing. For example, an Event might be a scheduled phone call or an appointment, or an Event might be a letter that is automatically sent. The Events page enables you to specify these activities.

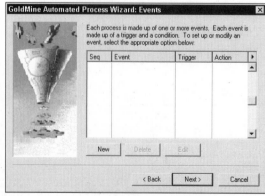

Figure 25-4:
The AP
Wizard's
Events
page.

4. Click the New button if you are creating a new Automated Process.

The Event Properties dialog box appears, as shown in Figure 25-5. The "Programming event properties" section, later in this chapter, describes the options in the Event Properties dialog box.

5. Set the options you want for your Automated Process and click OK.

6. Click the Finish button.

The AP Wizard brings you back to the Automated Processes Center window, as shown in Figure 25-6. This window contains all the events you designed into your new Automated Process.

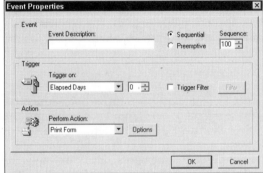

Figure 25-5:
The AP
Event
Properties
dialog box.

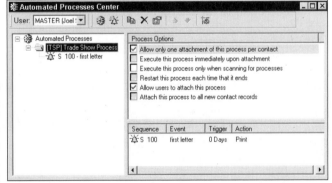

Figure 25-6:
A typical AP
events
summary
window.

Programming event properties

The Event Properties dialog box (refer to Figure 25-5) contains important options for setting up your Automated Processes. The dialog box's options are divided into three groups: Event, Trigger, and Action. The following sections describe the options in each group.

The monitor track: An elegant approach

If you're going to have more than one Automated Process (and you should assume you will), then using a monitor track is a clever way to implement your system. The *monitor track* (also referred to by some consultants as an *observer track* or a *watchdog track*) is the only track that records are ever attached to. In fact, the monitor track should automatically be attached to every record. Then you won't ever have to worry about attaching records to tracks at all.

The monitor track is like the traffic cop for the whole Automated Process system: It watches out for all the possible conditions within a record and directs each record to the appropriate track or tracks. Because one track (the monitor track) can call another track (for example, the trade-show track), using the monitor track is an elegant programming approach to developing a very sophisticated series of processes.

Preemptive events

Two kinds of events exist in GoldMine: preemptive and sequential. Every track can have many of each kind of event, but each track must have at least one sequential event. Every event is given a numerical sequence from 0 to 999.

Preemptive events are conditional statements, or more simply, they are IF statements. For example, if you want to send a notice to all customers that have not purchased anything in the last three months, you can put in a preemptive statement that says, "If there is a sale in the last 3 months in their History, then remove this track from the record."

You can only number preemptive events from 0 to 99 and, therefore, they are always at the beginning of the track. When you initially number your events, do not use consecutive numbers; allow some space to interject another event later. As a guideline, number your preemptive events 5, 10, 15, and so on.

Usually when you program preemptive events, you're trying to eliminate records from contention. Thus, try to create the logic within your preemptive statement to eliminate the record, rather than to confirm that this process is appropriate for this record.

Sequential events

Sequential events are always numbered from 100 to 999, and you must always have at least one sequential event in each track. Because the sequential events actually perform actions, if you didn't have at least one, the track would never do anything.

Just as with preemptive events, you should allow some room for growth, and make sure to number them in increments of 5 or 10. Sequential events are programmed into the system with the same procedure you use for preemptives. The only difference is in the Event Properties dialog box, you select the Sequential radio button rather than the Preemptive radio button.

Choosing a trigger

A *trigger* is the condition within the contact record's data that determines what action should be taken. For example, this might be an amount of time that passed since the last time this client was visited, or perhaps a scheduled activity that requires a notice being sent to a manager.

In the Event Properties dialog box, the Trigger On drop-down list enables you to choose from the following seven options to trigger an activity:

- ✔ **Elapsed Days:** This trigger activates as soon as the number of days you enter has gone by since the last event was processed; or if this is the first event in your AP, since the track was attached to this account.

- ✔ **Immediate:** This trigger sets GoldMine to immediately execute the action associated with the event.

- ✔ **Detail Record:** This trigger looks for the addition of a specific Detail, Document Link, Referral, or Other Contact. Don't be confused by the name Detail Record. This Detail Record can trigger on almost any kind of new supplemental information.

- ✔ **History Activity:** This trigger looks for the existence of a specific type of history record in order to activate — for example, the completion of a sales call with a result code of INT, indicating that it's an initial sales call.

- ✔ **Scheduled Activity:** This trigger looks for a specific type of calendar activity. For example, it may look for a scheduled training class before reserving a projector.

- ✔ **dBASE Condition:** This one is triggered by a dBASE expression you build using the GoldMine expression builder.

- ✔ **Disabled:** This option turns off the trigger for this event. Without a trigger, the event will never happen. This can be used to document, to debug, or simply to space things for easier reading.

Actions speak louder than words

The Perform Action drop-down list in the Event Properties dialog box (refer to Figure 25-5) supplies you with many options to choose from. These options are actions that will be performed when the trigger event you choose from the Trigger On drop-down list occurs, as discussed in the previous section. The actions you may choose from are as follows:

- ✔ **Print Form:** Prints or faxes a merge form when the event is triggered.

- ✔ **E-mail Message:** Generates and sends an Internet-based e-mail template when the event is triggered.

✔ **Print Report:** Prints a report when the event is triggered. Some reports, like the Address and Phone Report, print the entire database every time. Make sure not to have your AP print this report, or similar ones, for every record it scans.

✔ **Schedule Activity:** Schedules a calendar activity for a selected user when the event is triggered.

✔ **Create History:** Adds a history record to the contact record when the event is triggered.

✔ **Create Detail:** Adds a detail record to the contact record when the event is triggered.

✔ **Add to Group:** Adds the contact to a specified group when the event is triggered.

✔ **Update Field:** Updates one of the fields in the contact record with the result of a dBASE expression when the event is triggered.

✔ **Remove Track:** Removes the track from the contact record when the event is triggered, thus ensuring that no further actions will be taken for this account.

✔ **Add a New Track:** Attaches a new track to the contact record when the event is triggered. See the sidebar, "The monitor track: An elegant approach," in this chapter for some thoughts on when to use this approach.

✔ **Branch to Event:** Directs GoldMine to proceed to a specified event, and uses the code numbers of the events as a reference.

✔ **Run Application:** Starts an external application (for example, a Visual Basic program) when the event is triggered.

Executing a Process

Remember that processes, however well designed, will not work unless they are attached to records and then told to run. I discuss attaching records in the "Setting process options" section, earlier in this chapter. To run a process, follow these steps:

1. **From the main menu, choose Tools⇨Automated Processes⇨Execute Processes.**

   The Automated Processes Execution dialog box, shown in Figure 25-7, appears.

2. **Attach one or more records to a track by selecting the Attach Track to Selected Contacts option and choosing from the drop-down list.**

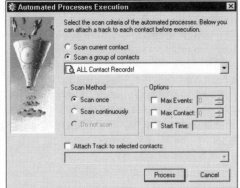

Figure 25-7:
Choose
which
processes
to execute.

3. **Click the Process button.**

   This causes the Process Monitor window, shown in Figure 25-8, to immediately appear.

Figure 25-8:
The Process
Monitor
window.

The upper pane of the Process Monitor window displays the elapsed time, the record currently being processed, the total number of records scanned, the number of events that have been triggered, and the title of the track currently being processed.

From the Process Monitor window, you can

✔ **Stop all processes** to stop all processing for all contacts.

✔ **Stop selected processes** to stop the current track for the current record from processing.

 ✔ **Copy logs to Windows Clipboard** to copy the log entries in the lower pane of the display to Windows Clipboard. From there, you can paste the information into your word processor or into a spreadsheet for further reporting.

Automated Processes are the most powerful features in GoldMine. Any contact management system can keep track of names, addresses, and appointments. But these Automated Processes, when properly implemented, are like a Marketing department in a box. Putting this together properly will easily pay for the whole installation of GoldMine, so don't neglect it.

Chapter 26

Using My GoldMine

In This Chapter

▶ Accessing your My GoldMine window

▶ Configuring your My GoldMine window

GoldMine is integrating more and more with the Internet. Like many other Internet-focused applications, GoldMine now has a special page to keep you abreast of things of interest to you from the wide world of the Web, as well as critical information stored right in your GoldMine data.

This facility, which is new to GoldMine 6.0, is a single window called My GoldMine. You can configure this window to provide news from a variety of Web sites of your choosing, as well as, for example, activity-based information from GoldMine. A special, not-so-customizable section automatically sends you information that FrontRange thinks you need to know.

If you're used to seeing pages like My Yahoo! or My Outlook, then you will be right at home with My GoldMine.

In this chapter, you find out how to set up your My GoldMine page, and you may even get a few ideas for what to include in it.

Accessing the My GoldMine Window

To display the My GoldMine window, or any version of it that you create, choose View⇨My GoldMine from the main menu. GoldMine 6.0 comes with a predefined, sample My GoldMine window, as shown in Figure 26-1.

You can't view any information coming from an external Web site unless your computer is connected to the Internet. Developing any Web-related customizations isn't possible without an Internet connection, as well.

If there are hyperlinks within your My GoldMine window, you need to click each of them to receive and view the information.

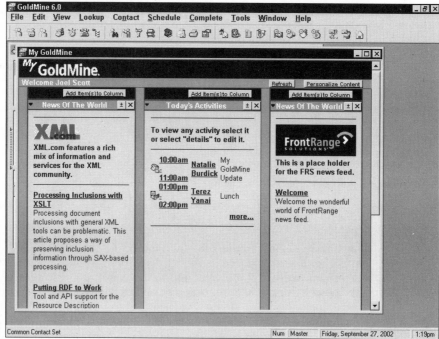

Figure 26-1:
The default
My
GoldMine
window.

Configuring the My GoldMine Window

The content of your My GoldMine window, as well as its appearance, is under your control. You modify this window from the main GoldMine screen by selecting File⇨Configure⇨My GoldMine. You then encounter the Configure My GoldMine dialog box, as shown in Figure 26-2.

The Configure My GoldMine dialog box contains three tabs that you can click to configure various settings. These tabs are described in more detail in the follow three sections.

The Layout tab

The Layout tab of the Configure My GoldMine dialog box, shown in Figure 26-2, allows you to control the page styles and the types of columns that are shown in the My GoldMine window. You have four options for layout: Default, Windows, Newspaper, and XP. Basically, each selection slightly modifies the background color and the font in which the text displays. The default layout is the most colorful and eye-catching, so I use that layout. Which one you use is really just personal preference — each layout option displays the same information. If you get tired of one layout after a month, you can change it without affecting the data.

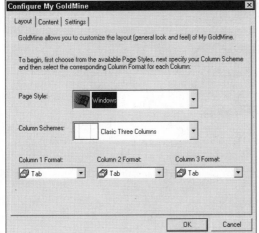

Figure 26-2:
Use this
dialog box
to change
how you
view the My
GoldMine
window.

You have a choice of three different column settings. If you choose the Even 2 Columns option or the Even 3 Columns option, you get either 2 or 3 evenly spaced display areas. With the Classic 3 Column display, the middle column is the widest, the left-most column is slightly narrower and the right-most column is narrower yet by a little. If you are concerned about one kind of display that takes a little more room than your others, use the Classic layout, putting that data in the middle.

For each column, you can also select either the Box View option or the Tab View option. In the box view, each item in the column is displayed. If you have a lot of text, this could create a very long column that requires a considerable amount of scrolling. In the tab view, only one item is displayed at a time, but you can select additional items from the list at the bottom of the column.

Mixing and matching box and tab views might not be the best approach. If you have one column in box view with a lot of data in it, you will need to scroll to the bottom of the page, possibly through a lot of blank area, to access the items listed in the tab view. Users not familiar with your layout may never see these additional items.

The Content tab

The Content tab of the Configure My GoldMine dialog box, shown in Figure 26-3, allows you to add to or edit the information in My GoldMine.

The Content tab allows you to add, remove, or reposition items that have been made available for My GoldMine. The right-most column contains information from FrontRange, such as announcements and links to its Web site. You can't remove or change this as you can with the other items displayed in My GoldMine.

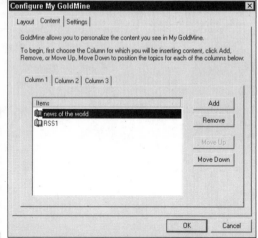

Figure 26-3:
Managing
content that
appears in
the My
GoldMine
window.

The Settings tab

The Settings tab of the Configure My GoldMine dialog box, shown in Figure 26-4, controls how often the My GoldMine window is refreshed. If you are using My GoldMine to monitor weather conditions in your area, you might want it to refresh every hour. If you are using it to monitor the stock market, you probably want to refresh more frequently.

The refresh rate can also be set right from the My GoldMine window using the Refresh button at the top right of the window.

Figure 26-4:
Setting the
refresh rate
for the My
GoldMine
window.

Chapter 27

Setting Up and Using the GM+View

• •

• •

*E*very record in GoldMine 6.0 contains the new, HTML-based GM+View tab, which stores customized Web pages. These pages, or views, can include rich content, such as text and graphics.

The GM+View tab is particularly useful when you have a variety of graphics associated with your accounts. For example, a recruiter or a talent agency could use the GM+View tab to store a photo of each client with that client's record. A real estate agency may use it to store a photo or a series of photos of each property it has listed. Going a step further, for particularly high-valued properties, a real estate agency might want to store an entire walk-through video tour with sound on the GM+View tab.

Basically, you can think of the GM+View tab as a customized Web page for each account in GoldMine. Any type of information you have ever seen on a Web site can probably be housed in the GM+View tab.

A key to making good use of this tab is to understand how flexible it is. You can have many different views set up, and the view shown for any particular account is controlled by rules that you set up. The data in a particular field can also determine what view is displayed, or you can use a dBASE expression if a single field is not sufficient to control the view. Finally, you can leave it up to the user to determine the view when he or she activates a record and wants to see what's on the GM+View tab.

In this chapter, you find out how to access information in the GM+View tab and how to set up some simple views.

Displaying the GM+View Tab

Every GoldMine record has its own GM+View tab. By default, the GM+View tab is the third tab from the left in the first bank of tabs. By simply clicking that tab, you see what information is associated with that particular record. Figure 27-1 shows a sample of a GM+View tab with three pictures associated with the active GoldMine record. A real estate agent might find a display like this to be helpful.

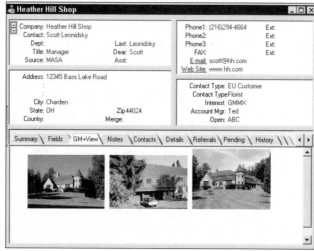

Figure 27-1:
A sample
GM+View
associates
photographs
with the
record.

Each GM+View tab can have one or more links to Web sites. The links in the GM+View tab are like hyperlinks on a Web page; just click the link to go to that Web site. For example, you might have a link to a mapping system, such as MapQuest, that displays the exact location of the active account, or perhaps gives you the driving instructions. You need to click that link to display the map or instructions.

Creating GM+View Templates

Only users with Master rights can design or even edit GM+View templates. The template contains all the instructions needed to actually display a series of graphics or links. To create a GM+View template, follow these steps:

1. **From the main menu, choose File⇨Configure⇨GM+View Tab.**

   The GM+View Tab Settings dialog box appears, as shown in Figure 27-2. All the existing templates appear in the upper-left box. You specify the default template by selecting it from the drop-down list on the upper-right part of the dialog box. The default template shows up automatically for every record in the database, unless some rule you have set countermands that. In the lower panel, you can see a preview of each template to get a feel for what it will actually look like.

Figure 27-2:
Create a
template for
GM+View
in the
GM+View
Tab Settings
dialog box.

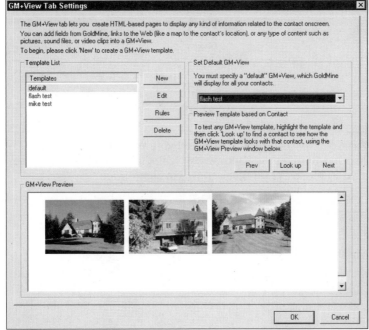

2. **Click the New button to display the Edit GM+View window, as shown in Figure 27-3.**

   Enter a descriptive name for your new template.

3. **Position your cursor wherever you want text or a graphic to be displayed and right-click.**

   Your choices for adding text, graphics, or links are shown in Figure 27-3. Right-clicking anywhere in the initially blank area accesses this shortcut menu.

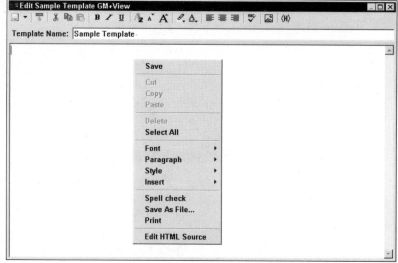

Figure 27-3:
Adding
features
to your
template.

After you have properly positioned your cursor, you can place fields or text files anywhere on the window. By right-clicking and selecting Insert, you get three additional choices, as shown in Figure 27-4.

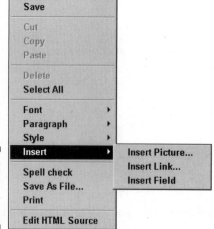

Figure 27-4:
Inserting a
picture, link,
or field.

Inserting fields and text files

When you right-click and choose Insert⇨Insert Field, you get yet another menu, as shown in Figure 27-5. The Contact Details menu choice gives you most of the critical fields from the upper portion of the main GoldMine screen. These fields are usually on display right in front of you anyway, so I'm not sure why it would be necessary to repeat them in this view. However, if you select the Include a Text File choice, you can have an associated file readily displayed in addition to the standard GoldMine fields.

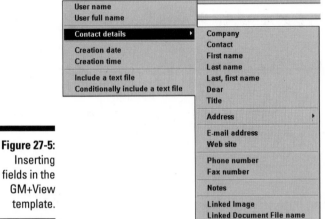

Figure 27-5:
Inserting
fields in the
GM+View
template.

Inserting links

Links, I believe, are more useful to have in the GM+View tab. By inserting a link, you can associate a GoldMine record with one or more Web pages. For example, you can include a link to a map with or without driving instructions. You could have a link to a weather site showing the weather forecast for this location. Perhaps more significantly, you could have a link to a news service or credit bureau Web site showing the latest news about each of your accounts.

Inserting pictures

Inserting graphics is a third and powerful choice. This seems like an obvious one for real estate agencies, talent agencies, and recruiters. But the possibilities for using photographs are endless. You may want to have photos of equipment that each account has on its shop floor, for example. Insurance companies might want photos of damaged cars and buildings to assist in claim evaluation.

You can insert one or more graphic files into a template and then manipulate its positioning and alignment by following these steps:

1. **From the main menu, choose File⇨Configure⇨GM+View Tab; click the Edit button on the GM+View Tab Settings dialog box.**

2. **In the Edit GM+View window (refer to Figure 27-3), click the Insert Picture icon on the local toolbar.**

   The Picture dialog box appears, as shown in Figure 27-6.

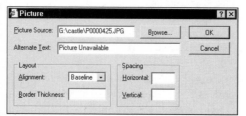

3. **Click the Browse button and locate the picture you want to insert.**

4. **In the Alternate Text field, type what text you want shown if the picture can't be displayed.**

   The alternate text selection allows you to specify some standard text in the event that your primary source is unavailable. This could happen, for example, if you are disconnected from either a disk drive housing the graphic or if you are disconnected from the Internet.

5. **Set the alignment of your picture, the border thickness, and spacing; click OK when you're done.**

   The layout and spacing sections of the dialog box allow you to position your pictures relative to the borders of the tab view and in relation to other pictures and text you may be displaying.

Selecting Your Template

Regulating who sees various templates requires Master rights. The starting point for template selection is the GM+View Tab Setting dialog box (refer to Figure 27-2). You can set up any template as the default template by selecting that template in the drop-down list in the upper-right part of the dialog box. Then, unless overridden by some other instruction, every user will see the default template associated with every record.

If you want to be cleverer, you can set up rules that govern the display of various templates. These rules can be based on the following:

- ✔ The value in one particular field
- ✔ A dBASE expression that might be a function of several fields
- ✔ User selection

The following steps show you how to set up these rules:

1. **From the main menu, choose File⇨Configure⇨GM+View Tab.**

   The GM+View Tab Settings dialog box appears (refer to Figure 27-2).

2. **Click the Rules button.**

   GoldMine displays the dialog box shown in Figure 27-7.

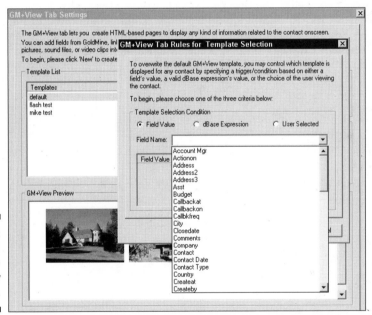

Figure 27-7: Using a field to determine a GM+View template.

3. **Select an option to determine the template selection condition.**

   You can choose to have the template selected based on the field value, a dBASE expression, or to allow users to select the template themselves.

For example, you might select the Field Value option and choose Account Mgr for the field name. Then, by clicking the New button, you are led through a series of selections.

In this example, you are shown a listing of all the Account Managers in your company. Select one. By doing this, you can now have separate templates for each Account Manager. Moe and Larry will each see potentially different aspects of each account's business.

4. **Click OK when you're done setting up your rules.**

Changing the rules so that different GoldMine users see different GM+Views might be relevant in the financial services arena, where investment bankers and stock brokers are not allowed to see any aspect of each others' business.

If you don't need to be so restrictive, you can have multiple templates and allow each user to decide which template he or she needs to see at any time. In the GM+View Tab Rules for Template Selection dialog box (refer to Figure 27-7), if you select the User Selected option, all templates become available to each user. When Moe brings up a particular GoldMine record, he can right-click in the GM+View Tab area and select from the entire list of templates. This is a great way to organize a large amount of graphic data that might be too confusing to display all in one window.

Chapter 28

Integrating with Outlook and Handheld Devices

In This Chapter

▶ Creating and using Outlook profiles

▶ Creating and using Palm Pilot profiles

GoldMine has its own built-in e-mail system. Many of the really focused GoldMine dealers believed it was almost heresy for their clients to use any other system. The problem was that Outlook was included with Microsoft Office, and almost every company had Outlook. Mysteriously, some companies and people just refused to stop using Outlook, even after installing GoldMine.

After several years of resisting the will of the marketplace and after merging with a company that itself used Outlook, GoldMine finally took an if you can't beat 'em, join 'em attitude and decided to integrate with Outlook.

Now GoldMine allows you to synchronize with Outlook by using either GoldMine's built-in synchronization or by using iCal meeting requests. This chapter discusses how you can happily coexist with all those Outlook stalwarts. You'll even be able to live with yourself if you are one of them.

Handheld devices, such as Palm Pilots, Pocket PCs, and various clones, are becoming increasingly popular. Clearly, many road warriors prefer the smaller, lighter, and handy handhelds to their laptops. I once found myself stranded in an airport and late for an appointment. It took me forever to boot up my laptop, start up GoldMine, and locate the account. Then I had to balance my laptop on my knee while using a pay phone. I became a believer that day. Now I have a combination digital cell phone/Palm Pilot. This chapter also focuses on using the most popular Palm Pilots with GoldMine.

Creating and Using Outlook Profiles

You will want to set up an Outlook Synchronization Profile if you use Outlook and GoldMine, or if you need to coordinate your GoldMine system with someone who primarily uses Outlook.

You may already be familiar with the concept of profiles from synchronization or from data importing. A *profile* is a set of instructions that describes how you want two programs or two sets of data to interact. After you have set up a profile, you can use it again and again without having to think about it too much.

To set up an Outlook Synchronization Profile, follow these steps:

1. **Choose File⇨Synchronize⇨Synchronize with Outlook, as shown in Figure 28-1.**

   The Outlook Synchronization Wizard begins.

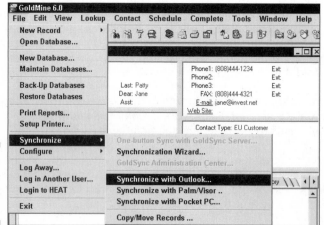

Figure 28-1: Beginning an Outlook Sync Profile.

2. **Select the Start a New Session option and then click Next.**

   The wizard next asks you to select how data should flow between GoldMine and Outlook — from Outlook to GoldMine, GoldMine to Outlook, or both, as shown in Figure 28-2.

3. **Click the Advanced button (shown in Figure 28-2) to access more options.**

   This selection brings up the Advanced Options dialog box, as shown in Figure 28-3. The General tab allows you to set the date range to ensure that you are sending all the information that may have been previously scheduled in Outlook. To avoid confusion, you should understand that this window regulates the transmission of appointment data that has been entered into Outlook and is being transferred into GoldMine.

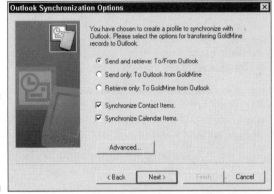

Figure 28-2:
Choose a send and retrieve option.

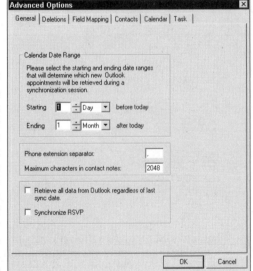

Figure 28-3:
The Advanced Options dialog box enables you to select a range of dates for synchronization.

For your first sync session, you may want to set the Starting Date back a considerable time to make sure that all your contact data from Outlook is sent over to GoldMine. From the second time on, you can set the starting date much closer to the current date. Resetting the date after the first session decreases the amount of time a sync session takes.

The five other tabs on the Advanced Options dialog box (shown in Figure 28-3) enable you to choose from more options as follows:

- **The Deletions tab:** Allows you to delete a record in Outlook and have that same information deleted in the related GoldMine record. Conversely, you can select the option to have deletions in GoldMine cause information in Outlook to be erased. Going a step further, you can remove all the data in Outlook that has ever been sent via GoldMine.

- **The Field Mapping tab:** Correlates GoldMine fields with their corresponding Outlook fields.

- **The Contacts, Calendar, and Task tabs:** Allow you to direct data to the correct Outlook folder. This is important if you have a custom installation of Outlook, if your Outlook is on a network drive, or if you've created your own folder structure in Outlook.

4. **When you are done with the Advanced Options dialog box, click OK; click Next to proceed to the next section of the wizard.**

   The Record Selections part of the Outlook Synchronization Wizard appears, as shown in Figure 28-4.

Figure 28-4:
Choose
which
records to
send to
Outlook.

You will probably want to carefully regulate which records are transferred to Outlook. For example, if you are one salesperson among many, you will probably want to restrict your Outlook synchronization to just your own records. You do this by selecting the Contacts in Current Active Filter/Group Changed Since Cutoff option. Make sure you set a cutoff date that is realistic.

5. **Click Next.**

   The wizard next asks you to select which Calendar records you want to send to Outlook, as shown in Figure 28-5. You probably want to synchronize only your own calendar. Keep in mind that the more calendars you choose, the longer the sync session will take.

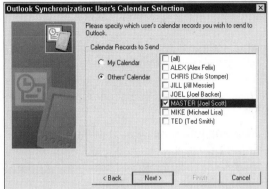

Figure 28-5:
Send your
Calendar or
another
user's
Calendar to
Outlook.

6. **When you are done selecting a Calendar, click Next.**

   The last thing the wizard asks you to do is to name your Outlook Sync Profile.

7. **Type a good name for your profile and click Finish.**

   GoldMine immediately begins processing your profile, and you can watch the progress of the synchronization in the process monitor.

You can access this synchronization profile as often as you want by choosing File⇨Synchronize⇨Synchronize with Outlook. You will then see the profiles you have already defined. Pick one (if you have more than one) and click Finish.

Creating and Using Palm Pilot Profiles

Creating profiles for PDAs is analogous to doing it for Outlook, but there are a couple of fundamental differences. For one thing, a Palm Pilot has a physical limit to the amount of data it can hold. Secondly, the software that connects GoldMine to a Palm has an extra component called a *conduit,* which directs the flow of your Palm data to a place and with a format that GoldMine can handle.

This section discusses the built-in integration between GoldMine and the Palm Pilot. GoldMine inherently can connect to the Visor as well as to several other Palm Pilot clones. In addition, GoldMine can handle the Pocket PC. I am limiting the discussion to the more popular Palm Pilot, although other hand-held devices synchronize in a similar manner.

Many users have found that an add-on product called CompanionLink enhances the integration experience. I mention this in case you are a serious

PDA and GoldMine user. You might want to check out this add-on, but this section focuses strictly on GoldMine's own link to the Palm.

The Palm Synchronization Profiles are accessed just as the Outlook syncs are — by selecting File⇨Synchronize⇨Synchronize with Palm/Visor. The first several sections of the wizard to set up Palm profile definitions are virtually identical to those of the Outlook Synchronization Wizard. There are, however, some noteworthy exceptions and issues.

When selecting which Calendar records to send to your Palm, you should select the My Calendar option. Otherwise, you may be sending more information than your Palm can swallow. Make sure to assign a filter (or group) within GoldMine before running the sync to further limit the quantity of data. See Chapter 12 for detailed information on filters and groups.

The conduit

The Palm Pilot comes with software called Palm Desktop Software. GoldMine sometimes also refers to this software (or the link) as the Palm/Visor Conduit. The Palm Desktop Software transfers the data in your Palm to and from your desktop computer. GoldMine, however, doesn't know anything about Palm Desktop Software, so a conduit is used to link GoldMine to the Palm Desktop Software.

If you have to reset your Palm (for example, if you leave your Palm in your car for a couple of days when it's 95 degrees, and the batteries die), you will need to uninstall the GoldMine conduit as follows:

1. **Start the sync wizard by choosing File⇨Synchronize⇨Synchronize with Palm/Visor.**

   The Palm/Visor Synchronization Wizard starts up.

2. **Click the Advanced button to display the Advanced Options dialog box.**

3. **Click the Conduit tab, and then click the Uninstall Conduit button, as shown in Figure 28-6.**

4. **Open your Palm Desktop Software and run a Hot Sync from there.**

   You will not be able to sync with GoldMine until you do this uninstall and resync. Then you can reinstall the GoldMine conduit and run your sync profile.

Doing a Hot Sync may create records on your Palm Pilot that are already in GoldMine. Therefore, you need to select the Purge tab in the Advanced Options dialog box and check the check boxes to delete any data that's already in the Palm. This will prevent further duplication in GoldMine.

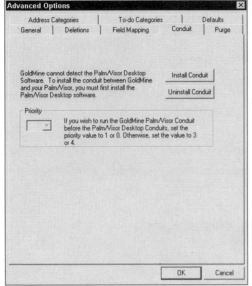

Figure 28-6:
Uninstall the
conduit
in the
Advanced
Options
dialog box
if you have
to reset
your Palm.

Advanced Palm Pilot options

A useful sync option is to identify which category of contact records in your Palm you would like to share with your GoldMine database. Each record in your Palm has a category designation located in the upper-right corner of the Palm screen (when you are in Address View). The default category is unfiled. The category option has a drop-down list containing Business, Personal, QuickList, Unfiled, and Edit.

After you have designated specific records as Business, for example, you select this category from the Address Categories tab in the Advanced dialog box in GoldMine's Palm Sync Wizard. The subsequent sync allows only Business contacts to move from the Palm to your GoldMine database.

Another advanced option is to have GoldMine delete an appointment from your Palm after it has been completed in GoldMine. This option also deletes contacts from your Palm if they've been deleted in GoldMine, so use this option with caution.

On the Deletions tab in the Advanced dialog box in GoldMine's Palm Sync Wizard, you can delete contacts and/or activities. When you perform the sync, contacts are deleted from the Palm if they have been deleted in GoldMine. Conversely, if you delete a contact in the Palm, the synchronization will then delete it in GoldMine. Activities can also be deleted, but it is completed activities rather than deleted activities that bite the dust. The two windows, shown in Figures 28-7 and 28-8 work together to control these options.

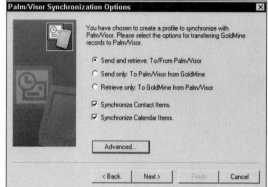

Figure 28-7:
The
Palm/Visor
Sync
Options
wizard.

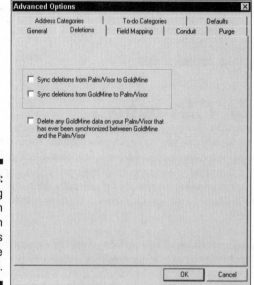

Figure 28-8:
Regulating
the direction
in which
deletions
are
performed.

Part VIII
The Part of Tens

The 5th Wave   By Rich Tennant

"This part of the test tells us whether you're personally suited to the job of network administrator."

In this part . . .

This part contains some of the most important information in the book. You can multiply the value of GoldMine many times over by interfacing it with some of your other applications. I searched the world, far and wide, for some of the best add-on products to discuss in this part.

GoldMine 6.0 has some great new features that weren't in previous versions of the product. In Chapter 30, I describe ten of the most useful new features in GoldMine 6.0.

Chapter 29

Ten Great Add-On Products

$\bullet\ \bullet$

*O*ne of the smartest things FrontRange did was grant outside developers access to its file structures. Doing so has spurred the development of many useful third-party products, bringing more and more power to the original system. Literally hundreds of add-on products exist. GoldMine dealers developed most of the add-on products. New products show up all the time, while existing products often disappear from the horizon.

Make sure you check whether a particular add-on supports your version of GoldMine before you buy it. Just because a product is discussed in this chapter doesn't imply an endorsement, although my company actually uses most of the products in this Top Ten listing. You have the freedom to determine whether a particular add-on is appropriate for your application. And just because an add-on product isn't discussed in this chapter doesn't imply that it's no good. I had to omit many good and useful products due to space constraints, ignorance, and/or neglect. I focus on products that either my clients or I use and find valuable.

Crystal Reports

Crystal Reports from Seagate and Stonefield Query from Stonefield Systems Group (see the section, "Stonefield Query," later in this chapter) are two reporting tools you can use in addition to the report-generating system built into GoldMine already.

Crystal Reports is a well-known and well-established general reporting tool. Crystal Reports can access data from a wide variety of formats. It just so happens that GoldMine data, whether in dBASE format or the more sophisticated SQL version, is perfectly compatible with Crystal Reports. Not only can you develop almost any kind of custom report you might want using Crystal Reports, but it's so well integrated with GoldMine that you can even include the Crystal Reports you have built right in the list of GoldMine's other reports. GoldMine users running reports will hardly know the difference. You may want some training before attempting to develop anything very sophisticated in Crystal Reports, and you will certainly need a good understanding of GoldMine's underlying file structure. See Chapter 19 for details on the built-in reporting system.

Recently, however, there have been some issues with integrating Crystal Reports and GoldMine. Each time a new version of GoldMine comes out, it seems that the current version of Crystal Reports doesn't integrate any more. This is a fluid, dynamic situation, and you should check with a dealer or with FrontRange to find out what the situation is at the moment you are contemplating matching these two products.

Details Plus

The Details tab in GoldMine is a powerful, relational section of the system. On this tab you can track, for example, each of the components of the computer you sold to a customer. Because the Details tab is relational, you can keep track of each of the computers you sold to that client.

While GoldMine allows you to track these components, you can't have more than about eight such components. Details Plus, a product of Solica Consulting, allows you to add an additional four fields. You can also have an extra note field. And, best yet, it's compatible with GoldSync, so your remote people can also take advantage of this increase in capacity. Sometimes, this is just what the doctor ordered.

Manufacturer: Solica Consulting, www.solica.com

Distribution: Most experienced GoldMine dealers

GoldBox

GoldBox is one of the most widely used tools within the GoldMine dealer community. GoldMine officially recognized it as one of the leading add-on products time and time again.

Initially, GoldBox was just a utility to expand and speed up the GoldMine importing and exporting functions. GoldBox was particularly useful for importing data into the secondary Contact, Detail, Pending, or History sections of GoldMine. GoldBox also enhances the GoldMine reporting and updating capabilities. The GoldBox merge/purge capability compares favorably with GoldMine's.

Most significantly, GoldBox has expanded into the area of custom views. With GoldBox, you can now have real-time links to outside tables. Every record in GoldMine can link to one or more tables of data. This could be useful for viewing accounting information or inventory. This feature, which now competes with Details Plus (see the "Details Plus" section, earlier in this chapter), further expands GoldMine's relational capabilities. In short, if you need to do anything with GoldMine data, chances are GoldBox can make it happen.

Manufacturer: Redstone SoftBase Company, `www.goldboxonline.com`

Distribution: Any knowledgeable GoldMine dealer

HEAT

GoldMine's merger with Bendata created a new product line for the company. Bendata came to the party with a product called HEAT. HEAT is a help desk program and is designed to allow you to monitor incoming service requests as well as to track the handling of these problems. With this program, you can better allocate your personnel and get a better handle on the types of problems that may need a different type of response. Actual colored gauges on the managers' screens give you graphic information about call volumes and resolution rates.

HEAT is intended for both internal and external help desks and call centers. In other words, you can use it for both incoming and outgoing calls, and it really doesn't matter if those calls are coming from your own staff or from outside customers.

With the current release, there is a version of GoldMine called *Sales and Marketing* (a beefed-up version of the standard GoldMine) that interfaces with HEAT (sort of). You need to contact FrontRange or check its Web site to find a dealer certified to demonstrate or sell these products. They are not distributed through any mass-market channels. You can contact FrontRange at 800-654-3526 or visit its Web site at `www.frontrange.com`.

KnowledgeSync

KnowledgeSync from Vineyardsoft is one of my personal favorites. GoldMine by itself is an excellent repository and organizer of all your data, but it doesn't really do anything unless you implement GoldMine's Automated Processes to cause activities to actually happen. KnowledgeSync, however, brings much more to the table.

Vineyardsoft advertises KnowledgeSync as an Alert Technology product. As such, it allows you to specify conditions in your database that automatically trigger an action. So a simple alert in KnowledgeSync might send an e-mail or pager message to the account manager the moment his or her biggest prospect calls with an issue. Or you might set it up to notify the sales manager whenever sales are lost, closed, or forecasts change.

But truthfully, KnowledgeSync can do a lot more than that. First of all, unlike GoldMine's Automated Processes, KnowledgeSync can look at many different databases at the same time. For example, it could look at GoldMine and at your accounting database and notify the salesperson that the forecast she just entered would put the client over his credit limit. Almost any database is a candidate for KnowledgeSync's scrutiny.

With a little assistance from Visual Basic, KnowledgeSync can also write to GoldMine fields. My company used this feature, for example, to create a system to automatically manage the responses from e-mail blasts. When an e-mail message is undeliverable or the recipient asks to be removed from our marketing campaign (what are they thinking?), KnowledgeSync can do this automatically and thus eliminates a great deal of time-consuming manual work. In addition, KnowledgeSync can be the basis for implementing many business processes within your company. Examples might be found in lead distribution, personnel management, marketing campaigns, and more.

Manufacturer: Vineyardsoft Corporation, www.vineyardsoft.com

Distribution: Sold through a select group of GoldMine dealers

LaserFiche/GoldFiche

GoldMine has the ability to link records to a variety of documents. It is a bit of a manual system and retrieving a document based on your limited recollection of the content is sometimes quite a challenge. If you really want to go paperless, you need to scan your documents, attach them to appropriate records, and be able to easily retrieve them based on a variety of search criteria.

The best system I have found is a combination of LaserFiche document management software and the GoldFiche integration. For the sake of truth in advertising, I have to tell you that my company created the GoldFiche system that connects LaserFiche to GoldMine.

Setting up a scanner on your network and implementing LaserFiche/GoldFiche could allow you to almost completely eliminate the need to store paper or buy file cabinets. LaserFiche could potentially allow even remote users access to corporate documents. LaserFiche complies with all known security rules and confidentiality requirements, particularly as they relate to the healthcare and financial services industries.

Manufacturers: Compulink Management Center, Inc., www.laserfiche.com; Computer Control Corporation, www.ccc24k.com

Distribution: LaserFiche dealers and Computer Control Corporation

Netilla

For a relatively small upfront setup fee and an ongoing monthly charge, you can have a Netilla-based system allowing anyone with Web access to access not only GoldMine, but also any other application you have running on your Windows 2000 server. Rather than getting just a subset of GoldMine, Netilla allows you to use GoldMine remotely pretty much the same way you would use it in the office. This system works well and has a considerable amount of security built in. The pricing structure makes it less desirable for small groups (ten or less) than it is for larger groups. Also, it tends to be a little slow, particularly when running GoldMine.

Manufacturer: Netilla Networks, www.netilla.com

Distribution: Through a network of dealers throughout the United States

OmniRush

OmniRush is a fax, e-mail, and print automation system that integrates with GoldMine. By itself, GoldMine can't fax anything. GoldMine requires an outside utility such as OmniRush, RightFax, or WinFax to transmit a fax document. Z-Firm, the developer of OmniRush, has won numerous awards from GoldMine and FrontRange and is a well-recognized and much-used product.

After you install OmniRush, you refer to it as if it's a user within your GoldMine system. That is, you schedule print or fax tasks for it just as if OmniRush were your assistant. OmniRush fully integrates with the GoldMine's Automated Processes and macro buttons. In addition, even remote users can use OmniRush and send documents from headquarters just as they would schedule anyone else for some activity.

You can use OmniRush to fax one document at a time, or you can set up fax broadcasts based on filters or groups of records. Because scheduling is an intrinsic part of using OmniRush, you can schedule documents to go out at night or on weekends to take advantage of the lower long distance telephone rates at those times.

One of the clear advantages that OmniRush enjoys over the other faxing solutions is its complete integration with GoldMine. When OmniRush sends a document, it logs that activity directly into the History tab with the time, date, and list of documents sent. If a transmission problem occurs, it's also recorded in GoldMine.

OmniRush is compatible with all versions of GoldMine — from 2.5 DOS to the current GoldMine 6.0.

FaxRush, the predecessor of OmniRush, is no longer supported by GoldMine 6.0, so you need to upgrade to OmniRush if you use GoldMine 6.0.

Standard fax modems (for example, Hayes or U.S. Robotics) are supported by OmniRush. Brooktrout fax cards are also supported on Windows NT 4 and are highly recommended. You need Microsoft Word, which should also be installed on the OmniRush server. OmniRush is compatible with all networks on which GoldMine runs.

OmniRush, in addition to having all of FaxRush's features, also handles credit card processing, UPS and FedEx shipping, and voice messaging. (About the only thing it can't do is make toast.) Plan on using the Brooktrout modem with OmniRush.

Your OmniRush license must match or exceed the number of licenses you have in your GoldMine system. Watch out for this! If you have a 25-user GoldMine license, you need at least that many OmniRush licenses, even if only two of you use OmniRush. In addition, OmniRush is not so simple to install and configure. Many, many options exist, and knowledge of hardware and networking is required. Using it is easy if it's set up correctly. I recommend having an authorized and experienced dealer install and configure OmniRush for you. Do not try this at home.

Manufacturer: Z-Firm LLC, www.faxrush.com

Distribution: Most authorized GoldMine dealers also handle OmniRush.

Quask

Collecting information from prospects and clients is a simple matter with an electronic survey system from Quask. The Quask system allows you to easily develop and distribute rather sexy survey forms that generate higher than usual response rates. Quask is fully integrated with GoldMine, allowing the returned document to automatically attach itself to the appropriate record in GoldMine. You can even set up custom fields within GoldMine and map the survey responses directly into those fields for further analysis and processing.

Sending surveys and acting on the results are cornerstones of any good continuous improvement or client retention program. The Quask system is ideal for this. I have used these surveys as a precursor to and as a follow-up on our training programs, for checking on the quality of our sales calls, project implementations, and service calls. In my office, Quask is now married to a series of Automated Processes within GoldMine that automatically follow up on responses out of the ordinary.

Manufacturer: Quask LLC, www.quask.com

Distribution: Computer Control Corporation, www.ccc24k.com, (North America); opportunIT, www.opportunit.co.uk, (Western Europe)

QuoteWerks and QwikQuote

QuoteWerks and QwikQuote are the two leading quotation systems that integrate with GoldMine. They both work well and allow your sales people to create sales forecasts and to produce customized quotes that attach themselves to the appropriate GoldMine accounts.

GoldMine's sales forecast section unfortunately lacks any ability to track the profit you will make on a particular sale. Each of these quotation systems fills that void.

Because each of these packages also integrates with accounting systems, your quote can be automatically turned into an invoice and/or a purchase order.

For those in the computer industry, QuoteWerks integrates nicely with the major hardware distributors, allowing you instant access to their pricing. While the two products are similar in nature, QuoteWerks was initially developed for computer dealers and, if that's your field, choosing between the two should be easy.

Manufacturers: Aspire Technologies, Inc., www.quotewerks.com; QwikQuote Development Corporation, www.qwikquote.com

Distribution: Almost any experienced GoldMine dealer

Stonefield Query

Stonefield Systems Group has developed a tool called Stonefield Query. This is really an alternative to Crystal Reports. Stonefield Query has a simple wizard interface. After selecting a report from the list of available reports, you can select the sort order, enter filter conditions, and select where the output should go (to a printer, disk file, spreadsheet, on-screen preview, and so on).

In addition to running predefined reports, you can create your own quick reports in just minutes. Simply select which fields to report on from the list of available fields (full English descriptions rather than cryptic names and symbols), and you're done! You don't have to know complex stuff like join conditions; Stonefield Query takes care of that for you.

Crystal Reports manufacturer: Seagate Technology LLC, www.seagate.com

Stonefield Query manufacturer: Stonefield Systems Group, Inc., www.stonefieldquery.com

Distribution: Most experienced GoldMine dealers handle Crystal Reports and/or Stonefield Query. Crystal Reports is also available through most major computer hardware and software distributors and even mail-order houses.

Terminal Services

Windows 2000 or Windows NT with Terminal Services enabled allows remote users with Terminal Services licenses to access applications remotely. If you already have this configuration or are planning to upgrade to this, then you have everything you need to access GoldMine from home, the road, or the moon. And what's really appealing to me is the cost — nothing. And the speed is excellent.

My company has used virtually every technology to connect remotely to GoldMine. We implemented Terminal Services in the summer of 2002 and haven't looked back. I highly recommend this solution, although you may need the services of an experienced network/Internet technical person to configure it.

Terminal Services, or parts thereof, is included with your operating system, assuming you have at least Windows 2000. You may very well need some assistance in setting it up, so plan on some consulting from a qualified network engineer.

Chapter 30

The Ten Most Important New Features in GoldMine 6.0

● ●

*B*eauty is often in the eye of the beholder. Ask ten knowledgeable people for the ten best of anything, and you will probably get a hundred answers.

The question most often asked by existing GoldMine users is, "What's in the new version that makes it worth the price to upgrade?" Well, that's the question this chapter addresses: Here are my top ten choices.

Backup/Restore Functions

Both the Backup and Restore functions are available under the File main menu selection. Users with Master rights as well as undocked, remote users can make use of this new feature. Version 6.0 incorporates a wizard allowing you to back up all or just selected GoldMine files. Of course, the Restore function offers that same selective or all-inclusive ability. Figure 30-1 shows the beginning of the Backup Wizard.

Figure 30-1: The Backup Wizard helps you back up your data.

Backing up or restoring while users have dBASE files open is a baaad thing. Therefore, the Backup Wizard gives you the ability to force active users to log out and get coffee.

GoldMine allows multiple databases, although only one can be active at any time. The Backup Wizard handles multiple databases, attachments, reports, templates, and linked documents.

While you can use the Backup function to create copies of your database(s) onto the same hard drive, please remember to make a copy on some type of removable media and store that backup somewhere off-site. Fires, floods, robberies, and hard drive crashes don't happen all that often, but when your hard drive is suddenly gone, you'll be sorry if your original and your only backup went with it.

Custom Field and Label Expressions

Virtually all the standard fields and any custom fields you create can take advantage of GoldMine's new custom field and label expressions. One of the most significant features within this new facility is the ability to have field labels automatically change based on the data in one or more other fields. For example, if the Contact field contains a military ranking such as Pvt. or Cpl., the Title field label changes to the Rank field.

With this new methodology, the data in one or more fields can actually control the appearance of the entire screen. Figure 30-2 shows one of the pertinent windows for customizing labels and data. Suddenly a record for a vendor can look very different from that of a prospect or an employee. This has major implications for the flexibility of GoldMine 6.0 and beyond.

Field label expressions can be used for all fields. A similar facility exists to populate the actual data in a field, but this is restricted to non-indexed fields.

Field label colors are also individually programmable. In the database my company uses, we have a field showing how many hours of support a client has available. Should those hours go into the negative, GoldMine can now turn the label red — a great warning sign to our support people. I'd love it if the label or data could be made to flash, but I haven't figured out how to do that yet. If you're especially clever, you can essentially make fields invisible on-screen by making the label and/or the data field match the color of the screen background.

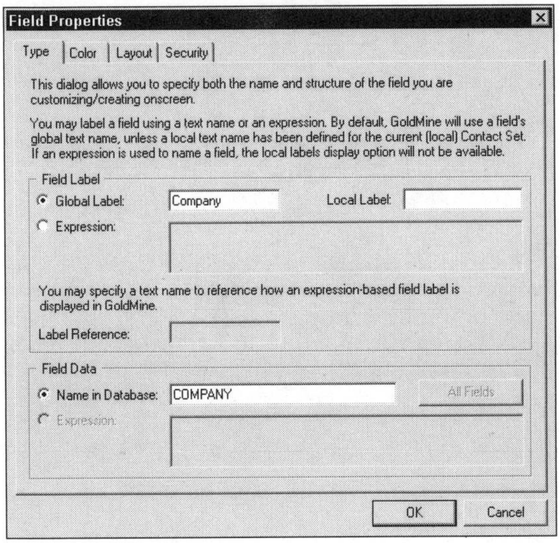

Figure 30-2:
Customizing
field labels
and data.

GM+View

Each contact record (account) has its own GM+View tab. This completely customizable tab supports the display of HTML documents that can house all kinds of data, including GoldMine fields, text, images, WAV files (sound bites), and other types of rich content, as shown in Figure 30-3. You can think of this new tab as a custom Web page specific to each account. To customize the GM+View tab, from the main menu choose File⇨Configure⇨GM+View Tab. You must have Master rights to create or edit the GM+View tab, but anyone can view the tab.

Different contact records can display completely different GM+View tabs based on a field's value, an expression's value, or a user's selection. In the simplest sense, you can use the GM+View tab to store a picture or several pictures. If you are a real estate agent, for example, you might have a contact record for a homeowner whose property you have listed. In the GM+View tab for that record, you can store one or more pictures of the house. And each house that you have listed can have its own set of pictures.

I use the Details tab to store driving directions to my accounts. Now, I can also store an actual map within each GM+View tab.

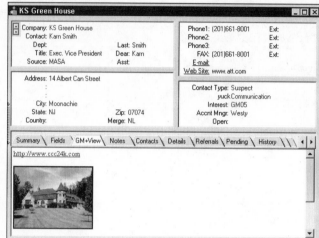

Figure 30-3:
A
customized
GM+View
tab.

Meeting Requests

GoldMine 6.0 can import and export iCal-based meeting requests. This means that GoldMine's calendar can communicate with any other scheduling program that uses the iCal format. For most of us, this translates to Lotus Notes and Outlook, which, along with GoldMine, are the only iCal-based systems I am aware of.

The real power here is the ability to have some team members using GoldMine and others using Outlook. From GoldMine, you can send a meeting request to multiple contacts and/or to multiple users. If you are scheduling a meeting, you don't have to worry about whether the attendees are using GoldMine, Outlook, or Lotus Notes.

For example, if you use GoldMine and you need to have two of your internal GoldMine users, one of your remote salespeople (who insists on using Outlook), your corporate attorney (who uses Lotus Notes), and a client (who uses Outlook) attend a meeting next week, you can easily send a request to everyone, knowing that they will all receive the meeting request without fail. It works in the other direction as well — Outlook users can generate meeting requests and receive responses from GoldMine users.

The power of this approach is that it reduces the need for an entire organization to switch from Outlook to GoldMine. Those who are on the periphery of the GoldMine user community (perhaps some managers, administrators, or some remote people) and who maintain a quasi-religious devotion to Outlook can keep running with that without feeling too guilty about not switching completely over to GoldMine.

My GoldMine

My GoldMine is a new feature that allows each user to assemble and to customize a single window containing all of life's essentials.

With My GoldMine, you can either pull information or information can be pushed to you. *Pulling* information means, in this case, GoldMine goes out to some source, like the Internet, and displays some data. Examples of pulling information would be downloading or viewing stock market reports or a weather report.

Information can also be *pushed* at you, meaning that the information is uploaded to your computer without you requesting it. Your network administrator might want you to receive updated price lists. He could push the data to you, having the lists automatically sent or uploaded to the window that displays My GoldMine so that you would be almost forced to see the new information.

One Button Synchronization

GoldMine has had synchronization built in for many years. It has always been the most technologically challenging part of the system. In the early years, there may have been an actual bug or two or three. Over the years, the developers gradually plugged up most of the holes and turned GoldSync into a reasonably solid part of the overall GoldMine experience.

Still, problems lingered, such as mysterious and inexplicable holes in the data being transferred. No one could seemingly explain it, so the developers came up with the theory that any remaining problems were user errors. This wasn't necessarily true, but I think it made them feel better.

To eliminate you, my friends, as the possible source of any synchronization errors, GoldMine 6.0 makes synchronization foolproof. After GoldSync is properly configured, you have an extremely limited set of options. Click one button and off the data goes, untouched by human hands. You can't mess up and, therefore, any problems that remain gotta be theirs.

The vast number of different kinds of modems was also a challenge for synchronization. To eliminate problems associated with modem-based synchronization, GoldMine 6.0 has removed all support for dial-up modems in favor of Internet-based connections.

QuickStart Wizard

The new QuickStart Wizard simplifies getting GoldMine up and running. The QuickStart Wizard appears immediately after you install GoldMine and helps you set up all the critical operations you most likely need. You can use the QuickStart Wizard to configure the following:

- Your own personal user information, such as your name and title
- Security settings, such as user names and passwords
- E-mail accounts
- The link to Microsoft Word
- GoldMine's industry-specific templates, such as those for real estate or for financial services

Search Center

As GoldMine evolved over the years, there was a smorgasbord of methodologies for looking up contact records and developing and revisiting filters and groups. GoldMine 6.0 now has a single place to go for all of this — the Search Center, as shown in Figure 30-4.

The Search Center incorporates all the old facilities for looking up individual records and for creating filters and groups. None of the old facilities have been eliminated just yet, but as later versions of GoldMine come out, you will gradually be weaned away from the old ways and strongly encouraged to become comfortable with the new Search Center that has all the old stuff and some new capabilities as well. You might as well get used to it now.

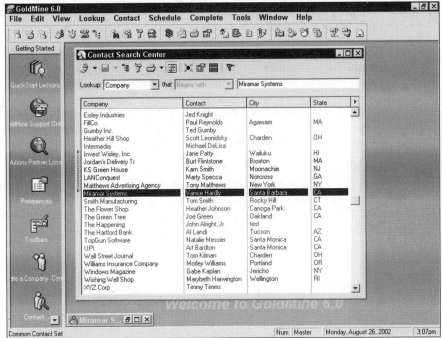

Figure 30-4:
The new
Search
Center.

Spell Checker

Spell checking has been requested since the earliest version of GoldMine I can remember. Finally, it's here.

The goal in developing GoldMine 6.0 was to make spell checking available for every notepad in GoldMine. As of this writing, the spell checker has been made available only for notes relating to scheduling and completing activities, for the body of e-mails, and in the InfoCenter.

Dictionaries are available in multiple languages, including English (US), English (UK), French, German, Spanish, Portuguese, Swedish, Norwegian, Danish, and Dutch. Legal and medical dictionaries are also available. Even Yogi would approve because all these dictionaries allow you to make up your own words and save them.

XML Import/Export

XML (Extensible Markup Language) is fast becoming the de facto industry standard for data exchange. GoldMine 6.0 extends your options for sharing data with those who do not use GoldMine with new XML wizards.

The XML Import Wizard enables you to define parameters for importing contact and activity data from an XML file. This means, among other things, that Pending and Historical activities can be gracefully imported.

The XML Export Wizard enables you to select the user and/or contact data to export. There is a wide range of flexibility covering almost every facet of GoldMine data, other than non-contact–related data. That means everything other than InfoCenter data and Automated Processes (pretty much) can be exported now.

Index

• S •